AF478653

The Dream of Chaucer

The Dream of Chaucer

Representation and Reflection in the Early Narratives

by Robert R. Edwards

Duke University Press   Durham and London

1989

© 1989 Duke University Press

Printed in the United States of America
on acid-free paper ∞
Library of Congress Cataloging-in-Publication Data
appear on the last printed page of this book.

For Emily

Contents

A Note on Texts

Quotations from Chaucer's poetry are taken from *The Riverside Chaucer,* ed. Larry D. Benson et al., which is based on *The Works of Geoffrey Chaucer,* ed. F. N. Robinson, 2d ed. Classical authors are quoted in the edition and translation of the Loeb Classical Library. Citations from the *Roman de la rose* use the edition of Félix Lecoy; translations of the *Rose* are taken from Charles Dahlberg's *The Romance of the Rose.* For convenience I have added translations of French, Italian, Spanish, and medieval Latin authors. For Guillaume de Machaut and Jehan de Froissart, the translations given are generally those in Barry A. Windeatt's *Chaucer's Dream Poetry: Sources and Analogues;* for Machaut's *Le Jugement dou Roy de Behaingne,* I have used the edition and translation by R. Barton Palmer. Other editions and translations are cited in the main entry for the author's name in the bibliography at the end.

Preface

This book is a critical study of Chaucer's early narrative poetry. It deals to some degree with Chaucer's lyrics, translations, and imitations, but the main focus is on a group of poems—the *Book of the Duchess, House of Fame,* and *Parliament of Fowls*—generally thought to have been written between the late 1360s and the early 1380s. Although the chronology for these poems, as for all Chaucer's poetry, remains somewhat uncertain, the internal evidence makes this sequence of composition plausible and indeed quite probable (Tatlock). Moreover, the three works form a cohesive ensemble, not the least in Chaucer's own representation of them. In the preface to the *Legend of Good Women* (F 417–21), written in the mid-1380s, Queen Alceste names the three poems, along with what may have been an early version of the Knight's Tale, as works that the poet has made to further Cupid's law and praise his name. They are works that emphatically connect the themes of love and poetic "making," as Alceste calls the poet's art of composition.

All three poems are written as dream visions, the narrative form which typically recounts a speaker's wondrous dream and so connects visionary experience with ordinary reality or, more precisely, with the stylized social reality of a poet addressing his audience in the here-and-now and giving it an account of dreams told in retrospect. The choice of this form locates the beginning of Chaucer's career as a narrative poet in literary conventions that, on the one hand, go back to classical and biblical models and, on the other, relate directly to the practice of his medieval contemporaries. Unlike the practice of many of his contemporaries, though, Chaucer's use of the dream vision to frame his narrative is predominantly secular, at least to the extent that a distinction between secular and religious values is possible in the later Middle Ages.

The three poems share, too, a common literary context. They were written for the English court of the later fourteenth century, taking court to mean the sociopolitical institution that encompassed royalty, aristocracy, magnates, and functionaries of the realm (Scattergood, Lenaghan). The *Book of the Duchess* was written to commemorate the death of John of Gaunt's first wife, Blanche of Lancaster, for whom Gaunt ordered a yearly memorial service that was observed on the anniversary of her death throughout his life. The *House of Fame* and *Parliament of Fowls,* according to most accounts, were probably written in connection with negotiations for Richard II's marriage in the period 1380–82. As Paul Strohm observes, "Chaucer's immediate circle was almost certainly composed of persons in social situations close to his own. Its members are to be sought among fellow knights and esquires of the royal household, and civil servants and lawyers of similar station in the London/Westminster area" ("Scene" 10). The figures named in Chaucer's later courtly works—Henry Scogan, Peter Bukton, Philip de la Vache, John Gower, Ralph Strode, and Lewis Clifford—give some sense of the audience. Educated and pragmatic, all serve in the milieu of royal administration. In addition, the circle must have included educated women, such as Queen Philippa and later Queen Anne, who plays the role of Alceste in the Prologue to the *Legend of Good Women.*

If the later evidence of Chaucer's audience is a reliable guide, the early poems are necessarily highly constrained in style and theme, and they function within a notably self-conscious environment where social values and behavior share the same language as poetic fiction. In theory, social life and literature are facets of courtly discourse (Zumthor). The social context does not, however, determine the meaning of the poems. There is nothing equivalent to the scene in John Gower's *Confessio Amantis* where Richard II commands the writing of the poem, nor is there a counterpart in Chaucer to the dedications that Gower makes to Richard II and later Henry IV. Nonetheless, the social context grounds the poems in a particular literary environment. The consolation of the black knight in the *Book of the Duchess,* for example, depends as much on ethical and social persuasion as on an appeal to the private experience of loss. The *House of Fame* depicts, among other things, the turbulent fate of reputations at court. Much of the comedy in the debate presented in the final section of the *Parliament of Fowls* is based on the social types associated with classes and estates.

Chaucer's own place in this environment is surprisingly well documented. From at least 1367, and possibly as early as 1360, he was a member of the royal household. He remained so for all his life, while continuing to enjoy Gaunt's patronage (Crow 19, 21). During the period in which he composed the group of dream visions, he held a number of official positions, the most important of them comptroller of customs from 1374 to 1386. In addition, Chaucer participated in various capacities in a series of diplomatic missions. He journeyed to Spain in 1366 and probably several times to France by the end of the 1360s (he had briefly been held prisoner by the French in 1359–60). He was sent abroad on a mission in 1368 and granted a letter of protection for traveling overseas in the king's service in 1370 (the nature of the service is not specified in either case). In 1372–73 Chaucer made his first recorded visit to Italy as part of a mission to Genoa and Florence, where he possibly met the great literary figures of the day, Petrarch and Boccaccio. He was sent on secret missions for the king in 1376–77. In 1378 he traveled to Lombardy on a royal mission to Bernabò Visconti, lord of Milan, concerning the prosecution of the Hundred Years' War. Chaucer's public life in this period is largely continuous with the social context of his poetry; the court is in a sense the audience and object of his early writing. The anomaly is that the evidence of the poems and the records of the life remain parallel but discrete; none of the biographical data refer to the writing.

Chaucer's poetry comes on the scene at a crucial juncture in English literary history. During the middle of this decade and a half, the European figures who had dominated high literary culture for half a century died without leaving successors of comparable stature. Petrarch died in 1374, Boccaccio in 1375, Guillaume de Machaut in 1377. French poetry continued to have a powerful influence, as seen in the English careers of Jehan de Froissart and Oton de Grandson, though knowledge of the French language may have been less widespread than earlier.[1] The rise of social classes aware of the cultural prestige of French literature created an environment for translating works like the Old French *lais* and courtly romance.[2] Meanwhile, English poets were producing the major texts of their own tradition and advancing beyond earlier didactic writing and the tradition of metrical romances. The B-text of *Piers Plowman* appeared in the mid-1370s, *Sir Gawain and the Green Knight* around 1380. From 1375 onwards Gower was writing the Latin and French works— the *Vox Clamantis* and the *Mirour de l'omme*—that would provide the social and philosophical grounding for his treatment of love in the *Confessio Amantis* (1385–93).

Seen in this historical context, Chaucer's early narratives hold a special place, and their achievement extends well beyond the literary conventions they employ or the social occasions that may have given rise to them. The dream visions introduced a sophisticated and notably self-conscious mode of literary representation to English poetry. They brought a new kind of courtly writing into English, works of fashion that appealed to a social and political elite. Rossell Hope Robbins has argued in the case of Chaucer's lyrics that, despite the artistic merits of earlier collections like the Harley lyrics, Chaucer's lyrics rather than a native tradition determined the course of English lyric poetry up to the Elizabethan age ("The Lyrics"). A similar case can be argued for Chaucer's narratives, despite the achievements of Langland, Gower, and the *Gawain*-poet.

The legacy of what the Renaissance knew as "Chaucers Dreme" endured for two centuries, and even in its own day it established the conventions for court writers like Thomas Usk, Thomas Hoccleve, and Sir John Clanvowe (Miskimin). It may also have fostered, as James I. Wimsatt contends ("*Dit*"), a reciprocal influence on some contemporary French writing. Taken in its own scope, Chaucer's early narrative poetry is the most refined body of work in an emerging national literature. It is at once the means and product of an ambitious cultural and literary project, which is to create an equivalent in English of continental court poetry. Derek Brewer has rightly observed, "From the thirteen-sixties onwards the very existence of Chaucer's poetry proves that the language of the court was English, and that the standard of literary culture was as high as it has ever been in any English court, and a good deal higher than it has been in most" ("Relationship" 10). The poetry marks, then, a moment of cultural and literary inauguration that grows out of a sustained engagement with the rich and varied background of medieval literary tradition as a whole. And it is in that engagement that we shall find the evidence of Chaucer's art and poetics.

Most interpretations of Chaucer's early narrative poems have followed approaches that place the works in one of two broadly defined contexts. Wolfgang Clemen established the dominant mode of aesthetic criticism by viewing the poems under the rubrics of convention and originality. Clemen describes the commonplaces of literary representation that Chaucer inherited and signals the points where he diverges from convention or turns it to his own uses. With certain modifications of emphasis, Clemen's approach has been taken by subsequent critics such as J. A. W. Bennett, Dorothy Everett, Robert O. Payne, and Joerg Fichte. The second approach has been made largely within a discussion of genre. Constance Hieatt, James Winny, and A. C. Spearing read the poems within the framework of the dream vision and the extensive literary and philosophical tradition surrounding that form from late antiquity onwards. Whether dream poetry constitutes a genre in itself remains a debated issue (Kane), but in choosing the form Chaucer clearly locates the beginning of his career as a narrative poet within a richly developed register of expression.

For all their efforts to read the poems in an aesthetic and literary context, however, these approaches reflect the critical assumptions implicit in their methods. Clemen's opposition between convention and originality takes for granted an inherent dichotomy in aesthetic creation. His is a Romantic aesthetic carried back into the Middle Ages, and it fosters a kind of interpretive arithmetic: originality, which represents an absolute value in that aesthetic, is what remains when convention has been subtracted. But as Dieter Mehl has pointed out, "The concept of originality is a most unreliable criterion for judging works of medieval literature, and Chaucer would certainly not, any more than his contemporaries, have had any ambition of departing as far as possible from his models, from traditional standards or from the literary trends of his time in general" (*Chaucer* 23). Medieval poetry as a whole was remarkably conventional, and a writer's originality was most often established within a poetics of translation rather than as an act of unique literary creation (Muscatine). Similarly, the approach through genre does not give an adequate account of the subtlety of Chaucer's achievement. To be sure, Chaucer draws on well-developed conventions to convey the interior world of his dreamer, but the implications of his portrayal extend far beyond psychological representation or the circumscribed fiction of the dream world. The question is not whether Chaucer drew on the conventions but what he did with them.

What I intend to show in this book is that the early narrative poems are a complex but unified group of works that operate in two distinct but complementary domains. As mimetic art, the poems convey a visionary experience. Chaucer's first-person narrator has a vocabulary to describe that experience, and he has a sense of its difference from other kinds of vision. The imaginative realm of the poem lies beyond ordinary experience in what he calls "so queynt a sweven" (*Book of the Duchess* 1330). He insists that it is "so wonderful a drem" (*House of Fame* 63). Though the dream differs from biblical and classical models, it projects an interior realm with an intelligible structure, a formal order, for it is "so ynly swete a sweven" (*Book of the Duchess* 276). The poem's action, its narrative trajectory, is given by the shape of the dreamer's experience.

But at the same time that it describes the narrator's experience, the poem is, in equal measure, self-referential. The language of narrative description is also the language of critical analysis, the means by which the poet constitutes and questions his art. Spearing rightly points out that the artifice of the dream vision makes the poem aware of its existence as a creative fiction and the poet aware of his own authorship (51). I want to argue that the dream vision is finally more than just a metaphor for artistic creation and poetic fiction. The poems consistently explore the fundamental terms of literary representation and not just the exquisite fact of their self-consciousness and textuality. They represent a sustained reflection on the nature and devices of art.

I owe a large debt to Richard Fly, Winthrop Wetherbee III, and Robert Worth Frank, Jr., for reading this book in manuscript and making valuable suggestions for revision. I am grateful to Jorge Gracia for advising me on medieval philosophy. The readers for Duke University Press have also been helpful in their recommendations for strengthening the book, and Reynolds Smith has been a supportive and knowledgeable editor. The errors and misunderstandings that remain are of my own manufacture. An early version of the third chapter appeared in *New Literary History* 13 (1982): 180–204 under the title "The *Book of the Duchess* and the Beginnings of Chaucer's Narrative"; it is reprinted with the permission of the editor. Terry Martin and Thomas Berninghausen worked as research assistants at different phases of this project, and I am thankful to them for the effort they have put into the book. My thanks go as well to the staff of the libraries at the State University of New York at Buffalo. I am especially grateful to the National Humanities Center where the first full draft of the book was written; the fellows and staff created a superb environment for research and thinking. The dedication to my wife, Emily Grosholz, records another, still more profound debt, intellectual and personal.

Introduction

The major line of argument I want to develop is that Chaucer's early narrative poems have to do with both mimetic representation and aesthetic speculation. It is one measure of Chaucer's superb artistry that he joins these two domains so closely. His poems describe action in an imaginary world, while they explore the poetics that underlies their fiction. We can see an example of Chaucer's artistic economy at the very start of his career as a narrative poet, in the scene that begins the dreamer's visionary experience in the *Book of the Duchess*. The narrator has been kept awake by obsessive, melancholic thoughts, and he asks for a book to read in order to drive the night away. He reads Ovid's tale of Ceyx and Alcyone, then falls asleep on his book of "romaunce." In his dream he awakens to find himself in a chamber painted with the full text and complete glosses of the *Roman de la rose*. The glazed windows of the room, illuminated by sunlight, contain "hooly al the story of Troye" (326). Meanwhile, birds sing in a harmony that specifically recalls Guillaume de Lorris's description of the Garden of Deduit in the *Roman de la rose*. The dreamer does not linger in this marvelous room, for another sound calls him to a quest, the "hert-huntyng" which is at the literal and allegorical center of the poem; but it is clear that Chaucer has begun the dream by situating its action in a conspicuously literary locale.

The poet-narrator's dream is that he awakens in a structure which constitutes an ideal book. The chamber encompasses the two central topics of medieval courtly literature—love and war—as exemplified by the master texts that read the poets of classical antiquity through the values of medieval vernacular culture. The *Roman de la rose,* as Guillaume de Lorris conceives it, contains "al the art of love" (*Romaunt* 40); it assimilates Ovid's erotic lore and applies it to every department of human conduct. The "whole story of Troy" probably refers to the *romans d'antiquité* which extended the history of Troy beyond Homer to include the story of Thebes as background and the story of Rome as the historical aftermath (Wetherbee *Poets* 23). It is against this composite ideal structure that the narrator will resolve at the end of his poem "to put this sweven in ryme / As I kan best" (1332–33). The exquisite decoration of the chamber is the point of textual allusion where the dream's action begins, and it is an aesthetic standard set outside the action; it is a domain of pleasure in the poem and an objectification of the poet's desire for his work.

The scene of the dreamer's awakening in the *Book of the Duchess* exemplifies what I shall describe in detail in the next chapter as Chaucer's practice of literary theory. My contention is that, although Chaucer wrote no formal, discursive treatise on poetics, he conducted an extensive practice of aesthetic speculation. The poems are means of representation and artistic self-consciousness. But if what Chaucer has to say about art is always embedded in a poetic context, it follows that his critical reflections are necessarily part of the imaginative discourse of his poems. His practical theorizing incorporates a subtle and carefully balanced play of assertion and negation, and like the stories and characters depicted in the poems, it cannot be reduced to a simple or even a single meaning.

Chaucer's self-conscious textuality functions, then, within an economy of textual meaning. His speculations about the nature of poetry have the same rich, if often problematic, standing as the poetry itself. The theorizing does not, however, radically deny the possibility of representation and poetic meaning. The early narratives assert the mysterious powers of representation and meaning; and like the *Consolation of Philosophy,* one of Chaucer's most important sources for later poems, they dramatize the problem of the knower rather than the impossibility of the knowable. In this way the poems embody a profound commitment to critical analysis and reflection, to a process of understanding that goes forward amidst indeterminacy and partiality. As they tell the narrator's story of his dream, the poems explore the complications of aesthetic systems, including foremost those that Chaucer sets out for himself.

The practice of theorizing is a constant feature of Chaucer's poetry, of course. The narrator of *Troilus and Criseyde* is concerned with, among other things, the nature of authorship, the way language changes over time, and the moral consequences of his story of pagan antiquity. The Prologue to the *Legend of Good Women* is a dramatized commentary on the etiquette of a court poet. It speaks to the roles of experience, books, and memory; the poet's place in literary tradition and a social milieu; and the slippery linkage between intent and utterance. The *Canterbury Tales* offer, in their multiple speakers, a large-scale dialogue on the relation of language and truth. The importance of Chaucer's early narratives is not just that they begin this process but that they begin it with a distinctive cohesion. The three dream visions are an integrated collection of works that examine a common set of aesthetic problems. The works echo one another to a remarkable degree and employ a similar form. In addition, they share a common language, themes, and narrative devices. These links suggest that the poems are in dialogue with one another.

One example of this textual dialogue can be found at the end of Book I of the *House of Fame.* The dreamer has just left the temple of Venus, which is decorated inside with scenes from Vergil's *Aeneid.* Chaucer's *ekphrasis* of the scenes inevitably recalls the episode of the dreamer's awaking in the painted chamber in the *Book of the Duchess;* at the same time it pays homage to Vergil's own use of the rhetorical *descriptio* in Book 2 of the *Aeneid,* which is in turn a recognition of Homer's verbal portrait of the shield made by Hephaistos for Achilles (*Iliad* 18). Now the ideal book represented in the *Book of the Duchess* contained a full text and all the glosses to the *Roman de la rose;* it was, in other words, a text capable of prodigious amplification. In the *House of Fame* Chaucer achieves a similar effect of amplification by elaborating the story of Dido and Aeneas: proverbs, rhetorical complaints, and historical exempla shift the accent from the grandeur of epic deeds and historical necessity to the private domain of erotic betrayal. The dreamer tells Vergil's story in the manner of the *Roman de la rose* and thereby enacts the method of reading imagined in the earlier poem.

The purpose of Chaucer's elaborate recollection in the *House of Fame* is to evoke and then amend the poetic method set out tentatively in the *Book of the Duchess.* Both poems are absorbed with the power of "thoght," the mind's capacity to project images and represent action through them. The source of images is distinctly verbal and literary: linguistic signs rendered as "portreytures" and "figures" (*House of Fame* 125–26). But at the end of the dreamer's account of the *Aeneid* in the *House of Fame,* Chaucer discovers, in a counter image, what such a concept of poetic imagination finally entails. The dreamer leaves the temple and beholds an immense desert of sand, which symbolizes the limitless domain of images and of texts amplified by resemblance and secondary meanings. It is a barren vista of signs multiplied without concrete referents, much like the state of psychological quandary that the narrators describe at the beginning of both dream poems. At this moment, however, Jupiter's eagle descends to grasp the dreamer and carry him into the sky, where he is to learn "tydynges" about love. Chaucer borrows the eagle from Dante's *Purgatorio,* and though he uses the figure to quite different ends from Dante's, the borrowing affords a commentary on the *Book of the Duchess.* We can see that Chaucer has developed the action and themes of the *House of Fame* so that they recreate the problem of the imagination as it was formulated in the earlier poem. The eagle intervenes to wrest the dreamer from repetition; as it happens, he also carries him to a more radical experiment in theorizing about art and language.

The self-reflexive theorizing embodied in the two examples I have mentioned evolves coherently in the dream visions, for Chaucer's aesthetic speculation reflects a conceptual unity rather than a diffuse thematic treatment. The three poems recall one another at significant places through iterations of language and a network of intertextual references, both to themselves and to other works. Chaucer has, as we shall see, an extensive practice of autocitation. Furthermore, his speculation is organized around a set of terms that lend a structural coherence. These terms are drawn from the principal categories of medieval faculty psychology—imagination, memory, and intellect—and Chaucer uses these so-called "internal senses" as a framework in which to deliberate about the status of poetic representation.

"Sapiences three"

The doctrine of the three faculties evolved, as Murray Bundy and others have shown, from a well-developed philosophical tradition, aided in some details by the works of medical authorities. In the first half of the thirteenth century Bartholomaeus Anglicus offered a summary of the doctrine in his popular and influential encyclopedia *De proprietatibus rerum,* a work that sought to guide university students through the new learning discovered in Aristotle and the Greek and Arab writers. Bartholomaeus writes (29):

> Sensus vero communis siue interior diuiditur in tres partes
> secundum tres cerebri regiones. Nam in cerebro tres sunt
> cellule: scilicet anterior, in qua virtus ymaginatiua operatur,
> que quidem ea que sensus extrinsecus apprehendit interius
> ordinat et componit, vt dicit Johannicius; est et media cellula,

> scilicet logistica, in qua sensibilis ratio siue estimatiua virtus
> dominatur; et iterum et tertia postrema, que est memoratiua,
> que ea que apprehensa sunt per ymaginationem siue rationem
> in thesauro memorie retinet et custodit.

In the fourteenth century John Trevisa translated Bartholomaeus. His rendering of the passage removes some of the technical vocabulary while presenting the main points (2:98).

> The innere witte is departid aþre by þre regiouns of þe brayn,
> for in þe brayn beþ þre smale celles. þe formest hatte *yma-*
> *ginatiua,* þerin þingis þat þe vttir witte apprehendiþ withoute
> beþ i-ordeyned and input togedres withinne, *vt dicitur Jo-*
> *hannicio I.* þe middil chambre hatte *logica* þerin þe vertu
> estimatiue is maister. þe þridde and þe laste is *memoratiua,*
> þe vertu of mynde. þat vertu holdiþ and kepiþ in þe tresour
> of mynde þingis þat beþ apprehendid and iknowe bi þe yma-
> ginatif and *racio.*

The main outlines of the doctrine that Bartholomaeus and Trevisa describe are as follows. The senses impress on the imagination to produce visual images (*phantasms*) which stand as signs for things in the world. The imagination, as Aristotle defined it (*De anima* III.3), is a movement produced by sensation in action. Like all artificial signs, the images created by this movement are arbitrary and mediate between the knower and the world; they are individual as well, and their appeal is to man's appetitive nature. Aristotle points out, further, that the imagination involves the will, and so an image can be produced in the absence of sensation. The epistemological problems are thus twofold. First, the imagination constructs figures that are derivative and removed from the direct experience of the world by the senses; and second, the images are either reproductive or constitutive. That is, they can be produced by sense impressions or by the imagination's capacity to generate visual images on its own. Consequently, the visual figures shaped by the imagination always have a problematic status in representation. The imagination may provide a basis for belief and opinion; it is a necessary but not a sufficient ground for knowledge.

The intellect, the second of the internal faculties, works by abstracting from the images produced by sensation or the will; it derives the universal nature (intelligible species) from the individual image based on its common properties. By this process of abstraction the individual becomes knowable in an objective realm of experience, for its common nature is discovered amid its singularities. The operations of the intellect give rise, of course, to the much-debated question of universals. What is the status of these common natures? Are they mental constructions or substances existing at some level of reality? William C. Dampier gives a convenient summary of the problem and the positions open to medieval thinkers (79).

> Why is it that we are able to classify? Are individuals the only realities, classes or universals existing merely as mental concepts or names, as the nominalists maintain, or have they a certain independent reality, existing in and with the objects of sense as the essence of those objects, as Aristotle taught? Or, on the other hand, have the ideas or universals a quite separate existence and a reality apart from the phenomena or the isolated beings, as Plato held in his idealist philosophy, which had come to be called realism? For instance are Democritus and Socrates realities, and humanity only a name? Or is man a species with a reality of its own, receiving here and there certain forms which make it Democritus or Socrates, accidents of the real substance, humanity? Are we to say *universalia ante rem* with Plato, *universalia in re* with Aristotle, or *universalia post rem* with the nominalists?

Taken in its own terms, the problem of universals was perhaps the most difficult question of the high and late Middle Ages. As a practical matter, though, most thinkers in the high Middle Ages followed some version of Aristotle's notion of abstraction, regardless of whether they had access to his texts (Knowles 115).

The third faculty is memory, which conserves the products of imagination in a storehouse (*thesaurus*), a repository of images. Sensitive memory preserves the physical image, while rational memory preserves the form abstracted by the intellect. Here the tradition admitted a diversity of sources and positions. The Platonic doctrine of reminiscence held that the ultimate reality consisted in Forms or Ideas, of which man preserved traces in his memory. It is along these lines, for example, that Augustine argues that at the core of all memory is the memory of God (*Confessions* 10). Memory thus represents not only the sum of individual experience and general categories but also a source of spiritual wisdom. On a practical level memory also developed, through rhetoric, artificial techniques for using images to retain the ordering and contents of discourse beyond one's innate capacity to remember.

Two works composed early in Chaucer's career show his familiarity with the general framework of the three faculties and demonstrate his active engagement with the tradition. In the Second Nun's Tale, which

Queen Alceste groups among Chaucer's didactic writing (*Legend of Good Women* F 424), Saint Cecilia interprets the three psychological categories in man as a figure of the Trinity. She explains to Tiburce, her brother-in-law, who is undergoing instruction in the Christian faith:

> Right as a man hath sapiences three——
> Memorie, engyn, and intellect also—
> So in o beynge of divinitee,
> Thre persones may ther right wel bee.
> (viii.338–41)

Chaucer's source for the passage is Jacobus de Voragine's *Legenda Aurea,* the great medieval compendium of saints' lives. In translating Jacobus, however, Chaucer imputes through his phrasing somewhat more autonomy to the faculties than does his source. The point of the original comparison is that the human mind is a microcosm of the mystery of the Trinity, and the logic of the comparison requires a corresponding unity between man and the godhead. Jacobus makes this correspondence explicit: "in una hominis sapientia sunt tria, scilicet ingenium, memoria et intellectus" (in the one wisdom of man there are three things, namely, imagination, memory, and intellect, 774). Chaucer's comparison suggests a subtle difference. Man's three faculties stand as relatively independent powers in contrast to the "o beyng" composed of three persons.

Chaucer's "sapiences three" may be simply a misreading of the line in Jacobus ("sapientia sunt tria"), but it suggests that in some way Chaucer regards the faculties as separate powers, hence as potentially independent sources for interpreting experience. This is the impression given, too, by Chaucer's translation of the passage in the *Consolation of Philosophy* where Lady Philosophy explains to Boethius the powers of cognition that allow man to know things in the world (*Boece* 5.pr4.132–217). "Wit" (the senses) operates on the material level; "ymaginacioun" understands the figure of things. "Resoun," she says, is a "universel lokynge" that extracts the species from the individual. "Intelligence" knows things in "same symple forme" residing in "devyne thought." The categories differ from the conventional divisions of faculty psychology in that Boethius offers a Platonizing version of Aristotle's *De anima.* ("Intelligence" is the agent intellect taken as a counterpart of the ideal Form.) Still, the insistence on the separation of cognitive powers remains the same. Lady Philosophy stresses that the hierarchy of cognition extends from the material to the divine in well-delineated levels and that man's knowledge comes from "his propre power" and not from the powers of the things he knows.

J. D. Burnley has rightly argued that Chaucer does not systematically follow any single model of cognition (103). Chaucer's terms for the visual figures created by the imagination vary, for example, and memory appears to be sometimes an independent faculty, sometimes a subdivision of imagination. The essential point is that the faculties serve Chaucer as topoi for discussing the nature of poetic creation. In the dream visions Chaucer integrates the three psychological faculties into the fabric of the narratives. The *Book of the Duchess* opens with an explicit discussion of imagination, and the extended dialogue between the dreamer and the black knight, which is the source of the poem's ostensible consolation, operates on the play of visual images and memory. Within the elaborate structure of the dream vision and through the conventionalized language of complaint and consolation, Chaucer dramatizes the mind's capacity to generate reproductive and constitutive images from reading and experience.

The *House of Fame* retains the focus on imagination and memory in its celebrated Proem on the status of dreams and in the narrator's description of the temple of Venus in Book I. Both passages address the truth value of images for cognition and representation. Book II explains the nature of language, which is the source of imagination in the system Chaucer has been setting out, and gives a particular emphasis to the fact that linguistic signs are constructed arbitrarily. In the final part of the poem Chaucer intensifies his speculation by juxtaposing the arbitrary and generative power of language and imagination to the functions of memory. He turns notably to the device of artificial memory as a means for organizing a continued reading of literary texts, which are sources for an experience of the world. But it is, as he reminds himself, an attenuated experience, for the stability of meaning that he finds in the *auctores* who act as the pillars of "Fames halle" (1357) stands against the frantic transformation of images and language elsewhere in the poem.

Chaucer uses imagination and memory, then, as topoi for aesthetic speculation. The two categories provide a critical language which allows him to reflect on the nature of poetry and to write his reflection into the poems as part of their narrative action. It is not that Chaucer programmatically reproduces these categories, nor does he shape the poems merely as allegories of imagination and memory. Rather, the poems use the functions of these two internal senses to formulate a series of questions about the truth conditions of the writer's craft. How do images and linguistic signs refer to things? Does language necessarily distort representation? Does the written word endure, or does poetry need rewriting to withstand oblivion? Given the arbitrary nature of signs and their interweaving of truth and falsehood, how can authority function to enforce distinctions and secure the possibility of knowledge over and against rumor and opinion? The epistemological problems for the philosophers are taken over as the aesthetic problems of the poet.

In articulating these questions Chaucer makes a further and still more problematic use of the traditional faculties, one that offers a means for understanding the concerns that lie at the center of his poetics. He suggests that poetry assimilates in a strong sense to the operations of the mind. Consequently, poetry is not an analogue or product of perception but an essential element. Within the subjective framework of the dream vision this formulation is thoroughly self-consistent, of course, for imagination and memory are the axis along which the poet-dreamer moves: the narrative line of the dream vision is a sequence of images, and the poet describes them from retrospect, thereby distancing and reshaping his visionary experience. As a general proposition, however, the association of poetry with cognition is necessarily limited, since it implies that the poet can know nothing outside the circularity of his own perception.

This line of reasoning obviously leads to an impasse, shown pragmatically by Chaucer's abandoning the *House of Fame* at precisely the point where a man of authority appears in the House of Rumor. At the end of this poem Chaucer clearly had to decide between two alternatives for handling the story: either to deconstruct authority into the arbitrary play of signs or to expound a position in which authority remains intact despite the alloy of truth and falsehood in language. (With the second alternative he would have to show, too, how such authority can escape ironically reproducing the arbitrary meanings of language, in short, how authority can be either transcendent or immanent with respect to language.) Chaucer did not—evidently could not—make this artistic and philosophical decision, but the problem remains and in various ways continued to inform his speculations about the nature of poetry.

At issue in the first two poems, then, is the epistemic status of poetic representation. The faculties of imagination and memory give a formal account of the ways in which poetry creates imaginative structures, such as the dreams he recounts. Like the imagination, poetry reproduces images from experience or creates them by themselves; like memory, it invokes the past and often draws on artificial constructions to order its parts and elements. But neither faculty offers a substantive account of poetic representation. Imagination and memory may help to describe how poetry operates, but they do not define what it is about. Chaucer's aesthetic speculation in the first two poems works to the limit of the conceptual topoi; it is a thoughtful and sophisticated examination of the continuities between poetry and thought. Nonetheless, it reaches a dead end.

In psychological and philosophical terms, the problem posed at the end of the *House of Fame* is the problem of the intellect. How does the mind abstract intelligibles from substances and the accidents of substance, the universal from the particulars of imagination? In poetic terms, how is poetry about the world and truth and not just about signs and the arbitrary images that the mind creates? If the question has the sound of modernity to it, it also has a venerable history. The tradition goes back as far as Plato's *Timaeus* (76e), but the most influential discussion is in the third book of Aristotle's *De anima,* which attempts to distinguish the ways in which the mind comes to grasp the essential form of things and thereby passes from opinion to knowledge. Arabic, Jewish, and Christian thinkers debated Aristotle's formulation of the issue extensively in the Middle Ages, and philosophers in Chaucer's day argued whether an intelligible species, a universal class of essences and forms, existed between words and things. Chaucer writes this general problem into the very beginning of the *Parliament of Fowls,* though as before the psychological category serves him as a topos for aesthetic speculation. Building on the characterization he has established of himself in the first two poems as a bookish servant of lovers, he describes his reading as a search "a certeyn thing to lerne" (20). He wants to find, in other words, something beyond the immediate and specific experience of the works, much as he wants to reach beyond the subjectivity of dreaming. The search that he dramatizes in the poem is concerned with abstracting a moral and philosophical meaning from images, reading, and sensation.

The path of this search leads through Cicero, Boccaccio, and Alan of Lille. Chaucer presents all three writers as authorities who investigate the nature of love, and by working through their positions he arrives at a sense of the meaning of the subject matter which has been at the focus of his own works. His resolution is, to be sure, not a precept about the nature of love but a heightened understanding of its implications for the individual and society. The poem ends with a debate and dispersal that recall but at the same time correct the final phantasmagoric scene of the *House of Fame.* The formel eagle does not choose her mate, but the other birds find theirs; and so the poem ends not in silence but song, a roundel addressed to Saint Valentine but sung to honor and please Dame Nature. The poem returns, in other words, to the particulars that constitute practical deliberation and lived experience.

If Chaucer works toward discovering something like the intelligible species of love, he finds in the meantime that his own vocation as a poet is linked fundamentally to what he seeks and writes about. The eagle in the *House of Fame* had described him as one who has served Venus and Cupid "withoute guerdon ever yit" (619), a distant observer whose service only magnifies his distance from love. But the dreamer in the *Parliament of Fowls* comes to understand that his writing participates in what he describes. The "certeyn thing" that the poet thinks he lacks at the beginning is part of what he has been producing all along, for the process of writing is an aspect of the generative power of love and so must be situated within it.

The Aesthetics of Medieval Lyric and Narrative

In tracing Chaucer's speculations through the topoi of imagination, memory, and intellect, I want to insist that he is developing a poetics that applies particularly to narrative. J. A. Burrow has pointed out that "Ricardian" poetry is mostly narrative (*Ricardian* 47). One may dispute Burrow's label for the period, but his point stands. In the three retrospectives that Chaucer incorporates in his work, it is clear that he regards himself predominantly as a narrative poet. Alceste divides his work into four groups in the Prologue to the *Legend of Good Women.* Cupid rebukes the poet for his "translacioun" of the *Roman de la rose* and *Troilus and Criseyde,* but Alceste points to his four narratives in praise of love, "many an ympne for your [Cupid's] halydayes" (F 422), then "other holynesse" (that is, *Boece,* the life of Saint Cecilia, which becomes the Second Nun's Tale, and Origen's homily on Mary Magdalene), and finally "many a lay and many a thing" (F 430).

Later, when the Man of Law speaks in the *Canterbury Tales* of Chaucer's crafty rhyming (II.46–89), he has in mind the treatment of Ovidian stories, and he refers directly to the Ceyx-Alcyone tale from the *Book of the Duchess* and to the stories in the *Legend of Good Women;* he also goes on to contrast Chaucer's narrative themes with John Gower's stories of Canacee and Appollonius of Tyre in the *Confessio Amantis.* Chaucer's Retraction at the end of the *Canterbury Tales,* the third of these retrospective passages, recalls the categories in Alceste's list, but with a different spiritual emphasis. The "books" he names as "translacions and enditynges of worldly vanitees" (x.1085) are all narratives. They stand in contrast to the translation of Boethius and "othere bookes of legendes of seintes, and omelies, and moralitee, and devocioun" (x.1088); everything he lists is narrative and discursive writing. The lyric element of his work is mentioned, as before, only by genre: "many a song and many a leccherous lay" (x.1087). The overwhelming sense of these lists, compiled at the middle and end of his career, is that Chaucer defines himself as a narrative poet. Lyric poetry is a consistent feature of his writing—indeed it probably figured large in his courtly production and it has, as we shall see later, an important influence on the creation of a narrative persona—but when Chaucer seeks to describe his work he does so by reference to narrative.

Modern critics have often discussed Chaucer's early poetry along the lines of a narrative model. Robert O. Payne identifies the structure of the visions as Chaucer's first structural model (*Remembrance* 112–45). Burrow says Chaucer and his contemporaries write poems with carefully articulated divisions, circular structures, varied levels of detail, and a tendency toward exemplification (*Ricardian* 47–92). Derek Brewer observes that Chaucer's poems develop out of encountering an obstacle or contradiction. "Chaucer tends in his earlier poems to embody a problem in narrative," he says, "with his own self as questioning and questing within the poem. That a narrative conveys a problem is a likely rule in Chaucer's poetic" (*Poetic* 20). The "individual narrative strategy" that Dieter Mehl finds in the *Book of the Duchess* (28)—Chaucer's "love of wide-ranging exposition and of seemingly aimless digression, and a deliberate delaying of the climax"—can be generalized to the other early narratives, as can the use of an abrupt ending. It might be added that Chaucer's most frequent practice is to work from an earlier text, and so a poetics of translation is implied in his art of narrative.

My emphasis on narrative as the object of Chaucer's critical reflection in his early poems follows from the divergent ways in which lyric and narrative poetry were regarded by aesthetic theorists of the Middle Ages. In the formulations of Boethius and St. Augustine, lyric functions within the domain of music. This means that lyric poetry is a rational form whose formal order reflects the ascending orders of harmony and mathematical proportion that were thought to underlie music. In Boethius's *De musica,* which represents the main development of classical and medieval theory, the relation of sounds (*musica instrumentalis*) is connected to "ethical" relations like body and soul (*musica humana*), and these are related in turn to the movement of the heavens (*musica mundana*). Poetic structure is a mirror of the providential order that contains these levels of relations.

In the first five books of his *De musica,* which is essentially a treatise on poetry, Augustine describes the means by which rational order governs poetic rhythm and meter. He shows how patterns of equal measurement and division reflect the mathematical structure of poetry, and he uses the metaphor of numerical ratios to connect the sensible domain of poetry to the powers of the soul, especially to the workings of cognition. In the sixth book he turns to the ethical considerations that bear on poetry. Augustine is especially concerned about the capacity of a rational, mathematically based form to produce images that threaten to become objects of appetite and that have an indeterminate relation to reality. The reproductive and constitutive images produced by poetry exist, he says, "at the very entrance of error" (*De musica* 356).

The musical aesthetic of lyric remained a powerful model in poetic theory throughout the Middle Ages. Boethius's formulations are repeated in later authorities like Guido of Arezzo and Hugh of St. Victor, and the speculative theory regularly introduced—and so justified—the practical teachings expounded in handbooks of music. In Chaucer's day the *ars nova* began to divide the speculative and practical domains of music. John Stevens points out, however, that for a poet-composer like Guillaume de Machaut the rhetoricity of music means meter and rhyme rather than figures of speech. Even Eustache Deschamps's much-discussed distinction between artificial and natural music involves not a wholesale abandonment of the numerical basis of lyric but rather an insistence on the "sweetness" (*douceur,* 'harmoniousness') inherent in the spoken line that employs fixed forms ("Music" 120). It is this mathematized view of poetry to which Chaucer refers in the Nun's Priest's Tale when the fox flatters Chauntecleer by saying, "ye han in musyk moore feelynge / Than hadde Boece, or any that kan synge" (vii.3293–94).

Lyric poetry, as conceived in medieval aesthetics, envisions harmony and proportion as the basis of artistic composition. The aim of lyric is not to create imaginary worlds or self-consistent fictions but to express an antecedent and objective formal order that extends from the sensory experience of words and sounds to the metaphysics that governs creation. Narrative poetry by contrast is concerned precisely with representation, and its conceptual framework is established in classical rhetorical categories. Isocrates and Aristotle associate narrative chiefly with judicial rhetoric: a brief, clear, and plausible description of events. The most important formulation for the Middle Ages comes from nearly identical passages in Cicero's *De inventione* and the pseudo-Ciceronian *Rhetorica ad Herennium,* the so-called First and Second Rhetorics. These works preserve Aristotle's focus on forensic rhetoric as the primary mode for narrative, but they make a distinction that subtly redefines and expands the scope of narrative discourse. Cicero (1.19.27) defines narrative as "rerum gestarum aut ut gestarum expositio"—an exposition of events that have occurred or are supposed to have occurred. The central ambiguity resides in the phrase *ut gestarum.* In the context of law courts, it carries the force of allegation ("things that are supposed to have occurred"), but it combines fact and hypothesis when applied, as it was, to a general theory of narrative discourse. Narrative becomes an account of events or of things that could have happened.

The rhetorical categories used to define medieval narrative thus present history and fiction, fact and probability as alternatives to one another. In the fourth century Victorinus noted this structural equivalence in his commentary on Cicero, and he tried to reassert Cicero's separation of legal and historical events from descriptions of the imaginary and hypothetical. Priscian, Cassiodorus, and Alcuin likewise attempted to distinguish *res gesta* from *ut gestarum,* the real from the fictitious or hypothetical. All these later authorities were constrained, however, by the distinctions expounded in the *De inventione.* Cicero had divided the judicial *narratio* from literary narratives; then subdivided literary narratives into accounts based on character and plot; and further divided narratives based on plot into fable (an invented story), history (actual events remote in time), and argument (fictitious though probable events). The problem with this systematizing is that, although the objects of representation can be distinguished, the mode of representation is the same. Narrative discourse itself cannot reproduce the differences among fable, history, and argument. Consequently, by the high and late Middle Ages, writers like John of Garland describe narrative as a form in which the real and the imaginary share the same properties.[1]

Chaucer's poetry develops against and within the question of narrative that medieval literary theory poses. As he sets out the possible worlds of his fiction, Chaucer incorporates the means to assess their claims of representation. He offers within the works a thoughtful and sustained reflection on the place of narrative fiction and on its capacity to represent experience. I am not arguing, however, that the poems are really about poetry, that their concern is simply or exclusively metacritical. My thesis is that critical reflection is embedded in literary representation. Furthermore, the power and seriousness of that reflection prepare for what critics like Glending Olson ("Making") and Winthrop Wetherbee (*Poets*) take as the decisive transition in Chaucer's career. Chaucer shifts from poetic "making" (the technical composition of verse, especially in a courtly context) to poetry (the full realization of the moral dimension of linguistic art). But it is his awareness in the early narratives of what is at stake in the poet's office that sets the conditions for creating works that can hold an equal footing with the *auctores* of the past and the few contemporary writers (Dante, Boccaccio, and Petrarch) who dared vie with them.

The chapters that follow offer a close reading of the texts and their sources which will show that Chaucer not only established a practice of sophisticated narrative poetry but also provided a way of imagining and talking about it. The first chapter describes the techniques of Chaucer's theorizing and his use of medieval literary theory and translation. The next chapter focuses on the creation of the narrator, tracing the figure from continental sources and showing the emergence of the persona with a distinctive poetic voice in Chaucer's courtly lyrics of complaint. The second half of the book concentrates on the narrative dream visions. Three chapters treat the *Book of the Duchess, House of Fame,* and *Parliament of Fowls* as works of representation and reflection, and they map the development of a poetics within the categories of imagination, memory, and intellect. In the final chapter I shall indicate how the aesthetic issues that emerge in the early narrative poems affect our understanding of the later works, the masterpieces on which Chaucer's reputation justly rests.

The Practice of Theory

Chaucer was by no means the first sophisticated or self-conscious poet to write in English, but he was the first to present himself consistently as such to his audience and readers. By dramatizing his poetic office and making that dramatization an essential part of his work, he inevitably raises questions about the aesthetic conceptions underlying his art. Although we have from Chaucer no strictly discursive statements about his poetics, the poetry speaks continually to the critical questions this self-presentation evokes. These are always embedded, however, in the contexts of narrative action and characterization.

Here the contrast with Dante is instructive: there is no formal treatise of vernacular poetics like the *De vulgari eloquentia;* no analyses of specific poems, as in the *Convivio* and *Vita Nuova;* and nothing comparable to the conceptual exposition of the *Commedia* given in Dante's "Letter to Can Grande della Scala." The closest point of comparison is the extended treatment of reading, aesthetic creation, and artistic succession in *Purgatorio* 21–26. It is not until Sidney's *Apologie for Poetrie* (1580) that a major English poet will undertake a direct commentary on the theory and practice of his craft. And yet the conscious artistry and literary allusions of Chaucer's poetry make it apparent that he thought deeply and abstractly about his art, that he adapted the conceptual models of medieval culture to examine the assumptions and possibilities of poetic creation, and that formal traditions of aesthetic speculation figure large in his conception of what poetry is and is about. Although Chaucer wrote no discursive account of literary theory, he has left an extensive practice of aesthetic reflection.

This practice is a constant feature of Chaucer's writing, and, as Joerg Fichte concludes in a recent review of modern approaches to Chaucer's poetry, "we have to use the clues implicitly contained in Chaucer's poetry" to understand his poetics (18). In some essential way for Chaucer, thinking about poetry is inseparable from writing poetry; reflection is inscribed in creation. In his early narrative poems Chaucer's practice of theorizing takes two important forms: reference to his own works and the use of poetic emblems. I want in this chapter to describe Chaucer's autocitation and his reliance on emblems in the dream visions. The extent of his intertextual and self-reflexive references will demonstrate that the dream visions are a body of closely linked works that both represent narrative action and offer a reflection on the nature of poetry. Then I want to set this practice in a broader literary context showing the relation of Chaucer's aesthetic reflections to medieval poetic theory and theories of translation.

Chaucer's Autocitation

Chaucer's narrative poetry begins with a conscious intertextual citation. The opening lines of the *Book of the Duchess* quote the beginning of Jehan de Froissart's *Paradys d'Amours,* and throughout his work Chaucer refers to classical and vernacular writers. At the same time Chaucer alludes to his own writing through verbal repetitions, shared motifs, and common themes. His allusions and echoes suggest the unity of his artistic vision and the coherence of the poetic assumptions behind his works. The dream visions in particular set out a network of intertextual references that offer a way of understanding the artistic project that the early narratives represent and of tracing the development of Chaucer's concerns in later works.

In the *Book of the Duchess,* where Chaucer is clearly writing within a courtly context, his poem naturally evokes the kind of lyric that courtier-poets composed within a literature of polite entertainment. Though Chaucer begins the *Duchess* by signaling his debt to Froissart, he adds to Froissart's motif of insomnia his own remark that "agaynes kynde / Hyt were to lyven in thys wyse" (BD 16–17). The same motif, with the distinguishing reference to natural law (*kynde*), appears in the first lines of the early experimental poem "A Complaint to His Lady," which is generally associated with the conventions of contemporary French lyricism.

> The longe nightes, whan every creature
> Shulde have hir rest in somwhat as by kynde,

Or elles ne may hir lif nat longe endure,
Hit falleth most into my woful mynde
How I so fer have broght myself behynde
That, sauf the deeth, ther may nothyng me lisse,
So desespaired I am from alle blisse.

(1–7)

Chaucer will return to this motif and phrasing in Anelida's complaint in *Anelida and Arcite* (written between 1378 and 1382), yet the resemblances between "Lady" and the *Book of the Duchess* are telling on several points. The speakers in these two poems begin by focusing on their inner lives; each is obsessed with the mental world of "thoght," which stands as a term for poetic imagination. In "Lady" the work of imagination is consuming: "This same thoght me lasteth til the morwe / And from the morwe forth til hit be eve" (8–9). In the *Book of the Duchess,* the narrator is consumed by "so many an ydel thoght / Purely for defaute of slep" (4–5) that his other powers of discrimination fail. Anelida, by contrast, is kept awake by the image of a repentant Arcite which she projects on her own and by the tears "this wonder sight" (333) elicits from her.

The "Complaint of Venus," adapted in the mid-1380s from three ballades by the French poet Oton de Grandson, elaborates on the predicament of the narrator in the *Book of the Duchess* while substituting a female voice for the conventional male speaker of the lyric complaint. Venus's description of the allegorical figure Jelosie serves to explain the effect on sensation produced by the narrator's "sorwful ymaginacioun" (14) in the *Book of the Duchess.* Love, says Venus, often gives "withouten ordynaunce, / As sorwe ynogh and litil of plesaunce, / Al the revers of any glad felyng" (38–40). The *Duchess's* narrator, in lines which again have no counterpart in Froissart's *Paradys,* complains, "Al is ylyche good to me— / Joye or sorowe, wherso hyt be— / For I have felynge in nothyng" (9–11). In addition Venus's account of how one behaves under the influence of Love's "nobil thing" (26) resonates with the man in black's highly figurative account in the *Duchess* of what he experiences when "fals Fortune hath pleyd a game / Atte ches with me" (BD 618–19).

As wake abedde and fasten at the table,
Wepinge to laughe and singe in compleynyng,
And doun to caste visage and lokyng,
Often to chaunge hewe and contenaunce, . . .

("The Complaint of Venus" 27–30)

The same vocabulary and the same figures of antithesis express, in the one case, the lover's infatuation and, in the other, the knight's loss of his lady to death.

In the ballade "Womanly Noblesse," which may date from the mid-1370s, we can find enumerated the qualities that the man in black ascribes to White, who is the locus of ethical values in the *Book of the Duchess*. The "stidefast governaunce" (2, 32) and "trewe perséveraunce" (8) that the lyric speaker celebrates echo the knight's recollection of White's "stedefast perseveraunce / And esy, atempre governaunce" (1007–08), lines that Chaucer adds to the passages he borrows from Guillaume de Machaut. It is this notion of erotic "governaunce" that also describes Venus's beneficent effects on Mars in "The Complaint of Mars": "Who regneth now in blysse but Venus, / That hath thys worthy knyght in governaunce?" (43–44).

I mention these links between the lyrics and Chaucer's first narrative poem not merely to suggest sources. The chronology of Chaucer's lyrics is, if anything, probably more vexed than the dating of the narrative poems. Nevertheless, the lyrics reflect the literary conventions of the court environment for which, as Alceste says, Chaucer "useth thynges for to make" (LGW F 364), and we know he wrote lyrics throughout his career. The lyrics serve in many respects as a poetic commentary on the narratives. What is especially interesting about the citations of the *Duchess* that Chaucer makes in these poems is that they point to the central aesthetic issues of his narrative. In the *Duchess,* as in "Lady," the narrator initially defines the workings of imagination through the dialectic of thought and absent sensation. But his definition, which is repeated by the man in black's description of himself as a young lover, lacks an object and a direction. It is the social and moral virtue ascribed to White that confers, as the lyrics reiterate, an ethical dimension to the imaginative powers that love and poetry share.

I shall argue later that the *Book of the Duchess* is a work of poetic beginnings that consciously rewrites authors like Ovid, Froissart, and Machaut. In a number of ways the *House of Fame* and the *Parliament of Fowls,* like the lyrics, refer back to this inaugural poem. The glass temple of Venus in Book I of the *House of Fame,* which conserves the text and illustrations of Vergil's *Aeneid,* recalls the luxuriously decorated chamber in the *Book of the Duchess,* which is covered with the text and glosses of the *Roman de la rose* and the Troy Book. The narrator of the *Duchess* and Creusa in the *House of Fame* lose their way "at a turnynge of a wente" (HF 182; cf. BD 398), and the narrators of both poems awaken to their dreams. The desert which the narrator enters after leaving the temple of Venus is a counterpart to the barren, dark valley of the underworld that Juno's messenger visits in the *Book of the*

Duchess. Both poems make a point of explicitly discounting the reliability of biblical and classical authorities to interpret the narrator's dreams. "Thoght," "wonder," and "fantasy" stand at the core of perception in the two poems, and constitute both the poet's material and the language for understanding his craft. They are the terms that describe the operations of imagination and memory.

The *Parliament of Fowls* continues the pattern of intertextual references, citing the *Book of the Duchess* and the *House of Fame* by repeating their language and themes. The *Parliament* opens with an elegant transposition of the craft of poetry and the art of love: "The lyf so short, the craft so long to lerne" (PF 1). The conceit harkens back to the man in black's definition of himself: "I ches love to my firste craft" (BD 791). The lovesick narrator of the *Duchess* says to himself, "I have felynge in nothyng" (BD 11); in the *Parliament,* the power of love is overwhelming, and "my felynge," the narrator says, "Astonyeth with his wonderful werkynge" (PF 4–5).

In the *Book of the Duchess,* "ydel thoght" had rendered the narrator "a mased thyng, / Alway in poynt to falle a-doun" (BD 12–13); and in the *Parliament* the effect of love is so great, he says, that "whan I on hym thynke, / Nat wot I wel wher that I flete or synke" (PF 6–7). The narrator hears birds singing in the *Parliament's* love garden "with voys of aungel in here armonye," and he listens to the "ravyshyng swetnesse" of instrumental strings playing "in acord" (PF 191, 197–98). The general source for the description is Boccaccio's *Teseida* (7.51–53), but Chaucer's phrasing goes back to Boccaccio's own source in the *Roman de la rose,* which is also the source for the description of the chamber and garden in the *Book of the Duchess* where the "swetnesse" of the birds' song, "al of oon acord" (BD 305), makes the narrator think "hyt had be a thyng of heven,— / So mery a soun, so swete entewnes" (BD 308–9).[1]

The dreamer's painted chamber in the *Book of the Duchess* is "ful attempre ... / For nother to cold nor hoot yt nas" (BD 341–42). The *Parliament's* narrator finds the same environment in the paradisiacal garden: "Th'air of that place so attempre was / That nevere was grevaunce of hot ne cold" (PF 204–5). White, whom the lamenting knight in the *Book of the Duchess* describes as the social objectification of "mesure" (881), "resoun" (922), and "governaunce" (1286), is an adumbration of her maker, the goddess Nature in the *Parliament,* who embodies divine order and works through "mesure" (300), "governaunce" (387), and "ryghtful ordenaunce" (390).

A comparable network of citation and allusion links the *Parliament of Fowls* to the *House of Fame.* In a sense, the *Parliament* redeems the truncated ending of the *House of Fame* by introducing its own figure of authority, Scipio Africanus. Scipio, like the docent eagle, sees the poem's narrator as a bookish drudge who is untouched by love yet still deserving of some recompense to "quyte" him (HF 670, PF 112) for his "labour" (HF 666, PF 112). Writing is a cause for the eagle's comic diminution of "Geffrey" in the *House of Fame* (614–71), and it becomes the purpose of the dream vision in the *Parliament.* Scipio tells the narrator, "And if thow haddest connyng for t'endite, / I shal the shewe mater of to wryte" (167–68).

Venus' temple reappears in the *Parliament,* changed from the historiated text of Vergil's *Aeneid* in Book I of the *House of Fame* to Boccaccio's brass temple supported by "pilers greete of jasper longe" (PF 230), which recall the pillars of Fame's palace. The message about the disastrous conclusions of love remains the same as in the retelling of Dido's story. Inside the temple the narrator sees "peynted overal / Ful many a story, of which I touche shal / A fewe, as of Calyxte and Athalante" (PF 284–86). Here, too, are present the acoustical images of sound, no longer scattered capriciously as they had been by Fame but now driven purposively by Jelosye: "of sykes hoote as fyr / I herde a swogh that gan aboute renne, / Whiche sikes were engendered with desyr" (PF 246–48). The barrenness that lies outside Venus's temple in the *House of Fame* (482–91) lends the compelling motif of sterility to the warning carved above the gate to the love garden (PF 137–39). Chaucer had used the term "sond" to pun on the barrenness of the desert and the empty sounds of speech reduced to a physical property (HF 486); it is specifically added in the *Parliament* to Boccaccio's description of the "Pazienza palida" sitting with the allegorical figure of Peace at the entrance to the temple: "Dame Pacience syttynge there I fond, / With face pale, upon an hil of sond" (PF 242–43).

The narrator of the *Parliament* apostrophizes Venus in the role of Cytherea as a source of poetic inspiration. "So yif me myght to ryme, and endyte!" (119), he asks. Earlier, "Geffrey" had invoked Cipris's help "to endite and ryme" (520) at the beginning of Book II of the *House of Fame.* The celestial journey that the narrators of both poems undertake in imitation of "Daun Scipio" shows them "helle and erthe and paradys" (HF 918, PF 32–33: "hevene and helle / And erthe"). It also joins them in the common error of supposing that Cicero's mention of the "infernal regions" (1.11.5) refers to the divisions of a Christian cosmology. J. A. W. Bennett observes that the two poems vary considerably in tone: "Whereas the lesson of the *Somnium,* as Chaucer construes it in the *Parlement,* is that we should not in the world delight, the *House of Fame* is flooded with ecstatic pleasure in the visible universe" ("Second Thoughts" 136).

Whatever the differences in outlook, the poems share the same quandary about dreams. The Proem to the *House of Fame* shows the irrelevance of Macrobius's categories for deciding the causes of dreams, and the narrator of the *Parliament* admits at length that the reasons for his dreaming are still indeterminate: "Can I not seyn if that the cause were / For I hadde red of Affrican byforn" (PF 106–7).

It might be argued that the close verbal echoes merely reflect Chaucer's rich and allusive language, his characteristic diction and style of speech. Alternatively, his reliance on imaginative devices such as the dream vision or the love garden might entail certain lexical choices that are bound to recur in successive poems, much as the choice of certain rhetorical commonplaces determined the linguistic register of many medieval lyrics. Cogent arguments have been made, too, for seeing similarities in poetic structure, and these may have an influence on language. A. C. Spearing (89) notes that the *Parliament* and the *Book of the Duchess* each have a preliminary section describing a dream-place and then come to the real subject of the poem. He sees a larger resemblance between the *Parliament* and the *House of Fame* in their presenting a long introductory section with the narrator awake. All three poems are constructed so that each successive structural unit is longer than the one that precedes it.

If we study the patterns of citation and allusion, it becomes clear, however, that the poems are linked not simply by a common set of lexical choices dictated either by authorial style or literary conventions, nor again are they joined principally by resemblances in structure. Rather, the intertextual patterns reveal a sustained engagement with several key issues: the nature of love and art, the poet's relation to his work, the problematic grounds for his knowing and interpreting experience. These are Chaucer's principal poetic concerns, and they inform his narrative poems as poetic themes and sources of aesthetic theorizing.

Poetic Emblems

Poetic emblems are narrative elements of the text—often visual or iconic images—that function as parts of the story but present at the same time a self-reflexive statement about poetic art. Robert W. Hanning ("Poetic Emblems") has shown that emblems are important devices in medieval vernacular literature, where in the absence of a formalized poetics they provide a means for poets to comment on their art. I have discussed in the Introduction how Chaucer situates one such emblem at the very outset of his storytelling. That is the figure of the dreamer's chamber in which the narrative action of the *Book of the Duchess* begins; it is this figure which he evokes and then modifies with the icon of the desert of "sond" in the *House of Fame.* Later in the *House of Fame* Chaucer presents another emblem of poetic art. He places Fame's palace on a rock of ice. Names are chiseled in the ice, but some of them, warmed by the sun, have melted into illegibility. Here the image makes a dual statement. It expresses at one level the transience of fame; at another, it shows the impermanence of writing and by extension the fragility of art works as a source of knowledge and memory. The narrator observes in a remark that applies equally to the story and his own efforts to tell the story, "This were a feble fundament / To bilden on a place hye" (1132–33).

Poetic emblems operate as parts of the text, parts of its imaginative economy, and our understanding of them depends, as elsewhere, on interpretive reading. What they have to say abstractly about poetics grows out of concrete literary symbolism and poetic language. Architectural structures in particular lend themselves to symbolically representing the artifice of poetry. The insomniac narrator of the *Book of the Duchess* playfully promises the gods, Morpheus above all, everything appropriate to a chamber: "and al hys halles / I wol do peynte with pure gold" (258–59) and cover with matching tapestries. Immediately thereafter he awakens in the room which embodies the *Roman de la rose* and the Troy Book. In "The Complaint of Mars" the emblem reappears as the site of erotic consummation and the place where Phoebus violently intrudes to part Venus and Mars: "The chambre ther as ley this fresshe quene [Venus] / Depeynted was with white boles grete" (85–86). The image of Taurus, which depicts Jupiter's ravishing Europa, conveys the mingling of desire and violence that animates the poem. The *House of Fame* is organized around a succession of emblems—the glass temple, the chiseled rock, Fame's palace—which culminates in the labyrinthine House of Rumor. In the *Parliament,* the temple of Venus, imported from the *Teseida,* is an emblem that demonstrates the profound ambivalence of passionate love, and thus it stands as a representation of the conflicts that underlie Chaucer's office as a love poet.

One of the most versatile emblems of poetic art is the figure of Morpheus. In retelling the story of Ceyx and Alcyone, Chaucer uses him to thematize the problem of representation, and Morpheus serves as the transition to the poet's own dream. In the *House of Fame,* the first of the poem's three invocations addresses the god of sleep through a highly nuanced reference of Morpheus that again calls forth the powers of poetic representation: "Prey I that he wol me spede / My sweven for to telle aryght, / Yf every drem stonde in his myght" (78–80). Later in the poem the eagle reveals that words have the power to take the shape of their speakers (1068–83). Though it has parallels in Boethius, Dante, and Vincent of Beauvais, the eagle's revelation describes the same kind of scene as the one in which Morpheus appears before Alcyone in imitation of Ceyx.

Finally, the dream itself is the most powerful emblem for poetic creation. In classical antiquity it served Plato and Cicero as a structure for symbolic action and philosophical speculation. The Bible, too, offers a network of dreams and visions and draws attention to the problem of interpreting symbolic content. For the Middle Ages the most important authority—and the one whom Chaucer cites even before he reads him— is the fourth-century Latin writer Macrobius, whose Neoplatonic commentary on the dream of Scipio Africanus, which appeared at the end of Cicero's *De re publica,* set out the essential protocols for distinguishing categories of dreams.

Macrobius, drawing on the Greek writer Artemidorus, classifies five main types of dreams—enigmatic, prophetic, oracular, nightmare, and apparition—but the fundamental difference is between prophetic dreams (the first three) and those without significance (the last two). There are abiding contradictions in Macrobius's taxonomy, however, and medieval commentators on his commentary were sensitive to the difficulties of distinguishing types of dreams. The enigmatic dream, for instance, is "one that conceals with strange shapes and veils with ambiguity the true meaning of the information being offered, and requires an interpretation for its understanding" (Stahl 90). The definition succeeds, of course, in reproducing the difference that Macrobius intends to explain, and the subdivisions that he appends to it continue in a steady logical regression.

Despite these contradictions, Macrobius's categories remained highly influential. We shall see later that Guillaume de Lorris's adaptation of Macrobius at the beginning of the *Roman de la rose* is something like an originary text for Chaucer. In the high and late Middle Ages, attention focuses on the categories of dream that Macrobius dismisses as "not worth interpreting." Medieval Latin poets, the Neoplatonic theorists of the school of Chartres, Guillaume, Jean de Meun, and Chaucer employ these sorts of dreams as a way of talking about the status of poetry, the truth value of artistic representation, and the place of subjective experience as a form of knowledge. The cognitive model of the dream vision becomes a model of aesthetic perception.

Medieval Poetics

The evolution of Chaucer's poetics can be traced through the evidence of the poems, but it is embedded at the same time in a complex literary-historical context. A native tradition of narrative poetry preceded Chaucer and found an audience in the aristocracy and merchants outside court circles. Elements of that tradition remain visible in Chaucer's writing, as for example in the metrics and some of the diction of the early narrative poems and in the battle descriptions of the Knight's Tale (i.2601–16) and the *Legend of Good Women* (629–53); they are visible, too, in parodies like Sir Thopas and the Parson's protest, "I kan nat geeste 'rum, ram, ruf,' by lettre" (x.43). But the tradition itself was largely isolated from the main stream of medieval poetic theory and especially from the much-debated question of vernacular literature. The latter was an important element in theorizing about poetry and fiction from the twelfth century onwards.

The question, briefly stated, was whether the European vernaculars were adequate vehicles for serious poetry. Of course, the issue was decided almost as soon as the question could be formulated. Chrétien de Troyes and Marie de France established the cultural prestige of chivalric literature; earlier the *romans d'antiquité* had created a vernacular equivalent to classical epic. Dante's focus on lyric poetry in the *De vulgari eloquentia* extolls the achievement of writers in the "illustrious vernacular," and the *Roman de la rose* and the *Commedia* are beyond doubt the central literary texts of the high Middle Ages.

The debate continued throughout the fourteenth century, however, and some of its most notable disputants—Petrarch, for one—judged wrongly, believing that Latin would endure as the principal vehicle of literary composition. That Chaucer's early poems earned him a place within the continental vernacular tradition is clear from Eustache Deschamps's ballade in 1386 praising Chaucer as the "grant translateur." And Chaucer's engagement with Latin, French, and Italian writers throughout his career offers strong evidence of his commitment to defining a body of poetic work within the vernacular tradition. Elizabeth Salter observes: "It is as if the situation of the English poet had to be seen to be broadly comparable with that of the greatest European vernacular writers: a relationship between a chosen language and the Latin of tradition—which was enhancing rather than exact in its implications" (126).

The aesthetic reflections that emerge from within Chaucer's practice take shape, then, in the foreground of his own writing and the middle distance of European literary tradition. The substructure of these reflections is to be found in the *artes poeticae,* which were compiled by Latin theorists in the twelfth and thirteenth centuries from the teachings of ancient grammar and rhetoric. The poetics they formulated offered medieval writers the procedures to invent, order, and adorn a literary work in fitting style. The doctrine was centered on the three internal parts of classical rhetoric, relegating the two external parts (memorization and delivery) to second position.

Chaucer's allusions to the thirteenth-century rhetorician Geoffrey of Vinsauf in *Troilus and Criseyde* (1.1065–71) and the Nun's Priest's Tale (VII.3347–52) are evidence of his familiarity with the standard doctrines of composition. The ironies and dislocations of his allusions demonstrate, however, that Chaucer views established poetic doctrine as an unstable body of precepts open to change and new formations. His reference in the *Troilus* associates poetic invention with the project of seduction, and "Gaufred, deer maister soverayn" (VII.3347) is apostrophized in the Nun's Priest's Tale to witness his own exaggerated lament on King Richard's death and the poet's satiric employment of the devices of amplification that Geoffrey taught. Chaucer's acknowledgment of poetic theory thus points to a creative tension and revision rather than a simple assimilation of its doctrine.

The poetics to which Chaucer alludes in these passages is, as James J. Murphy (*Rhetoric*) remarks, highly prescriptive, and it generally reflected the aesthetic values of Latin high culture in the universities. The texts that transmitted the doctrines of composition answered the needs of specific audiences and the demands of pedagogical systems. No theorist before Dante wrote of poetics in general. Though they claim to be a general theory of discourse, the precepts embody a particular compositional slant, and they are constrained by the social contexts of the works.[2] Generalizing from the *artes,* Edmond Faral held that medieval poetics was largely given over to concerns with stylistic ornamentation. Though Faral's view has subsequently been modified by later scholars who object that he accorded a privileged place to style within a broader domain of aesthetic issues, the teachings of medieval poetics remained overwhelmingly technical rather than speculative.[3] Dorothy Everett ("Love Visions"), among others, has placed great emphasis on Chaucer's rhetorical dexterity and especially his use of technical devices such as *digressio, sententia,* repetition, and *contentio* (antithesis).

Although it fails to render a full account of artistic creation, medieval poetic theory nonetheless offered a vocabulary for defining the process of creation. Beyond showing which figures to use in composition, the doctrine described the means for setting out the imaginary architecture of a work. In particular, discussions of rhetorical invention offered techniques for discovering and selecting the conceptual order of the poet's materials, and it is within the domain of invention that poetic theory attains its fullest conceptual expression in the Middle Ages.

The procedures of invention depend on what Matthew of Vendôme in his *Ars versificatoria* (c. 1175) terms the "inner meaning" (*interior sententia*) and "the conceptual realization of the meaning" (*sententiae conceptio*) of a work. The most celebrated figure for this process is the architectural metaphor that Geoffrey of Vinsauf introduces at the beginning of the *Poetria nova* (43–48), which compares the poet to the builder of a house who first plans the work in his imagination and then executes it.

> Si quis habet fundare domum, non currit ad actum
> Impetuosa manus: intrinseca linea cordis
> Praemetitur opus, seriemque sub ordine certo
> Interior praescribit homo, totamque figurat
> Ante manus cordis quam corporis; et status ejus
> Est prius archetypus quam sensilis.

> If a man has a house to build, his impetuous hand does not rush into action. The measuring line of his mind first lays out the work, and he mentally outlines the successive steps in a definite order. The mind's hand shapes the entire house before the body's hand builds it. Its mode of being is archetypal before it is actual.[4]

Peter Dronke finds in this passage an "insistence on the organic nature of a work of art" ("Rhetoric" 327). A fourteenth-century commentary on the *Poetria nova* explains that this description of invention is what is meant by *poesis,* "the art of the poets" (Woods 16).

In addition to these general precepts, medieval literary theory envisioned two practical approaches to invention. Poets could find their sources, it was said, in materials that had already been versified (*materia exsecuta* or *pertractata*), or they could find new subject matter (*materia illibata* or *remota*). In setting out this distinction the theorists followed and amplified Horace's admonition, "Aut famam sequere aut sibi convenientia finge" (Either follow tradition or invent what is self-consistent, *Ars poetica* 119). Either choice involved the practice of topical invention, by which the poet would devise his work according to the commonplaces (topoi) that were connected with the materials. It was thus that the primary act of conceiving a work took place not only within the imagination but also within a closed discourse. The world of the poem is set out within the limits of the topoi, and these—as in the highly differentiated symbols for persons, places, and implements imaged by devices like the wheel of Vergil (Faral 86–89)—are associated with genre (epic, comedy, and pastoral).

When poets choose to use previous sources, as Chaucer does in most of his writing, the strictures are explicit. "Ne sequamur vestigia ver-borum," Geoffrey of Vinsauf exhorts in his *Documentum,* a school manual devoted to elaborating verse from existing materials: "let us not trace the footsteps of the words" (Faral 309). He goes on to counsel that writers, looking over the imaginative world of their source (*universitatem materiae speculantes*) want to speak where the earlier authors are silent and rearrange the order of the work: "ibi dicamus aliquid ubi dixerunt nihil, et ubi dixerunt aliquid, nos nihil; quod etiam prius, nos posterius, et e converso" (let us say something where they have said nothing, and where they have said something, let us say nothing; what they put first, let us put last, and vice versa, Faral 309–10). A process of creative elaboration and restructuring is thus already contained in the techniques of medieval poetic composition. In the Monk's Tale the retelling of Ugolino's tragic story, for example, suppresses the dream and cannibalism that Dante records in *Inferno* 33 and emphasizes the pathos of the situation. When we turn in subsequent chapters to a detailed examination of the dream visions, we will see that Chaucer plots the action of his narrative and signals his meaning by exploiting the possibilities of what remains implicit in his sources.

Later vernacular writers recognized that, in addition to an abstract plan of composition against which the fitness of topoi and figures of speech could be measured, the process of invention involved chance, the discovery of what is already virtual and immanent in perception though not yet articulated, the indeterminant and perhaps always elusive constituent of artistic creation. Much as Aristotle had to admit chance as a supplement to his theory of causality, a fourteenth-century poet schooled in the posthistory of the *artes* confronted chance within the compositional archetypes that were held to precede and enable his execution of a work. When he retells the tale of Ceyx and Alcyone early in the *Book of the Duchess,* for example, Chaucer finds in Alcyone's dilemma a complex analogy to his own situation and the distress of the man in black. His omission of the ending of Ovid's story shifts the accent to the emotions of pity and dread. The account of the *Aeneid* in the *House of Fame* dwells on Dido rather than on Vergil's epic themes. Similarly, Cicero's "Dream of Scipio" is given new emphasis in the summary presented in the *Parliament of Fowls.* In *Anelida and Arcite* Chaucer begins with an imitation of Boccaccio's epic style but finds that his subject is not military prowess but the "slye wey" (48) of Arcite, which he began writing about even before he realized it.

For Chaucer, as Donald Howard ("Idea" 42–43) points out, "The act of planning in his original becomes something much closer to a lucky accident, 'winning'—as we would say, 'getting' or 'catching'—something. And the thing caught is not the *archetypus* of his original but a 'purpose'—as we would say, an 'intention.'" The text that emerges has a double bond to this process: it is both an artifact of intention and a trace of the informing intelligence that "wins" its purpose. But Chaucer goes a step further, especially in the dream visions. By dramatizing his narrator he places a figure of this intelligence within the text. The poems stand as both the creations of a writer's imaginative process and the site of the "accidents" that attend his writing. They, more than any set of abstract principles, are the evidence of his theories and attitudes.

I have mentioned that Chaucer tends to work from *materia exsecuta,* materials that other poets have already used and that he gives a new configuration. Medieval poetic theory makes it clear that this kind of transformation depends on an understanding of the antecedent text. It follows, then, that Chaucer's poetic invention occurs in relation to entire texts and not as an isolated reworking of parts. Writers make their choices informed by the full scope of the original; they survey its conceptual order and set out a new disposition of its parts. The essential dialectic, as Geoffrey of Vinsauf explains it, is between speech and silence. Such a dialectic is possible, though, only to the extent that writers engage the source as a complete text. There remains, of course, a difference between the prescriptions of the *artes,* which are directed to exercises in composition, and the practice of an accomplished poet like Chaucer. But the habit of engaging the antecedent text rather than extracts is a consciously articulated principle of medieval poetics, and it is consistent with the practice of compositional modeling that Chaucer acknowledges in his poetry.

The protocols of invention described in the *artes* necessarily influenced Chaucer's view of poetic creation, and they ought to influence as well our historical understanding of the process underlying his poetry. The exhaustive source studies carried on since the nineteenth century have shown the wide range of Chaucer's reading and the diverse patterns in which he adapts other texts by allusion, citation, and reworking. Although few critics now debate whether Chaucer is imitative or innovative in these adaptations, the general assumption remains that the borrowings are limited and local, that Chaucer takes parts of other works which are distinctive and attractive and therefore offer him heightened possibilities of expression within his own poems.

For the dream visions the question of textual influence is deeply implicated in the practice and theory of poetic composition. B. A. Windeatt holds that Chaucer selectively and combinatively borrows parts of his sources, incorporating passages rather than whole texts or even the whole idea of a text (*Dream Poetry* ix). Windeatt sees the effects of such borrowing in Chaucer's coordinating new structures, and in this view he accepts Wolfgang Clemen's description of Chaucer's relation to literary tradition. Clemen writes of Chaucer, "He sets free much of what he borrows from the past by turning it to new uses. He disregards what had previously been the function of certain themes, and gives them a new connotation which often produces an ironic contrast between their former overtones and what they now imply and signify. With light-hearted dexterity he simply reverses the plus and minus signs in front of these traditionally conditioned themes, and fits them into a context which is the very opposite of their previous one" (3–4).

On this view, isolated borrowings and a pattern of aesthetic innovation can be accounted for simultaneously. However, Chaucer's adaptations cannot be both isolated borrowings and elements of a textual restructuring that takes its meaning at least in part from its divergence from the sources. The arguments are flatly at cross-purposes with each other. Windeatt's belief that meaning arises from deploying the sources in new settings, like Clemen's assertion that a "new connotation" arises from contrast with the original texts, indicates instead Chaucer's deep and thoroughgoing engagement with his sources. Like all great poets Chaucer makes informed and resonant use of other writers. Behind the selective borrowings and his reversals of themes implicitly stands a practice of critical reading, one that involves both antecedent texts and literary tradition.

We shall see in later discussion that the dream visions use earlier works not only as sources but also as symbols of meaning, which Chaucer contrasts and modifies in the course of his own narrative. Perhaps the most complex example of his critical reading occurs later in his career, in *Troilus and Criseyde*. Winthrop Wetherbee (*Poets*) contends that in *Troilus* Chaucer comes to the material of his courtly and pagan love story through the cultural reading of antiquity that was furnished by Dante and Dante's Statius. As Wetherbee explains, the radical extension of a tragic love story set in the pagan past requires the historical framework of an authoritative Christian poet before Chaucer in turn can transcend the attractions of the materials and see them for himself in their full dimensions. Like the works Chaucer reads for his earlier narrative poems, Boccaccio's *Filostrato* serves two facets of invention in *Troilus*—as a material source for Chaucer's poem and coevally as a text interpreted in the light of literary hermeneutics.

In its large dimensions the gesture of appropriating sources, as the theorists recommended, is not directed merely toward a collection of separate antecedent texts, each of them engaged independently as a source for composition, but rather toward literary tradition as a whole.

Chaucer's adaptation of his predecessors revives their work at the same time that it places his own writing within the context of serious writing. Much like Dante, whose installation in the *bella scuola* is recalled comically in the envoi to the book in *Troilus and Criseyde* ("kis the steppes where as thow seest pace / Virgile, Ovide, Omer, Lucan, and Stace," 5.1791–92), Chaucer wants to join the community of poets by placing his work among theirs—and theirs within his. He does so while claiming a status for his own vernacular writing that associates it with the other developed vernacular traditions. His ambitions, measured against the achievements of Dante and Petrarch, require both a distinguished body of work and a theory of poetry to define its nature.

"Grant Translateur"

The techniques of poetic invention that Chaucer follows in his early narrative are closely connected to the practice of translation. Although some critics argue for making a distinction between literary adaptation and translation, both activities exist on a spectrum defined by invention. Translation, like topical invention, uses strategies of embellishment, preservation, and intertextuality (Bruns). Windeatt, in his study of *Troilus,* finds that Chaucer uses at least three separate techniques of translation: rendering yet re-expressing the original, small additions of phrases and lines, and larger interpolated passages (*Troilus* 4). The effect is a transvaluation of Boccaccio's *Filostrato* that both conveys the sense of the original and registers the poet's distinctive response to the poem. Chaucer's earlier narratives employ the same techniques to a greater or lesser degree, and they operate within the rhetorical conventions that evolved from antiquity and the rise of Christian culture.

The governing strategy of medieval translation is given in Saint Jerome's dictum (*Epistula* 72.5.2) "non uerbum e uerbo, sed sensum exprimere e sensu" (interpret not word by word but sense by sense, 1:508). Jerome draws on Horace ("nec verbo verbum curabis reddere fidus / interpres," *Ars poetica* 133–34) and on the practice that Cicero describes in his approach to rendering Greek texts into Latin. Cicero intends to keep the same ideas and forms (or figures of thought) as in the originals, while observing the usage of his own language. "I did not hold it necessary to render word for word," he says, "but I preserved the general style and force of the language" (*De optimo genere oratorum* 5.14). Jerome's admonition is perhaps more a commonplace than a practical guide, and he makes an important exception by insisting on the need for literal translation in the case of Scripture.[5] For vernacular writers in the Middle Ages a crucial development is the assimilation of

the rhetorical functions of invention and interpretation within translation. Rita Copeland has proposed that, in addition to training the writer
in the resources of his own language (the pedagogical aim of Roman
literary education in Cicero and Quintilian), translation serves as a means
for discovering materials and establishing their meaning through a
literary hermeneutics.

In Chaucer's translations modern scholars have seen the practical
application of these principles. The A-fragment of the *Romaunt of the
Rose* and *Boece* remain close to the original texts from which Chaucer
worked, and Chaucer's literary achievement can be measured by his
success in appropriating the models. Caroline Eckhardt says, "The *Roman* has thus been transformed into an English near-equivalent that
still carries with it the prestige, sophistication, and courtliness associated
with its original, along with much (if we can hear it) of the actual sound
of the original words" (50). Tim William Machan believes that "writing
Boece was in part a way for Chaucer to examine language as language"
(127) and not just an exercise in refining his compositional skills. The
translation of the "lyf of Seynt Cecile" in the Second Nun's Tale offers
a clear case in which translation and invention have reciprocal functions.
The tale combines two sources, the *Legenda Aurea* of Jacobus de Voragine and a Latin life of the saint, and switches from one to the other
approximately midway in the story. The effect of manipulating the sources,
Sharon Reames observes, is to offer a more pessimistic vision of divine
power and man's free will than was portrayed in earlier versions. The
strategy of translation, like that of rhetorical invention, depends on an
interpretive reading of the sources.

Moreover, for Chaucer translation serves the aim of cultural appropriation and definition that it had earlier achieved for Roman writers.
Salter regards translation as a decisive gesture in the poetic project that
Chaucer's poetry represents: "Chaucer's very deliberate act of beginning
his poetic career by training his skill as a translator of French shows a
freshly awakened preoccupation with English as a fit vehicle for the
major works of European literature. It is impossible that Chaucer should
not have been familiar with the theory, and the practice, of the fourteenth-century Italians, such as Dante and Petrarch, on this question of
the use of the vernacular" (123).

The key text in this regard is undoubtedly the *Romaunt.* Chaucer's
translation of the *Rose* is the cause of Deschamps's extravagant praise
of Chaucer as the "grant translateur." For Deschamps translation means
both the rendering of the text and the cultural transference implied by
the text. It is *translatio* in the sense that Chrétien de Troyes (*Cligés* 24–
42) portrays the passing of chivalry from Greece to Rome and then to

France; the difference lies in the subject matter—love rather than war. Deschamps's praise is not for Chaucer's fidelity to the original or his refinements of his own diction and style. Deschamps sees Chaucer as the figure who has transplanted the *Rose* to English soil and made it flourish there. The major metaphor is insemination.

> Aigles treshaulz, qui par ta theorique
> Enlumines le regne d'Eneas,
> L'Isle aux Geans, ceuls de Bruth, et qu'i as
> Semé les fleurs et planté le rosier
> Aux ignorans de la langue pandras,
> Grant translateur, noble Geffroy Chaucier.

> Lofty eagle, who by thy science
> Dost illumine the kingdom of Aeneas,
> The isle of giants (those of Brutus), and who there hast
> Sown the flowers and planted the rose-tree;
> Thou wilt enlighten those ignorant (of French),
> O great translator, noble Geoffrey Chaucer.[6]

In succeeding stanzas Deschamps expands the metaphor so that Chaucer's translation becomes itself another version of the garden and then an authentic source to other writers. He says, with encomiastic exaggeration, "Et un vergier, où du plant demandas / De ceuls qui font pour eulx auctorisier, / A ja long temps que tu edifias" (And a garden, for which thou hast asked plants / From those who poetize to win them fame, / Now for a long time thou hast been constructing, 17–19). It is from this distant source rather than the original that Deschamps, the literary successor of Machaut and others inspired by the *Rose,* ostensibly takes his inspiration: "Requier avoir un buvraige autentique, / Dont la doys est du tout en ta baillie" (I ask to have an authentic draught, / For the spring is entirely in thy keeping, 22–23).

In a sense Deschamps's compliment to Chaucer's skill as an appropriator of literary tradition veils a claim to reassert the power of the original and the national tradition that created it in the first place. Chaucer may have carried off the rosebush and recreated the garden in Brutus's Albion, but lineage and priority, hence the literary authority of the original, are not seriously in doubt. For Chaucer the *Rose* is as close as anything to an originary text. By that I mean it is the mythological ground where he first discovers the condition of authorship already determined and the materials of invention ready for deployment. In a later chapter we will see how the *Book of the Duchess* functions as a work of conscious poetic beginnings for Chaucer's narrative art, a declaration of self-inauguration that breaks from its sources even while using them. By contrast, the *Rose* remains a source that cannot be abandoned by the poet's self-conscious historical breaks. It is the text he shares with Machaut and Froissart, even as he vies with them to establish the place of his own work. More important, he finds in the *Rose*—and shows in his translation of it—the aesthetic issues that inform his own early narrative poetry.

The essential issue for Chaucer concerns the truth value of poetry, the capacity of a fictional work to represent reality. This issue is the opening topic of the *Rose,* and Guillaume de Lorris remarks at some length on the reliability of dreams. Dreams are a figure for all poetic fictions, and the case Guillaume makes for them establishes by analogy the rationale for poetic representation. Guillaume finds his "garant" ("warraunt" in the *Romaunt*) in Macrobius but gives a notably incomplete account of Macrobius's doctrine, saying that he "halt nat dremes false ne lees" (*Romaunt* 8) when he sharply distinguished prophetic from unprophetic dreams. In fact Macrobius's discussion of the categories of dreams begins, "The last two, the nightmare and the apparition, are not worth interpreting since they have no prophetic significance" (Stahl 88).

In some measure Guillaume's misreading is a response to the problem of Macrobius's categories. Macrobius, as we have seen, differentiates dreams according to their truth value by separating those which prove prophetic from those that do not. The difficulty is that their truth can be established only afterwards, and so the categories and subdivisions he expounds are circular. This is the problem that Chaucer brilliantly anatomizes in the Proem to the *House of Fame* and makes the source of irony in the Nun's Priest's Tale. Guillaume rewrites the circularity of Macrobius's taxonomy into a flawed argument. He concedes that many people dismiss dreams as mere fables and lies but contends that some dreams can be dreamed which are not lies because they afterwards appear to be true.

> Aucunes genz dient qu'en songes
> n'a se fables non et mençonges;
> mes l'en puet tex songes songier
> qui ne sont mie mençongier,
> ainz sont aprés bien aparant. . . .
>
> Many men sayn that in sweveninges
> Ther nys but fables and lesynges;
> But men may some sweven[es] sen
> Whiche hardely that false ne ben,

> But afterward ben apparaunt.
>   (*Romaunt* 1–5)

Guillaume therefore asserts, against those who doubt dreams, that he is confident of the significance of dreams as signs of the good and evil that will befall men: "quar endroit moi ai ge fiance / que songes est senefiance / des biens as genz e des anuiz" (15–17). Thus he concludes that most people dream many things symbolically (*covertement*) which they later see openly (*apertement*): "que li plusor songent de nuiz / maintes choses covertement / que l'en voit puis apertement" (18–20).

Guillaume's argument is invalid, and the final conclusion he reaches is false. For an argument to be valid the truth of the premises must force the truth of the conclusion. What Guillaume does is to construct two related subarguments of which the first employs valid reasoning but the second does not; he thus gives the appearance of deductive rigor without being able to sustain it. The first subargument properly employs what medieval logicians called contradictories: the premise "some dreams are not false" forces the conclusion that it is not the case that all dreams are false. In the second subargument he tries, however, to relate opposing propositions that have no necessary logical relation to each other. The premise "some dreams are not false" does not force the truth of the conclusion "all dreams are not false," which is to say, "no dream is false." Quite apart from its logical structure, Guillaume's argument fails as a piece of informal reasoning. As in Macrobius the truth of the conclusion falters because there is no reliable way to distinguish false from prophetic dreaming.

Chaucer's translation makes it clear that he recognized precisely where Guillaume's argument turns from valid to invalid reasoning. Guillaume attempts to move from the acceptably true statement that not all dreams can be reckoned false to the general claim that (all) dreams are predictive of what will happen: "songes est senefiance / des biens as genz e des anuiz" (16–17). Chaucer translates the passage, however, so as to suggest that he sees the impossibility of making universal assertions from particular and merely probable statements. Following the line of Guillaume's argument and anticipating its next step, which is to conclude that most people have some significant dreams, Chaucer corrects the reasoning to emphasize the experience of many people ("many wightes") but not all people ("as genz").[7]

> For this trowe I, and say for me,
> That dremes signifiaunce be
> Of good and harm to *many* wightes
> That dremen in her slep a-nyghtes

Ful many thynges covertly
That fallen after al openly.
      (15–20; emphasis added)

Chaucer's translation is faithful to the diction and style of the *Rose,* but we can see that it also involves a critical reading of the text, which recognizes its inconsistencies. Translation serves a hermeneutic function and at the same time serves the purpose of poetic invention. Chaucer discovers in the logical weakness of Guillaume's argument an imaginative space for situating poetic fiction. Guillaume's confusion of the particular and the universal, the many and the all, defines the territory of the counterfactual and hypothetical. Chaucer in effect rejects the global theorizing Guillaume wants to impose on psychological and aesthetic processes. His translation of Guillaume's defense of visionary experience emphasizes what is not universal about dreaming, what remains idiosyncratic, though still accessible to understanding.

In this respect the *Romaunt* lays the aesthetic groundwork of the early narrative poetry. All the dream visions will reject the kind of determinate meaning that Guillaume wants to claim as a justification for his poem. Instead, they locate their materials and their poetic discourse in "wonder thinges" that fall outside systematic meanings. This choice entails other kinds of aesthetic problems, for the decisive tension in the early narrative poetry is between the particular and the general, but it is a choice that Chaucer makes clearly and consistently.

Chaucer's translation of the *Rose* discovers a second aesthetic issue in the theme of desire and in the relation of desire to poetry. The first narrative told within the framework of the narrator's dream is the story of Narcissus. Guillaume's handling of the story links the erotic and the aesthetic. His dreamer in fact reenacts the story he has recited, for he lets himself down beside the well to gaze at the water and the shimmering gravel. In the dreamer's story Narcissus is drawn to the well by thirst after a day of hunting; these two facets of appetite are ironically combined to represent self-infatuation as a search for an inner desire that cannot be satisfied. For the dreamer, who thinks to escape "scatheles, full sykerly" (*Romaunt* 1550), desire has to do specifically with representation. The "merveilous cristall" (1579) is a "mirrour perilous" (1601) that depicts the garden in full and accurate detail.

For ther is noon so litil thyng
So hid, ne closid with shittyng,
That it ne is sene, as though it were
Peyntid in the cristall there.
      (1597–1600)

The crystal is an emblem of the poem and of the art that conceives the poem, and it has the same power of representation that Guillaume ascribes to dreams. Just as dreams represent "ful many thynges covertly / That fallen after al openly" (19–20), the crystal creates images with unambiguous meaning.

> Ryght as a myrrour openly
> Shewith all thing that stondith therby,
> As well the colour as the figure,
> Withouten ony coverture, . . .
>
> (1585–88)

Chaucer signals that he recognizes Guillaume's references when he embellishes the couplet "et as cristaus, qui me mostroient / mil choses qui entor estoient" (1603–4) by translating it with the additional allusion to seeing openly: "the cristall in the welle / That shewide me full openly / A thousand thinges faste by" (1636–38).

The *Rose* elaborates the parallels between desire and representation in order to suggest that the erotic is constituted through the aesthetic. In the mirror provided by the well and the crystals, the dreamer sees a rosebush surrounded by a hedge, and he is seized by the "lust and envie" to look more closely and to pull a bud from it. The "rage" that overtakes him is not caused, however, by the object of desire but by the act of figuration; he sees the rosebush depicted in the mirror, and it is then that desire appears. In addition, the object of desire is itself remarkably indeterminate. Though he praises the particular rosebud above the others, the essential gesture is arbitrary: "Among the knoppes I ches oon / So fair that of the remenaunt noon / Ne preise I half so well as it" (1691–93). The rosebud cannot be differentiated by its intrinsic qualities, only by the dreamer's response to it; its value is a function of the dreamer's projection.

The scene thus contains a number of themes that will emerge in Chaucer's own writings—the arbitrary and solipsistic nature of desire, the role of artistic representation in constructing erotic attachments. The story of Narcissus, perhaps like the tale of Ceyx and Alcyone, stands as an example of Chaucer's first narrative. Its importance as a work of translation lies both in the technical skill it allowed Chaucer to develop and in the materials it helped him invent.

Chaucer's speculations about his art are written into his poems. His early narratives are self-conscious literary texts that are also conscious of one another as works that explore the nature of poetry. Within the poems Chaucer's practice of theory turns around autocitation and poetic emblems. But these devices are not isolated gestures of artistic definition.

Rather, they draw on the resources of poetic invention and translation to locate the matter and manner of writing. Though his contemporaries and Renaissance successors admired Chaucer for his style, his larger contribution lay in establishing the claims of English vernacular poetry to be a self-conscious art with a capacity for critical reflection. That achievement grows out of his creative dialogue with his own works and with his literary predecessors.

The Narrator in
Chaucer's Early Poems

No doubt one of Chaucer's great poetic achievements is the creation of his own narrative persona. The narrator, as Morton W. Bloomfield has remarked, is "the ubiquitous figure in Chaucer's poetry" ("Gloomy Chaucer" 61), continuous if not identical throughout all the works. Bookish, uncertain, flawed in his understanding yet responsive to the human situations he discovers, Chaucer's narrator stands at the beginning of every poem and thereby sets the conditions by which we learn the poet's stories. He is at once an imaginative source and a practical means of Chaucer's narrative art.

This chapter will discuss how the narrator operates within the textual economy of the early narrative poems. I want to propose that the invention of the narrator is a necessary condition of Chaucer's early narrative, for in subtle yet decisive ways it helps to constitute Chaucer's poetry. The narrative persona is not simply a disguise the poet assumes inside his fiction but a figure he must invent before the fiction can proceed. The narrator is the speculative agent, the self-reflexive critic, occasionally the fall guy, who thematizes the poet's efforts to establish the terms of his narrative art. He enacts the drama of imagination and memory that informs the earliest two poems and carries out the search for the intelligible species of love that marks the first important consolidation of Chaucer's poetics.

By foregrounding the figure of the poet, the narrator makes it possible to devise a comparatively decentered narrative. By that I mean that the poetry consists in self-conscious performance as well as a representation of action and events. Generally speaking, narrative is organized in mimetic and rhetorical dimensions, or along the axes of representation and presentation. As we saw in the last chapter, by means of invention and translation Chaucer discovers the poetic materials that his narratives portray through verbal imitation. His art as well lays a great stress on the rhetorical dimension; it is a poetry that describes conditions as much as events, and those conditions are defined in large part through the narrator, who makes the conveying of the story part of literary meaning. It is the narrative persona that serves, too, as the mediator between the imaginative world of the poem and its courtly audience, an audience that in certain respects Chaucer has to invent (Reiss 393).

To understand the complexity and significance of Chaucer's persona in the early poems we need to look first at the variety of functions which he serves. We shall turn then to the sources for representing personae in medieval literary theory and the practice of continental vernacular writers. Finally, we shall examine the ways in which the persona Chaucer projects in the courtly lyrics delineates his self-presentation in the dream visions and reflects the context of performance which the lyrics and the early narrative poems share.

A *"fictive person"*

A number of assumptions, all of them contested in one way or another, have attached to the narrator in Chaucer's early poems. The first is that, as Dorothy Bethurum and others contend, he is essentially a single figure acting under various guises.[1] The second, reading back from the debate over Chaucer the pilgrim and Chaucer the man in the *Canterbury Tales,* is that he must be either a fictional, poetic proxy or some version of Chaucer's actual social identity.[2] A third assumption is that within the poems themselves the persona is a consistent figure. In other words, he maintains a stable characterization, whether fictitious or historical. This leads of course to the much-debated question of the "obtuse" narrator in the *Book of the Duchess* and the *House of Fame* and to later inconsistencies, such as in the Prologue to the *Legend of Good Women,* where the dreamer praises Alceste but fails to recognize her.

The last of these is the key assumption, for it underlies the other two. Whether we see the narrator as fictitious or historical and whether or not that characterization is maintained from one poem to another, the essential point for most readings of the poems is that the narrator is portrayed consistently and so establishes a stable, if complex, point of view. It is in turn that viewpoint which determines a strategy for discussing the unity of the poems. The dream visions move through a series of heterogeneous narrative sections, but the narrator gives us a sense that everything is contained within his consciousness, hence that the experience is unified and intelligible. The alternative to seeing a consistent persona within the poem is to confront a style of narrative that diverges radically from our expectations of narrative poetry.

The assumption of a consistent persona faces significant challenges from contemporary approaches to representation and authorial portrayal. David Lawton has suggested that the narrator is radically unstable: he is an "open persona" or "apocryphal voice" that establishes a multiplicity of relations to his subject matter and audience. There is, Lawton contends, no single identity (fictional or social) represented by the poetic "I" but instead a modulation of tones presented through him. Robert M. Jordan likewise emphasizes the importance of presentational voice and rhetorical artifice over realistic characterization. "In Chaucer's dream visions," he says, "this voice always represents the poet in the first person, yet it is always distanced from him to some extent" (*Poetics* 114). The fundamental structure, he argues, is the relation of narrative discourse to the absent poet.[3]

Both these views were anticipated by Marshall McLuhan's observation that the narrative persona is manipulated for rhetorical emphasis. McLuhan does not deny the structural use of persona to establish a viewpoint for narrative, but he says, "The 'I' of medieval narrative did not provide a point of view so much as immediacy of effect. In the same way grammatical tenses and syntax were managed by medieval writers, not with an idea to sequence in time or space, but to indicate importance of stress" (166). The implication is that the narrator is not an object of imitation, much like the story he tells, but part of the narrative code; he serves to interrupt, punctuate, and intensify mimetic art. The rhetorical dimension stands, then, as a complement to the mimetic and representational facet of narrative poetry.

We can find a number of places in Chaucer's early poems where the narrative persona functions to lend rhetorical emphasis, even at the cost sometimes of consistent characterization. The narrator's identification with Alcyone in the *Book of the Duchess* leads him to an authorial comment which momentarily breaks the illusion that he is recounting a dream. Partway through the story, he interrupts his retelling of Ovid's tale to assert:

> Such sorowe this lady to her tok
> That trewly I, that made this book,
> Had such pittee and such rowthe

> To rede hir sorwe that, by my trowthe,
> I ferde the worse al the morwe
> Aftir to thenken on hir sorwe.
>
> (95–100)

The narrator never returns to this reference to the morning after; but he has clearly announced that sorrow is his theme, and that announcement intensifies the elaborate parallels drawn between the dreamer's experience and the classical heroine and later between the dreamer and the man in black. Rhetorical emphasis may account, too, for the most celebrated crux in the early poems. The narrator overhears the man in black's lament for the dead White, but continues the dialogue, apparently oblivious to the fact, until the man makes his climactic disclosure, "She ys ded" (BD 1309).

In the *House of Fame* the narrator's tone shifts markedly and ironically in the course of the poem's invocation. The narrator calls on the God of Sleep to help to tell the dream correctly, asks God to show grace to lovers who dream of their beloved, but ends by praying Christ to visit calamity and death on anyone who misconstrues the dream. Ann Watts remarks that we hear another voice, Chaucer's direct and earnest voice, at a point later in the poem where "Geffrey" is asked his name in Fame's palace, and he refuses to let "no wight have my name in honde" (1877); otherwise, she says, "the relationship between author and speaker may fluctuate considerably" (231). In the *Parliament of Fowls* the discrepancy between the narrator and the dream is perceptible. The voice that confidently opens the poem and summarizes the "Dream of Scipio," though it maintains the comic role of a bookish and unrequited servant of Love, speaks with a kind of authority that is hard to find in the character who is shoved into the garden by Africanus and resembles the Lover of the *Roman de la rose* in his wonder at what is contained inside.

These passages make it clear that Chaucer's early narratives cannot be approached simply as mimetic art—that is, as little more than the retelling of a dream vision as if it were an autonomous fiction unified by the poet's invention of his materials. Nor, alternatively, can we posit a thoroughly consistent narrator whose performance is the metafiction that the poem represents. Lawton and Jordan may overstate the argument for an unstable narrator (inconsistency is not identical to radical instability), but they refute the contention that the poetic "I" is the object of representation and therefore the source of artistic unity. The case is rather that the representational dimensions of the poems exist in a dynamic relation to the rhetorical dimensions, which emphasize the poet's mode and style of presentation. The narrator stands, albeit uncomfortably and perhaps uncertainly, at the point where mimesis and rhetoric converge. One of his functions is to assert the place of performance and presentation within narrative and so to establish a self-conscious art.

In this respect Chaucer's early narratives complicate and enrich some of the dominant aesthetic principles formulated in the Middle Ages. Foremost among these principles was the belief that the art work consists essentially in representation, and accordingly its coherence depends on a formal, mimetic order. To be sure, such a belief finds an explicit warrant in medieval aesthetic theory. Thomas Aquinas, for example, distinguished making (*facere,* an activity directed toward external materials) from doing (*agere,* something acting within consciousness, such as volition). Aquinas says that art is transitive; it is an operation for making things rather than a simple reflection of the maker: "Bonum artis consideratur non in ipso artifice, sed magis in ipso artificiato" (*Summa Theologiae* 1a2ae.57.5). The product of making incorporates an intelligible structure, such as the *archetypus* or *interior sententia* of poetic invention or even the chance "winning" of a "purpose," which is knowable on its own terms.

But if making (*facere*) is the primary aesthetic activity, it is never carried on apart from a purpose and a context; it always has an audience, and the art work, especially a first-person narrative, mediates between personal and cultural intentions, imaginary and social worlds, even when the social world itself encompasses a secondary order of fiction. Whatever claims we make on historical or aesthetic grounds for an art work's standing as a discrete heterocosm, it still draws on the radical particularity of a place and time. Furthermore, we know that the persona is artificial, but it is not arbitrary. Scholars may disagree about Chaucer's precise social status—whether he is bourgeois or well connected— and consequently about the degree of familiarity with ducal and regal audiences that his status afforded him early in his career. There is no disagreement, however, that his status bears directly on his representation of himself. The "I" of the poems, and in particular of the early narratives, must define itself in relation to a historical man, and the range of possibilities for that definition is socially determined and limited. The creation of a persona thus involves a principle of exclusion. (One choice for ironic self-impersonation is not, for example, John of Gaunt.) When he discusses his own "fictive person" in the *Confessio Amantis,* Chaucer's contemporary John Gower makes the point overtly: a persona cannot be built on an image far removed from the authorial image most people would see (Middleton 105–6).

Besides rhetorical emphasis and shifting narrative to encompass a performative mode, another function of Chaucer's narrator is to create a kind of perspectival art that had no full counterpart in English poetry. Earlier writers in the native tradition adopt the perspective of an omniscient narrator who describes action, reports speeches and the internal conflicts of his characters, and occasionally interjects a tone of foreboding. For the most part the narrator in these poems operates as a member of a community defined by kinship, nationality, or locale. The narrator of *King Horn,* the earliest English romance (c. 1225), carries out the duties of historical recollection without drawing attention.to his own role. *Havelok the Dane* (c. 1290) opens in the same mode: "Herkneth to me, gode men, / Wives, maidnes, and alle men, / Of a tale that ich you wile telle" (Sands 58). Although the narrator of *Havelok* intervenes to direct his audience's response and structure the narration (Barron 72), the imaginative world of the poem is built on values and assumptions that he shares directly with his audience. In tail-rhyme romances like *Sir Amadace,* description and speeches alternate; and when the poet speaks in the first person, he directs attention to the narrative rather than himself: "Thanne sir Amadase, as I yo say, / Hase ordanut him opon [a] day / Of the cuntray in a stownnde" (Mills 170). The poetic "I" is a subordinate mode within narrative discourse.

Chaucer's contemporaries achieve a remarkable perspectival art by the manipulation of viewpoint. In *Piers Plowman* Langland subtly juxtaposes richly detailed allegorical description, the poet's voice as Everyman, and the several identities of Piers. John Gower takes the persona of Amans at the beginning of his *Confessio Amantis* and emerges at the end as a figure close to himself, an old man released from Venus's service after discovering what he looks like in the mirror. By contrast the narrator of Chaucer's dream poems has neither Langland's vast social vision nor Gower's didactic intent, which makes it possible to subordinate tales from exemplary history to the purpose of moral correction. The sources for Chaucer's self-portrayal lie, as we shall see, in a medieval theory of poetic voices and in the practice of continental writers whose vernacular tradition is the context for the artistic project of Chaucer's narrative poetry. Chaucer's difference from his predecessors and contemporaries thus reflects a difference in milieu and cultural ambitions, and the narrator represents a gesture toward the court writers whom Chaucer emulates.

The conventional view is that Chaucer uses his narrator to achieve the effect of a self-conscious artistry that is taken as an end in itself. R. W. V. Elliott, who sees the pose of the slow-witted narrator adopted in all of Chaucer's work, believes, "the adoption of such poses enables the poet to dissociate his waking self from what happens, from what is said and done in the dream; to be both involved and on the fence, committed and non-committal" (57). Morton Donner formulates Chaucer's narrative perspective as a play of subjectivity and objectivity centered on the narrator: "Chaucer narrates subjectively through the medium of 'I' but objectively by de-emphasizing the role of 'I' in his narratives" in favor of ideas, characters, and actions presented for their own sake and speaking to universal values (190).[4]

The effect that Elliott and Donner describe differs, however, from the conventional use of viewpoint as a poetic technique. The narrator of Chaucer's early poems does not merely amplify the possibilities of perspectival narrative; rather, he uses self-conscious presentation as a means to establish a new form of narrative, one based on a sense of poetic indeterminacy. The poems are constituted within the dreamer's imagination and memory and enacted through an authorial voice with a wide range of tones. They insist on some kind of objective referent— an inverted subjectivity (as in the highly articulated dream-world), a realm of common experience (what "men may say"), or a figure like the anonymous "querulous objector" whom the speaker conjures up to demand a commonsensical explanation of things (Bloomfield "Gloomy Chaucer" 66). Nonetheless, the narrator's presentation of himself reminds us, as Clemen observes, that we are given "impressions, not facts" (116). The narrator speaks "as me thoght," as he has seen and now remembers. What he describes is contained within the figure he presents of himself, and it is contingent to the same extent as the poetic "I."

We can delineate the quality of Chaucer's indeterminacy by contrasting it to *The Parliament of the Three Ages,* a dream vision composed perhaps a generation before Chaucer started writing. Like Chaucer's dream visions, the *The Parliament of the Three Ages* contains a strongly sketched first-person narrator and employs a structure in which the first section dwells on the narrator (he is a hunter stalking deer) before turning to topics and subject matter that he describes in recounting his dream. The poem differs from Chaucer's visions, however, in that the dreamer is only a narratorial device and his dream only a frame for presenting the debate among allegorical figures for the three ages of man and for rehearsing the exempla of the Nine Worthies, well-known wise men, and famous lovers. When the dreamer awakens he returns home with a prayer to God and the Virgin. The narrative is fully contained within the dream, and the dream is recounted without gestures of performance. But there is no evidence that the visionary experience is problematic or that the narrator must struggle to understand his experience. We find no counterpart to the narrator's sympathetic identification with Alcyone in the *Book of the Duchess* and nothing like the moments in the *House of Fame* in which "Geffrey" is caught in his own creation. If there is a resemblance to the narrator's spectatorial role in the *Parliament of Fowls,* there is no corresponding determination in the end to continue reading so as to find a better dream.

Two other functions of Chaucer's narrator—authentication and textuality—are closely related. As Bloomfield observes, "We read a narrative not only for a story but for the authenticating voice. In one way or another a narrative must not only present a story but an authentication of that story. In other words, a story must also present a solution to its epistemological problem" ("Authenticating Realism" 339).[5] In dream poetry this function is clearly at the fore. Dieter Mehl proposes, "the endeavour to give authority to the narrator's message was most likely one of the reasons for the popularity of the dream-vision, and Chaucer's variations of this form show him struggling again and again with the problem of literary authority and the validity of personal experience" (15).

Chaucer's persona shares the function of authentication with the speaker of *The Parliament of the Three Ages.* The final words of the hunter-dreamer echo his opening lines and claim an experiential status for the dream.

> And in the monethe of Maye thies mirthes me tydde,
> Als I schurtted [amused] me in a schelfe [bank] in þe schawes
>   [thickets] faire,
> And belde me [built myself a blind] in the birches with bewes
>   [boughs] full smale,
> And lugede [sheltered] me in the leues, þat lighte were & grene.
>
>   (660–64)

But the narrators of dream visions, particularly Chaucer's persona, do not serve merely to authenticate some version of the imitative fallacy, for their narratives do not merely reproduce the sudden shifts and juxtapositions of dream structures. The epistemological problem that Bloomfield refers to is not solved simply by the device of a first-person narrator who claims to be retelling a dream; it has to do with the truth claims of poetic representation. Furthermore, in his early narratives Chaucer's poetic strategy is to go beyond the claims of describing a dream and to treat literary tradition as the referent of his writing. His bookish narrator, as the eagle in the *House of Fame* and Africanus in the *Parliament of Fowls* remark, seeks not admission to the love garden but contact with the text that describes it.

Chaucer's textuality in the early poems serves, then, as the structural complement to the narrator's authenticating voice. If the narrator recounts visionary experience, it is experience already constructed in other texts and taking its meaning by establishing a relation to them. That relation exists on two connected levels—the invention of material and the poet's role within literary tradition. As Piero Boitani notes ("Old Books"), the narrator signals the fact that the poem begins from antecedent texts and aspires to the status of a text itself. And here again it is important to distinguish Chaucer's practice from that of his predecessors. The poet of *Sir Orfeo,* for example, claims a warrant for his poem in the tradition of the Breton lay. The early fourteenth-century romance *Octavian* claims (10–12), "Yn bokys of ryme hyt ys tolde / How hyt befelle owre eldurs olde, / Well oftyn sythe" (Mills 75). These are formulaic phrases, much like the conventional appeal in the historical romance *Athelston* (777–79): "Whenne the King hadde said so, / A gret fir was maad tho, / In romaunce as we rede" (Sands 152). We have a stronger sense of textuality in *Sir Gawain and the Green Knight,* where references to the historical forerunners of the Arthurian court point toward epic and romance. The *Gawain*-poet makes his final appeal to literary tradition ("The Brutus bokez therof beres wyttnesse," 2523), but he locates the imaginative sources of Gawain's adventure within the poem itself.[6]

Chaucer's achievement in devising his narrator consists in aligning the traditional function of authentication with a notion of textuality. The narrator of the dream poems refers not to a private experience but to a poetic tradition that has shaped his experience and provided the materials for recounting it. In this, as in poetic invention, he is at once an innovator and translator of European conventions. We can assess his self-dramatizing persona by looking at its sources.

Poetic Voice
and Continental Prototypes

A theory of poetic voices was formulated in antiquity and disseminated in the Middle Ages by the grammarians and rhetoricians who established a general outline for medieval literary theory. It originates in Plato's reflections on the ambivalent nature of representation. In Book III of *The Republic* (392 D) Plato reasons that an account of an event will be presented either as simple narration or through imitation. A poet must therefore speak in his own voice in recounting, imitate the speeches of others, or use some combination of the two. Imitation (*mimesis*) here, as against Book X of *The Republic,* means copying and impersonation. Clearly Plato is interested in distinguishing modes of performance and communication rather than establishing the status of artistic representation, for the poet who speaks and the characters whose speeches he reports occupy the same ground and differ only in their forms of address. In some important way that remains implicit and is never analyzed fully in Plato's reflections on discourse, the narrator is thought to be continuous with the fiction he presents.[7]

In later antiquity Plato's distinctions become poetic styles (*characteres dicendi*) and a formalized system of poetic voices. The Roman biographer Suetonius connects these styles to poetic genre in his *De poetis*. Just as Homer is the reference point for Plato's distinction of direct and indirect discourse, Vergil is the main pattern for types of literary discourse. Pure narrative voice, Suetonius says, is illustrated by the *Georgics,* imitated speech by comedy and tragedy, and the mixed style by the *Aeneid,* which combines narration and mimesis. Commentators on Vergil's *Eclogues* reproduced these categories, and the fourth-century grammarian Diomedes elaborated them into a theory of poetic voices which he applied to both fictional and discursive writing.

The encyclopedists of the early and high Middle Ages incorporated the theory of poetic voices as part of literary theory, and the influence continued through the Renaissance.[8] The theory is a continuous feature of medieval literary theory; it is part of the analytical repertoire elaborated by a variety of authorities in the Latin high culture of the Middle Ages (John of Garland's *Parisiana Poetria,* for example). More important, it registers, in the kinds of distinctions it makes, a powerful ambiguity regarding poetic address and poetic fiction. The two domains are never sharply delineated, but shade into each other; and this ambiguity resides at the very root of the tradition of critical reflection about narration and poetic fiction.

The theory of poetic voices offers a conceptual framework for the style of mixed address that characterizes an important body of vernacular poetry in the high and late Middle Ages. We usually regard the *Roman de la rose* and the poems written under its influence, notably those of Guillaume de Machaut and Jehan de Froissart, as narrative poems. Though amplified by didactic digressions and lyric sections, the *Rose* and the later *dits* follow a plot structure and lead to a resolution of the story. The narrative is conveyed by a first-person speaker who establishes rhetorical emphases, viewpoint, and a sense of authentication. Yet this speaker, like the figures Plato discusses, occupies the same plane as the allegorical and historical characters he encounters. He is bound to the action as author and participant. Sometimes he must recount actions and speech deeply embedded in the discourse of others, such as the dreamer's report of Nature's confession in the *Rose,* in which Nature quotes the bedtime colloquy of a foolish husband and scheming wife

(Dahlberg 9, 277). Despite being at several removes, there is no lessening of immediacy. Moreover, the narrator is acutely aware of his work as a literary text, which is a product of writing and a means of connecting the author's work with antecedent texts.

The prototype of the first-person narrator for secular poetry in the vernacular is the Lover in the *Rose*. We have seen how Chaucer as translator responds to Guillaume de Lorris's apology for dream poetry, which is a claim for poetic authentication, and to the story of Narcissus, which serves as a model for self-reflexive narrative. James I. Wimsatt ("French Poetry" 114) believes, in addition, that the lover-narrator in Guillaume's portion of the poem is one source—but not the only one— for the naive narrator in Chaucer's poetry. John H. Fisher finds in the portrayal of the Lover "the same self-deprecatory tone as Chaucer's persona" and the same "confiding, personal, one-to-one voice" ("French Influence" 182). At various points in the early narratives Chaucer's persona shows his origins in the *Rose* by reenacting the Lover's experience. The garden depicted in the *Book of the Duchess* recreates the one that the Lover explores in the *Rose;* and the *Parliament of Fowls,* despite the Dantesque motif of the twin messages over the gate, reproduces a version of the same landscape, even to the point of going to Boccaccio's own sources in the *Rose.* The Lover's description of the devices on the wall surrounding the garden inspires Chaucer's anaphoric technique in the *House of Fame,* where the dreamer reports the sequence of what "I sawgh" in the temple of Venus.

Chaucer's own engagement with the text in the *Romaunt* shows his awareness of the role of the narrative "I." Caroline Eckhardt notes that Chaucer's translation increases the first-person vocabulary of the poem. The reason may be that Middle English syntax requires the first-person pronoun in instances where the Old French construction can often drop it. Eckhardt speculates, "Perhaps building upon this essential change, Chaucer seems to have found opportunities for heightening the narrator's presence in the poem" (52). An important instance of this revision, not mentioned by Eckhardt, involves the narrator's claim to authorship. Guillaume's narrator explains the title and subject matter of the poem: "ce est li *Romanz de la Rose,* / ou l'art d'Amors est tote enclose" (37–38). Chaucer shifts the passage, however, from the passive to the active, and makes explicit the narrator's role as the shaping consciousness of the poem: "It is the Romance of the Rose, / In which al the art of love I close" (39–40).

A number of Chaucer's authorial locutions and narrative gestures similarly derive from the *Rose,* or more precisely from Chaucer's treatment of Guillaume's text. The Lover asserts, "Now this drem wol I ryme aright" (*Romaunt* 31), and Chaucer echoes him, though in a different tone, in the invocation to the *House of Fame:* "Prey I that he [the god of sleep] wol me spede / My sweven for to telle aryght" (78–79). The original reads simply, "Or veil cel songe rimeer" (31). The qualifications and disclaimers that typically accompany the narrator's act of memory in Chaucer's poetry are prominent in the *Rose:* "Herafter shal I tellen right / The soothe and eke signyfiaunce, / As fer as I have remembraunce" (*Romaunt* 994–96). Prominent, too, is the countervailing sense of control; the Lover immediately adds, "All shal be seid, I undirtake, / Er of this book an ende I make" (*Romaunt* 997–98). At moments such as the one in which he amplifies Dido's complaint in the *House of Fame* and asserts, "As me mette redely— / Non other auctour alegge I" (313–14), this sense of the narrator's (and the poet's) control reveals itself.

Guillaume's narrator, as these passages indicate, insists on the textuality of the *Rose,* its status as a book written to stand as an object of knowledge about love and requiring interpretation. When Jean de Meun takes over Guillaume's love allegory, infusing it with encyclopedic interests in science and philosophy, he broadens the scope of the narrator's role as well as the poem's sense of itself as a text. Jean is a self-conscious and self-dramatizing appropriator of literary texts, vitally engaged with literary tradition and with complementing antecedent writers (Knopp 31). Jean has the God of Love ratify his succession as an author: "car quant Guillaumes cessera, / Jehans le continuera" (10557–58). Love addresses his counselors on the matter of literary appropriation and presides over the ritual of Jean's authorial installation.

> Por ce m'en veill ci conseillier,
> car tuit estes mi conseillier,
> si vos cri merci, jointes paumes,
> que cist las doulereus Guillaumes,
> qui si bien vers moi portez,
> soit secouruz et confortez.
> Et se por lui ne vos prioie,
> certes prier vos en devroie
> au mains por Jehan alegier,
> qu'il escrive plus de legier,
> que cest avantages li fetes
> (car il nestra, j'en sui prophetes). . . .
>   (10625–36)

"And I beg your grace with joined palms that this poor wretched Guillaume, who has borne himself so well toward me, may be helped and comforted. And if I did not beg you for him,

> I should certainly beg you at least that you give Jean the
> advantage of lightening his burden so that he may write more
> easily, for I prophesy that he will be born." (Dahlberg 189)

Jean establishes the poetic "I" as a translator who not only renders
earlier texts but confronts their authors and defines his own project by
his difference within a line of literary succession. His dramatization of
literary succession makes it clear that this reworking is also a dialogue
over time and over the disjunctions of time with the previous author
("anz trespassez plus de XL" [10560]), and to carry it on the poet must
locate himself within the imaginative world of the poem. Robert O.
Payne rightly contends that Chaucer addresses the same problem. Chaucer's solution depends on the creation of a narrative persona whose
rhetorical ethos as well as his invention serves as a point of contact
with successive readers. Payne says, "the Chaucerian speech/poem, like
all those the Eagle showed him in the *House of Fame,* is an initially
invented construct which, once committed to time, carries into the
stream of time some seeds of its speaker and its topics which germinate,
grow, bear fruit, and reseed themselves in successive generations of
hearer/readers" ("Realization" 285).

Jean's importation of encyclopedic learning into the *Roman de la
rose* has been described generally, if inadequately, as the imposition of
scholastic, Aristotelian naturalism on Guillaume's courtly, Platonic idealism. The effect of Jean's additions, apart from complicating the unity
of the original poem, is to establish the poet as a cultural figure committed to a wide range of learning and to integrating areas of knowledge
and experience within imaginative discourse. Though Dante and Boccaccio are more remote sources for Chaucer's narrator (Lawton 57),
they enhanced Jean's conception of the poet's office by their practice
within individual works and by finding in the total corpus of their own
work an accommodation between philosophical and poetic concerns.

Dante's prose writing treats poetry analytically and discursively; and
the commentary in the *Convivio* shows the incorporation of philosophical materials within the poetry. In the *De vulgari eloquentia* (2.4)
Dante declares that the poet (a term he extends to vernacular writers)
must possess grammatical art and a speculative appreciation of music,
and in the *Vita Nuova* (chap. 25) he scorns ignorant writers who "rhyme
stupidly," by which he means those who compose verse without the
conceptual sophistication of devices like allegory and personification.
In his extended comments on poetry in the *Genealogie deorum gentilium* (14.7), Boccaccio likewise stresses the importance of learning
for the poet. As in Dante's conception, grammar and rhetoric lie at the

basis of art, "yet over and above this," Boccaccio stresses, "it is necessary to know at least the principles of the other Liberal Arts, both moral and natural, to possess a strong and abundant vocabulary, to behold the monuments and relics of the Ancients, to have in one's memory the histories of the nations, and to be familiar with the geography of various lands, of seas, rivers and mountains" (Osgood 40). Dante and Boccaccio confirm what Jean demonstrates when he appropriates Guillaume's text: the poet who represents himself in his work is not just a composer but also a man of letters.

The second paradigm for Chaucer's narrator is the poetic voice that Machaut subtly elaborates in his lyrico-narrative *dits*. Though he recognizes the influence of the *Rose* on Chaucer's self-characterization, Wimsatt contends, "Machaut's narrator supplies easily the best precedent among Chaucer's sources—of whatever language—for his literary persona, an important aspect indeed of his literary art" ("French Poetry" 122). Chaucer may have come across Machaut's poetry while a prisoner in France in 1359–60 (Crépin 59), or he may have been introduced to it by Froissart in the 1360s (Wimsatt "Machaut's *Lay*" 16). Chaucer turns to Machaut throughout his career as a source for materials. And Machaut combines many of the features of the narrator's persona in Chaucer's early poems. Like Chaucer, he has a social status outside the circles of a court elite but earns his place because of skill and talent. Daniel Poirion describes his position as follows: "Attached to the court without really being part of it, Machaut makes himself at once the interpreter of the lives of others and of his own feelings: an attitude common to many authors but marked, in Machaut's case, by the assertion of the 'I' in face of the others. Assigned to sing the loves of princes, he is tempted to substitute himself ingeniously for them" (205 [my translation]).

Machaut is usually credited with inventing a new kind of narrative persona in his *dits amoureux* and with contributing to the evolution toward a subjective poetry. The common ground Machaut's narrator shares with his audience is the experience of the erotic, expressed most richly through the term *sentiment,* but the poet often finds himself separated from *joie.* Machaut's originality, Poirion believes, consists in distinguishing his own situation from that of the aristocratic protagonist whom he celebrates through the poem (198). The chief device for establishing this difference is comic reduction. The narrator portrays himself hiding in his chamber out of fear of the plague at the beginning of the *Jugement dou Roy de Navarre.* He is "plus couars qu'uns lievres" in the *Dit de la Fonteinne amoureuse* (92), imagining the lamenting voice he hears in the night to be a spirit come to murder him. (His obtuseness in later presenting a full transcription of the lament to its imagined aristocratic author is a forerunner of Chaucer's seeming obtuseness in dealing with the man in black.) In the *Jugement dou Roy de Behaingne* he lies hidden in bushes, overhearing the debate of a lady and knight, until the lady's dog reveals his presence.

Lawton, who mostly rejects the influence of Machaut on Chaucer's persona, suggests that Machaut's greatest contribution was to provide "a model for appearing comically as narrator *in propria persona* before a court audience" (50). But Machaut's poetic self-consciousness operates in another dimension as well. In the Prologue to his works Machaut stages his own inauguration as a poet by imagining that first Nature and then Love appear to him. Nature confers the instruments of his craft—Scens, Retorique, and Musique—while Love gives him his poetic *matière* in the form of Dous Penser, Plaisance, and Esperance. The first three gifts represent the formal aspects of poetry and the means to control the materials ("Scens y est qui tout gouverne" [159]); the second group turns sorrow to joy and implies an erotic ethic.

> Mais garde bien, sur tout ne t'enhardi
> A faire chose ou il ait villenie,
> N'aucunement des dames ne mesdi;
> Mais en tous cas les loe et magnefie.
>
> (21–24)

> But take care above all and do not be so bold as to do anything churlish, and in no way speak ill of women, but praise and magnify them in every case.

We shall see in the next chapter that Chaucer refers to the Prologue in defining his own poetic beginnings in the *Book of the Duchess;* in the *Legend of Good Women* he adapts the ethic to the injunction that the God of Love lays on him. The point I want to make here is that Machaut is not simply the source of a comic persona; he is also the source of a formalized reflection on the poet's craft.[9] The "I" of Machaut's narratives defines the ground of performance from which Chaucer begins to devise a sophisticated narrative poetry that can emulate its continental models.

Chaucer devises his persona, then, within a tradition that recognizes the fluid boundaries of narrative and performance. As a structural device the poetic "I" of the *Rose* and of Machaut's *dits* gives the possibility of a narrative constructed on both subjectivity and textuality. As a figure of the poet the persona attempts to locate poetic art within a tradition of learning. Chaucer discovers in his literary predecessors a role for the poet as a man of learning. It is that role which he cultivates within the milieu of the fourteenth-century court, while renegotiating the terms of the cultural equation between the aesthetic and the moral.

Court Poetry and Poetic Persona

The historical and social context for all of Chaucer's poetry before the *Canterbury Tales,* especially for his early poetry, is the English court of the later fourteenth century. Court, in this sense, means royalty, aristocracy, and the functionaries of civil administration. From perhaps as early as 1360 Chaucer was connected with the royal household (Crow 19, 21). He served from June 1367 (perhaps earlier) until the end of his life as an esquire in the *familia regis* (Crow 94n). The royal courts of Edward III and Richard II determined the elite literary values during Chaucer's poetic career and established a literary etiquette for both poets and poetry alike. The social life of the court, as Richard Firth Green has argued, revolved specifically around the king's chamber (*camera regis*); it was there that aristocratic taste was formed and a poet had to win his audience (38). Froissart tells us that the position of king's esquire obliged courtiers, among other things, to compose poetry for court entertainments. The Eltham Ordinance, to take another example, directed members of the royal chamber to entertain the king along with their other duties.

In the course of Chaucer's early poetic career, the court itself underwent a cultural change and even a change in style. The first stage had begun early in the century and involved a shift from Latin works and the vernacular "making" of minstrels toward a literary milieu composed of court amateurs and professional writers, such as Froissart and Machaut. Under Edward III the milieu was dominated by French letters. Froissart was Queen Philippa's favorite, and Juliet Vale has suggested that Philippa's death and Froissart's departure occur at the time of a rise in the English vernacular in court circles (47). The second stage involved the development of an international courtly society. Gervase Mathew traces the origin of this society to the Neopolitan court of Robert of Anjou, which fostered Boccaccio. Although V. J. Scattergood and J. W. Sherborne have disputed the extent of Richard II's cultural innovations, it seems clear that a highly sophisticated society evolved and that it valued extensive and self-conscious ceremony and a fashion not only for poetry but for the broader activities of humane letters. The English court, like others, came to reflect what Green describes as "the competitive courtly ostentation of the period" (25). Furthermore, as Patricia Eberle (169) suggests, courtly style was seen in political dimensions, such as Thomas Walsingham's denunciation of Richard II's courtiers: "They were knights of Venus rather than knights of Bellona, more valiant in the bedchamber than on the field, armed with words rather than weapons, prompt in speaking but slow in performing the acts of war."

Within these historical changes, social life and artistic creation invert and complicate one another. Writing of a "Chaucer tradition" that extends in an unbroken continuity to the Tudor court, John Stevens emphasizes the ludic role of social life and its organization around the game of love, which legitimizes secular experience and aestheticizes behavior: "It taught you how to behave to your peers when you all had time on your hands; not how to do them good, but how to make yourself desirable; how to 'commune,' especially in mixed company, and how to please" (*Music* 155). The literary products that reflect and at the same time help constitute the game are, in a sense, "stylized talk, idealized talk" (160). The subject of this talk is love, and the logic of social discourse is that "if you want to please, you must allow yourself to fall in love and remain in love" or at least act the part of a lover: "This is why the art of living approximates to the art of loving; and why the great first psychology of love, the *Romance of the Rose,* is also the source and pattern of 'courtesy' books" (155–56).[10] One of the poems representing the dominant courtly style in which Chaucer probably began his writing makes explicit the social aims of love (Wimsatt *"CH"* 12–13).

> Assez est assavoir
> De Bien Amer entrer en seignourie:
> De miex dire, de miex faire et valoir.
> S'est eureux qui a ce point s'allie.

> To enter into the lordship
> Of Good Loving, this is enough to know:
> To speak better, to do better, to increase in merit.
> He is happy who joins this life.

The court amateurs, as Glending Olson reminds us, were preeminently functionaries "playing important roles in the ongoing social rituals of their societies, to which their work might often simply be an appendage" ("Making" 288).[11] Their pose is that of an amateur furnishing polite amusement and on occasion offering serious advice to his superiors. Their work existed alongside the compositions of literary professionals who were skilled in other fields, such as historiography (Froissart) and music (Machaut). For both kinds of writers, however, poetry and social life are joined in a common, if not single or even singular, discourse. As Paul Zumthor has argued, the language of the court poet creates figures on the surface of reality but does not situate them in time and space, so that rhetorical "ornament is indistinguishable from substance" and the gestures of social life are coded actions (495). The governing tension of this cultural drama is between movement into elite circles and exclusion, which permits a ruling elite to consolidate and retain power.

Chaucer's position within this environment is usually described by social class. A capable civil servant and royal administrator, he is also a poetic correspondent with other functionaries—Henry Scogan, Sir Peter Bukton (or Sir Robert Bukton), Sir Philip de la Vache—and with Richard II ("Lak of Stedefastnesse") and Henry IV ("The Complaint of Chaucer to his Purse"). Scogan was the tutor to Henry's sons. His "Moral Balade" incorporates Chaucer's "Gentilesse," and the two poems announce the lesson that only virtue endures in a mutable world. The development of lay administration, as R. T. Lenaghan remarks, makes possible this kind of " 'lateral' reading" (157), in which Chaucer's verse finds part of its audience among other functionaries in the royal civil service.

Chaucer seems nonetheless to stand apart from the circle of court amateur writers. Clemen proposes that an "intermediate position between the middle-class and the aristocracy" leaves Chaucer "ideally fitted to portray different types and to offer a criticism of the social order" (20). E. Talbot Donaldson and Donald Howard, though they differ in their approaches to Chaucer's persona, characterize him as a bourgeois facing a not unfamiliar dilemma: "he does not want to appear bourgeois in the eyes of the upper class, but he knows that the most bourgeois thing he can do is to show discomfort about his status or, worse, attempt to deny it" (Howard "Man" 342). John Lawlor emphasizes that class distinctions shape the literary dynamic of Chaucerian performance: "The modern reader must see Chaucer standing in the circle of a small society, each known to him, and each his feudal superior. . . . His working principle is skilful opportunism, based upon a self-characterization which springs from the literary tradition in which he works—last and therefore decidedly least of those who re-tell the stories adorned by their great predecessors—and from his actual position, the humble servant of those who are his social superiors" (*Chaucer* 19–20).[12]

Lawlor grounds Chaucer's performance in a dialectic of literary self-consciousness and social inferiority, and on this view the persona Chaucer projects is distinctly the product of these forces. The persona allows the poet to participate in the constitutive fictions of social life, and it mediates between objective and artificial social roles. But it does so while redefining at least one of the essential terms: if the stylized environment of the court required something like the artificial personality of the lover, Chaucer created a fictional self in the guise of the failed lover who still remains a poet. His persona at once achieves inclusion and distance—a definition of self that allows the poet to participate in society and at the same time a sign of his difference from the circles in which he travels. In the voices that the poet adopts within the structure of social and literary impersonation, the roles of initiate and outsider interpenetrate.

What held these public and private facets together and lent them cohesion was a sense of style. Patricia Kean has called it Chaucer's "urbane manner," and she finds it exemplified in "a naturalistic, conversational" style and the use of literary convention to fill "the need to communicate directly with a clearly defined and known audience of a well-bred and sophisticated type" (1:32). In an early poem like "An ABC," supposedly translated for Blanche of Lancaster's private meditation, the open style is apparent in the rhetorical context. The poet addresses the Virgin, yet his words are directed beyond her to the noble patron who is the secular embodiment of all her virtues: "Thou art the bush on which ther gan descende / The Holi Gost, the which that Moyses wende / Had ben a-fyr, and this was in figure."[13] The subtlety and fine discriminations of "noble talking" can be seen, too, in the contrast with another style of presentation cultivated in the period. Formally, the characteristics of Chaucer's open style resemble many aspects of the "common voice" that Anne Middleton finds in the "public poetry" of contemporaries like Gower and Langland. But the styles diverge fundamentally in their rhetorical purposes. The openness of courtly speech is shared by a circle of initiates, with whom the poet has a subtly nuanced relation. The address of the "common voice" is directed across the various estates which comprise society and the political commonwealth.[14]

The lyric complaints which Chaucer wrote throughout his career and which serve as companion pieces to the early narrative poems show us isolated, though significant, moments in which the poet's persona defines itself through and against the social discourse of courtly impersonation. The complaints depict Chaucer's "fictive person" engaged in the game of love precisely at the point where self-presentation comes under the greatest pressure because, in the logic of the game, a lover's rejection forces either withdrawal from civilized life or an estrangement from the art predicated on "stylized talk." In "A Complaint to His Lady," an uneven, possibly experimental poem that employs three different metrical forms while expressing the conventions of courtly love, the speaker describes himself in relation to other lovers, presumably the court circle that constitutes the audience and judges of his poem. He is "leest worthy of alle hem" (67) and "unconnyng and unmete, / To serve" (69–70). Whatever his relative merits, though, he argues his way back into the game, telling his lady, "Now certes, and ye lete me thus sterve, / Yit have ye wonne theron but a smal" (106–7). This, like much of the language in the poem, is a commonplace in the rhetoric of courtly complaint, as Earle Birney (640) and Paul M. Clogan (187) have remarked. But Chaucer expands the commonplace here and elsewhere not simply to score a point in an imagined debate but to call into question the first principles of the social fiction.

The speaker of the complaint turns the tables on a woman who will cause his extinction merely because of his "good wille," and so he maneuvers her into taking responsibility for what will be the moral collapse of the love game. Her rejecting him, he argues, calls into question "al your wommanly pitee, / Your gentilesse and your debonairtee" (101–2), but more than that, it undermines the possibility of ethical discriminations, making "as good were thanne untrewe as trewe to be" (117). In asking finally to be granted "som drope" (125) of his lady's grace, the speaker transforms the conventional motifs of service and devotion to the concerns of his own poetic office. His comic reduction, ironically paralleled in the lady's capacity for pity, serves an aesthetic aim, but ironically liberates the speaker from the context in which poetry is supposedly subordinate to sentiment and behavior. For this indeterminate quantity ("som drope") of an undefinable quality ("your grace") allows him to preserve a form of social participation. Though presumably excluded from the role of lover as poet, he keeps his place within the domain of "noble talking" by dramatizing its absence.

Chaucer's lyric persona takes on an explicit poetic role in "The Complaint Unto Pity," with which "A Complaint to His Lady" is associated in the early textual sources.[15] The poet's lament is no longer a posture adopted in the abstract game but a formal text "writen in myn hond" (43), hence the objectification of court manners within literary discourse. As in the previous poem the speaker uses the most notable device of Chaucer's narrators, the figure of *diminutio,* to portray himself: "I be not konnynge for to pleyne" (97). But his reduction of himself is not directed toward his lady in this instance; it is not a pose struck in a localized dialogue with a woman whose refusal threatens to end the game. Rather, the speaker sees himself isolated from the universal attitudes which comprise social decorum at large and so underlie the game.[16]

Wolfgang Clemen notes that "The Complaint Unto Pity" is the only fully allegorical piece among Chaucer's shorter poems. It draws at least some of its personifications from the allegorical personnel of the *Roman de la rose:* Bounte, Beaute, Lust, Jolyte, Assured Maner, Youthe, Honeste, Wisdom, Estaat, Drede, and Gouvernaunce (179–81). These comprise an intelligible structure of attributes related to each other, "confedered both by bonde and alliaunce" (42). But the speaker sees them joined another way—"confedered alle by bond of Cruelte" (52). His isolation from the attributes of social life is intensified by his unique perception that Pity is dead and the virtues of courtly experience are all arrayed against him. The decisive element in the poem is not, as we might expect, the speaker's complaint against "the crueltee and tirannye / Of Love" (6–7), which has persisted, as in the *Book of the Duchess* (36–37), "be lengthe of certeyne yeres" ("Pity" 8); it is his composing the bill of complaint that separates him from the allegorized social world of the love court. This is the "wonder newe" (29), as the speaker calls it, using the vocabulary that elsewhere designates a dream vision. Within the lyric's stylized fiction about the death of Pity, which is the central virtue to which the courtly lover appeals, the complaint dramatizes the ambiguous position of the courtly "maker" and reveals the tensions within his disguise. His power of perception lets him write, but it is also the quality that removes him in some measure from the social world he writes about.

Another poem, probably written in mid-career, complicates the interchange of art and social life figured in the early courtly complaints. In "The Complaint of Mars," a Valentine's Day poem fraught with warning and disappointment, the speaker offers a form of multiple impersonation that again works to define his role within a common social and artistic discourse. The poem begins as an *alba,* a poetic dawn song. The poetic "I" addresses his audience—"hardy knyghtes of renoun" (272), ladies, and "ye lovers, al in-fere" (290)—as if they were actors in the drama of separation played by lovers who must part at the lark's morning song so as to avoid discovery and scandal. He evokes a framework of shared social and literary fiction much like the one supposed in the Prologue to the *Legend of Good Women* or at the end of the *Troilus.* "Ye lovers, that lye in any drede," he says, "Fleeth, lest wikked tongues yow espye!" ("Mars" 5–6). As the poem unfolds the identification is enriched by other associations. The conventional situation of the dawn song is read onto the mythological story of Mars and Venus, whose joy in bed is disturbed by Phoebus's invasive light. The scene recalls in some details the blissful consummation of Troilus and Criseyde, and the mythological context introduces a further range of astrological associations which describe erotic attraction and separation under the guise of physical laws and therefore as deterministic.

But if courtiers can be imagined as figures in a poem that reads classical mythology through the conventions of medieval lyric, the powers of the poet's art distinguish him from the court circle defined by those roles. Unlike the courtier-lovers awakened by the bird's song, the poet can sing "in my briddes wise" (23). And it is with this sense of a separate, though still fictitious, voice that he acts as a witness to recount the story and complaint of Mars. Chaucer's address then sets out two distinct functions in the discourse that joins the court poet and his audience. Writing "for the worship of this highe feste" (22), he defines the function of the courtly audience as imagination: they are to discover themselves in the multileveled roles of the poetic figures. His own function, though, is not imaginative identification but formalized memory: "what his compleynt was, remembreth me" (150). The work of memory is thus assimilated to poetic composition, as it is in Chaucer's dream visions. The poet's craft makes possible the rich overlay of associations—literary, mythological, astrological—that join the social and poetic fictions, but it is a craft undertaken with full cognizance of its occasion, constraints, and final difference from the social art with which it shares the same language. Consequently, the poet prefaces his recital of Mars's complaint with a poignant and revealing reservation: "therfore, in this lusty morwenynge / As I best can, I wol hit seyn and synge; / And after that I wol my leve take" (151–53). Self-cancellation is one of the conditions of his performance.

The self-conscious narrator who asserts the difference and limitation of his role is sketched briefly yet decisively in the complaints. Self-fashioning is a by-product more than an overt aim of composition, but it is also a necessary condition of writing. The figure of the poet emerges more fully, of course, in the dream visions. His mode of address remains the "conversational style" of the lyric, as he gives an account of his psychological state in the *Book of the Duchess* or explains his bewilderment at dream categories in the *House of Fame*. Even the elevated diction at the start of the *Parliament of Fowls* settles into conversation and familiarity: "On bokes rede I ofte, as I yow tolde" (16).

What the dream visions offer in contrast to the complaints is an expanded portrayal of the poetic persona engaged in his craft. Chaucer leaves behind the role of poet as lover to assume the role of love poet, the servant of those who serve the God of Love. The *Legend of Good Women* clearly reveals this break when Chaucer describes himself as one who comes after "ye lovers that kan make of sentement" (F 69); his composition depends on "glenyng here and there" (F 75) and rehearsing "that ye han in your fresshe songes sayd" (F 79). But the dissociation of social and poetic roles actually starts with the writing of narrative. The sleep-bereft narrator of the *Duchess* finds relief in the book of "written fables / That clerkes had in olde tyme, / And other poetes, put in rime" (52–54). As he recounts its chief story, the tale of Ceyx and Alcyone, the affective reader takes on a sense of authorship.

He quickly comes round to asserting his artistic and moral authority: "I, that made this book, / Had such pittee and such rowthe" (96–97). Pity and compassion allow his shift from empathy for the story to sympathy for the man in black, yet the narrative persona retains the aesthetic distance needed to "reherse" (474) the knight's complaint and the knight's "firste song" (1182) as a lover.

This awareness of craft—and of its separation from the lover's social role as poet—lies at the root of the narrator's persona in the *House of Fame*. Howard suggests that the "Geffrey" presented in the poem may be the first full artistic use of a persona in English ("Man" 340). If so, it is a persona that compels interest because of its absorption with the writer's craft. The eagle in Book ii delineates the poet's separation from "Loves folk" (614–40) and his assignment to writing and inditing in praise of Love and "in his folkes furtherynges" (636). Yet this comic reduction comes after the narrator has claimed his role and asserted his authority. For the dreamer recounts his dream "as I kan now remembre" (64), and his treatment of Dido's complaint, for example, is told "As me mette redely— / Non other auctour alegge I" (313–14). The frequent use of *occupatio* in retelling the *Aeneid* in Book i of *The House of Fame* refers the curious reader to the poet's sources—Vergil, Ovid, Claudian, and Dante—but there is no indication that the account given in the poem is felt to be inadequate. When the narrator invokes Apollo at the start of Book iii, he seeks aid to make the verse "sumwhat agreable" (1097) because his own "diligence" is directed to the "sentence" of the story, which "in myn hed ymarked ys" (1103). In the scene later at Fame's palace where the narrator is asked his name, he asserts his own capacity to recognize and claim a place within the overall disposition granted to man's reputation: "I wot myself best how y stonde" (1878). The source of this assertion, Chaucer makes clear, is the poet's art: "I wil myselven al hyt drynke, / Certeyn, for the more part, / As fer forth as I kan myn art" (1880–82).

A similar balance between dependence and assertion is apparent in *The Parliament of Fowls,* where the poet takes a stronger position toward the authority of other writers, including contemporaries like Boccaccio. The narrator builds on the role established by the earlier poems, and announces his removal from love and the fates of lovers, as if it were by now an accepted convention or commonly recognized gesture. The shove Africanus gives him as he deliberates the contrary messages above the gate is another instance of the sort of physical comedy begun by the eagle in *The House of Fame,* who snatches the bewildered dreamer from the desert outside the temple of Venus. For all the comic self-presentation, though, there is no doubt that the narrator in the *Parlia-*

ment is a figure directly associated with poetic creation. He prays Venus, "Whan I began my sweven for to write, / So yif me myght to ryme, and endyte!" (118–19). Africanus obliquely but firmly confirms his authorial role by seeming to call it into question: "And if thow haddest connyng for t'endite, / I shal the shewe mater of to wryte" (167–68). The wonders of the park and Venus's temple are seen under Africanus's Vergilian tutelage, but the main part of the experience—the assembly of birds held under Nature's governance—comes when the narrator is by himself: "Forth welk I tho myselven to solace" (297). Though still indebted here to previous writers such as Alan of Lille, the narrator has made a clear gesture of poetic independence, and the rest of the poem proceeds with direct narration and minimal intrusions of the poetic "I."

The pattern of periodic self-assertion in the dream visions suggests that beneath the comic persona there is an evolving figure of the poet, a character who speaks to the matter of his art and lays hold of a firm, though problematic, authorship. It is this figure who appropriates the texts of the poets and establishes the scope of artistic invention; he values "sentence" and "mater of to wryte" over the sheer technical skill of "art poetical" (HF 1095). It is this figure, too, who enlists the eagle to carry him inside the wicker house to realize "al myn entente / Me for to pleyen and for to lere" (2132–33), and who in the *Parliament* recognizes Dame Nature from his own reading. Far from being a passive observer of his own fantasies, he is the willing subject who acts decisively in the interest of his art. In the next three chapters we shall examine the framework and terms Chaucer uses to define the form and substance of that art. Throughout this process of aesthetic definition, the narrator's experience serves equally to project poetic fictions and reflect on the principles that enable such fiction.

Imagination and Memory (I):
The *Book of the Duchess* and
the Beginnings of Chaucer's Narrative

The *Book of the Duchess* is the most historically contextualized of Chaucer's early narrative poems. Chaucer himself connects the poem to the death in 1368 of Blanche of Lancaster, the wife of Edward III's son and Chaucer's patron, John of Gaunt. In the *Legend of Good Women* (F 418) Queen Alceste lists "the Deeth of Blaunche the Duchesse" among the poet's works which serve the God of Love, and in the *Canterbury Tales* (II.57), the Man of Law mentions the "Ceys and Alcione" which comprises one of the major sections of the poem. The testimony of later authorities also draws attention to the connection with Blanche.[1] John Lydgate says in his Prologue to the *Fall of Princes* (1.304–5) that Chaucer wrote "the pitous story off Ceix and Alcione, / And the deth eek of Blaunche the Duchesse." John Stowe is probably the author of note in the chief manuscript source which records that Gaunt commissioned the poem "pitiously complaynynge the deathe of the sayd dutchesse blanche" (Norton-Smith fol. 130).

These historical references have served as indications for a number of modern readers that the meaning of the poem must lie somewhere in the cultural environment that gives rise to it. D. W. Robertson, Jr., proposes ("Setting" 172) that the *Book of the Duchess* may have been written in connection with the yearly memorial service that Gaunt established at St. Paul's Cathedral to mark the anniversary of Blanche's death (September 12). James I. Wimsatt believes that the literary and social contexts of the poem are intertwined. The *Book of the Duchess* opens with an adaptation of the *Paradys d'Amours* by Jehan de Froissart, the favorite poet and secretary of Queen Philippa. Chaucer's proximate source for the story of Ceys and Alcyone is the *Dit de la Fonteinne amoureuse,* composed by Guillaume de Machaut for Jean, Duc de Berry, who was a hostage at Gaunt's palace at the Savoy. Machaut's *Jugement dou Roy de Behaingne* provides an analogue to the dreamer's over-hearing the Black Knight's complaint, and his *Remede de Fortune* is a major source for the themes of the knight's complaint. Wimsatt remarks, "The works [of Froissart and Machaut] with which Chaucer associated his elegy for Blanche were part of London court life and part of history, and perhaps it would not have occurred to the poet at the time to separate the spheres" ("*Lay*" 16).

Given this well-documented background it is surprising that the historical and social contexts shed so little direct light on the *Book of the Duchess.* Though they situate the poem in the milieu of Edward III's court, they offer no framework for interpreting the richly allusive texture of the poem. Instead the contexts have dictated an etiquette of interpretation. The task of modern criticism has been to try to reconcile the poet's seemingly desultory manner of exposition and his ironic self-presentation with the gravity of the presumed occasion of the poem and thereby to uncover a principle of decorum, if not artistic unity.

This need to resolve the dissonance of style and context within such a courtly poem ought to suggest that something beyond simple commemoration is involved in Chaucer's writing the *Book of the Duchess.* Much as it may be elegaic or occasional, the poem stands at the threshold of Chaucer's career as a narrative poet; it is at once example and paradigm—his first long poem and his first treatment of the aesthetic problems of writing narrative. As such the poem attempts to set out a particular mode of vision within the limits imposed by the topic and the social context. If its public and ceremonial purpose is to offer consolation, even "*consolatory entertainment*" (Birney 647), to John of Gaunt, the indwelling and complementary purpose is to examine and reflect on the poet's art. The poem is a work of artistic initiation, and its beginnings lie equally in the domains of representation and aesthetic speculation.

The poet's reflections on his craft counterpoint the narrative development in every structural unit of the poem. The opening description of the poet's insomnia, his reading the tale of Ceyx and Alcyone, and his later dreaming that he joins the emperor's hunt—all these are linked thematically to the elegy for Blanche that emerges in the dialogue of complaint and comfort with the grieving knight.[2] Chaucer announces a set of poetic issues in the early sections by portraying a psychological origin for literary imagination and examining the nature of images and representation. And in the dramatized encounter with the knight he poses questions about the adequacy of language and the play of imagination and memory in commemorative art. These concerns do not, however, form a subtext or hidden meaning discernible only through an allegorical reading; rather, they are implicit in the poetic materials. Inscribed in the work are terms which clarify and comment on its aesthetic process.

The narrative of the *Book of the Duchess* and Chaucer's reflection on poetics grow, moreover, from a sustained engagement with poetic authority. Chaucer relies on Ovid, Guillaume de Lorris, Machaut, and Froissart for the chief episodes of the poem and for details of phrasing, motif, and theme throughout the poem. His borrowings suggest that he read their poetry not simply for the topics of their *materia* but for the range of aesthetic possibilities that these earlier works evoke; he has a critical understanding of his predecessors, and he reconceives their works within his own.[3] It is in this reading that the complex nature of poetic invention becomes evident. While Chaucer follows the models of previous texts, as the rhetoricians had advised, he also discovers his own "purpose" in what they offer. Far from determining the narrative, his borrowings mark the points where chance and intuition operate within poetic composition. For example, Chaucer situates his "Ceys and Alcione" between the antecedent texts of Ovid and Machaut. Similarly, he complicates and makes problematic the conventional language of the black knight's complaint in a way not apparent in the sources and certainly not recognized in the Boethian values that have been taken to represent the cornerstone of the poem's consolation.

Chaucer's poem establishes a new order of meaning that transcends the conceptual and chronological differences in the sources, for in a sense the sources are all authorities, read without historical distance or perspective. It is as if they all belonged to a common literary discourse. Barbara Nolan has argued that in the *Book of the Duchess* Chaucer goes so far as to subvert his authorities in order to free his narrator from the pretentiousness of the French poets and establish him as an enigmatic figure (206). But the impulse in Chaucer's writing is more toward distinction than simple opposition. The narrative action and the poet's self-reflexivity evolve within a courtly milieu and antecedent texts, and the objective is to claim a place within tradition while testing its limitations.

Chaucer's borrowings imply, then, an active poetic dialogue with his contemporaries and predecessors. One dominant feature of that dialogue is a concern with poetic subjectivity, which proves essential for Chaucer's poetics. The determining opposition in Ovid and the French poets is not between reality and illusion but within the economy of subjective experience. Rather than focus on an experience of the world, these writers seek to refine forms of internal perception. Ovid's poetry is centered on interior experience—the emotions of mythological figures in the *Metamorphoses,* the poet's turbulent responses to love in elegiac works like the *Amores.* Guillaume de Lorris opens the *Roman de la rose* with a glossing of Macrobius that insists on the value of dreams as figures of truth. Machaut and Froissart locate the dreamer as the source and interpreter of action in their dream poems. Like these writers, and especially Machaut, Chaucer stresses poetic subjectivity, for it is both a technique for point of view narrative and a starting point for aesthetic creation (Poirion 191–92). More specifically, Chaucer's narrative art begins in the imagination and retains its locus there. The aesthetic problem he faces—and this is the critical project of the early narratives—is to find a means of externalizing interior experience, of transferring what exists within consciousness to an intelligible form that has a social and moral existence and is thus an object of knowledge.

Poetic Imagination

Chaucer signals his concern with poetic subjectivity by opening the *Book of the Duchess* with an account of the narrator's mental state. We might take this as the originary gesture of his narrative, for he explicitly identifies the narrator's interior world as "our first mater" (43) and "my first matere" (218). But the gesture is not made as a personal act of self-inauguration. The narrator's description of his emotional condition draws largely from Froissart's first lines in *Le Paradys d'Amour,* a poem written for Queen Philippa in the 1360s and reflecting in turn a strong debt to Machaut's *Remede.* Froissart gives the initial episode of Chaucer's poem, and his text stands as a metonymic figure for the style of court poetry that dominated the immediate literary and social milieu. Chaucer's beginnings as a narrative poet are thus encoded in both poetic subjectivity and authority.

Froissart opens his poem by presenting the melancholic, insomniac narrator that Chaucer recreates with greater complexity and nuance. The first-person narrator is for Froissart a device to introduce his dream of a paradisiacal garden, where he encounters the allegorical figures of Plaisance and Esperance, the God of Love, and finally his own lady.

> Je sui de moi en grant merveille
> Comment je vifs quant tant je veille,

Et on ne poroit en veillant
Trouver de moi plus traveillant,
Car bien saciés que par veillier
Me viennent souvent travillier
Pensées et merancolies
Qui me sont ens au coer liies
Et pas ne les puis deslyer,
Car ne voeil la belle oublyer
Pour quele amour en ce traveil
Je sui entrés et tant je veil.

(1–12)

I can only be amazed that I am still alive, when I am lying
awake so much. And one cannot find a sleepless person more
tormented than myself, for as you well know, whilst I am lying
awake sad thoughts and melancholy often come to torment
me. They bind my heart tightly, and I cannot loosen them, for
I do not want to forget the fair one, for love of whom I entered
into this torment and suffer such sleeplessness.

Chaucer makes a number of significant adaptations from the passage.
All of Froissart's highly crafted poem employs the diction of the courtly
love vision, except perhaps for a single line in which the poet's lady
asks whether he has composed any new poems: "Avés vous riens fait
de nouvel?" (Haven't you composed anything new? 1602). Derek Brewer
("Relationship" 9) has demonstrated that the style of Chaucer's translation relies, by contrast, on the diction of a native literary tradition to
achieve the effect of conversation: "I have gret wonder, be this lyght, /
How that I lyve, for day ne nyght / I may nat slepe wel nygh noght" (1–
3). Further on in the opening section Froissart's narrator prays to Juno
and Morpheus to grant him relief from his insomnia. However, Chaucer
sees a different possibility. He delays the prayers until later in the poem
and then divides them between his narrator and Alcyone, so as to reflect
the parallels between the dreamer's predicament and Alcyone's tragic
circumstances in Ovid's tale.

The most crucial adaptation is that Chaucer develops Froissart's "pensées et merancolies" into an examination of aesthetic form and imagination. A "defaute of slep" produces "so many an ydel thoght" (5–6)
that the poet-narrator can define the exterior world only by its absence
and negation. Chaucer uses "ydel" with two important connotations: his
thoughts are without practical effect, and they are devoid of moral
significance (MED s.v. "idel"). James Winny has argued that "thought"
includes the categories of imagination and fancy (34), but A. C. Spearing

points out that the term is restricted to the faculty which produces mental images—the imagination (223). "Ydel thoght" represents a process of imagination isolated from the external world and specifically isolated from questions of good and evil. The narrator carries the separation of mental life from sensation into a collapse of discrimination: "Ne me nys nothyng leef nor looth. / Al is ylyche good to me— / Joye or sorowe, wherso hyt be" (8–10). Amplifying Froissart's self-presentation, Chaucer thus situates the beginnings of the narrator's imagination in a play of images without limitation or overt purpose, of signs without referents.

For the narrator, the process unfolds within the polarity of image and "nothing." "I take no kep / Of nothing" (6–7), he observes, and "I have felynge in nothyng" (11). The flow of mental images, he proclaims, can exist independently from real objects and sense experiences. His remarks stipulate a kind of perception that contradicts the classical and medieval premise that ideas proceed from the senses; like dreams, the narrator's condition proceeds from imagination, though he denies sensation (Bundy 186). His "sorwful ymagynacioun" creates its own economy in the "fantasies [that] ben in myn hede." Brewer ("Relationship" 26), citing the usage in Froissart's *Chroniques,* glosses "imagination" as 'desire,' and Douglas Kelly shows that from the twelfth century onwards the term expressed the power to project abstractions and feelings (*Imagination* 45–56, 196). The loss of sensation and the resultant inward turn of the narrator preclude his recognizing a sequence in the images ("how hyt cometh or gooth"), and this disruption of sequence continues into a rupture of time. Although he knows he has suffered a "sicknesse" for eight years, its cause remains hidden and thus capable of an indefinite projection backwards. So, too, the remedy that would impose a term on distraction remains unattainable in the future: "And yet my boote is never the ner" (38).

At the same time that it establishes the narrator's subjective experience as the focal point of narrative, the opening of Chaucer's poem dramatizes the act of imagination and portrays its claims to representation as radically problematic. As in the lyric complaints, Chaucer represents his persona as a figure in isolation: he inhabits an indeterminate, negative space removed from the world, society, rational judgment, and time itself. In its extremity, this is a realm of distraction and obsessive rumination. Yet it cannot be reduced merely to psychopathology, for the terms of reflection and the discriminations of the narrator's imaginative experience are too rich and finely articulated. Nor does the poem's opening devolve to an elegant *captatio benevolentiae,* the rhetorician's gesture seeking the goodwill of his audience by offering a pleasing image of himself. Rather, Chaucer consciously locates the beginning of the poem and the beginnings of his narrative art within a realm of subjective experience that stands as a way of describing aesthetic creation. It is a conspicuously troubled description, though. He does not claim an absolute privilege for imagination and poetic subjectivity. In appropriating Froissart he offers a tacit critique of the French court poets, by reformulating the radical extension of subjectivity in their poems as a paralyzing solipsism at the start of his own.

The Prologue to Machaut's works contains an even more schematized version than Froissart's poem of the conventions within and against which Chaucer begins writing. Love and Nature appear before the poet to give him the content and form of his art. Love confers Machaut's *matière* (Dous Penser, Plaisance, and Esperance), and admonishes him to do no villainy, not to speak badly of women, but to praise and magnify them. Nature gives the means of poetic composition (Scens, Retorique, and Musique). She explains that Scens controls the poet's *matière* ("Car Scens y est qui tout gouverne," 159); Retorique is meters and fixed forms. She also discusses at length the role of the imagination.

> Car quant Souvenir recorder
> Fait l'amant par douce pensée
> Le très belle et la bien amée
> A qui il est mis et donnez
> Et ligement abandonnez,
> Plaisant ymagination
> Met en son cuer l'impression
> De sa douce plaisant figure
> Et dous Pensers qui la figure,
> Dont son fait cent fois embelist:
> Sages est qui tel vie eslist.
> (Hoepffner 1:8)

> For when Memory makes the lover recall by Sweet Thoughts
> the beautiful and much loved lady to whom he is bound and
> given and gently abandoned, Pleasing Imagination puts the
> impression of her sweet, charming figure in his heart and
> Sweet Thoughts shapes it there, which embellishes her face
> a hundred times: wise is the man who chooses such a life.

Chaucer's opening in the *Book of the Duchess* reverses the key terms of Machaut's Prologue. Machaut's "plaisant ymagination" becomes "sorwful ymaginacioun," and the impression given by Imagination, which unites erotic and poetic experience, is reduced to nothing. Machaut observes that a sad man using imagination is made impervious to joy, and he suggests that music is the remedy to melancholy (lines 85–95). Chaucer rejects this traditional therapy, however, and seeks his remedy in the fictional world of narrative rather than the proportions of music.

The book of "romaunce" which Chaucer's narrator orders brought to him to "drive the night away" (49) provides an alternative to distraction and to the poetics of courtly subjectivity. The "written fables" of the clerks and poets have two chief characteristics—their formal order and moral coherence. Shaped by the constraints of rhyme, the tales are the formal antithesis of the narrator's indistinct, disconnected images of melancholy. The stories they tell—"of such thinges, / Of quenes lives, and of kinges, / And many other thinges smale" (57–59)—treat events that occurred in a Golden Age "while men loved the lawe of kinde" (56); they are the ethical contrary to what the narrator describes as his living "agaynes kynde" (16). The narrator conceives of these fables as spatial, even geometrical. Their function is "to be in minde" (55)—that is, to introduce a formal order of imagination that supplants the "sorwful ymagynacioun [that] / Ys alway hooly in my mynde" (14–15) and "suche fantasies [that] ben in myn hede" (28). He argues, in other words, for the displacement of fragmented images by a complete artistic structure and the moral order of poetry. The romance contains the "beter play" by removing his thoughts from "nothing" to "a tale / That me thoughte a wonder thing" (60–61).

Chaucer emphasizes the contrast with Froissart by portraying the book as a means of psychological and moral rescue, and the contrast suggests that his beginnings involve some reevaluation of the craft of the courtly maker. Unlike the book crafted "in olde tyme" (53), Froissart's poem is conspicuously located in the tradition of the *Roman de la rose*. Its main action takes place in the paradisiacal garden (*clos d'Amours*) with the allegorical personnel surrounding the God of Love, and it is concerned with an erotic life that is equivalent to court life. Esperance tells Froissart's dreamer:

> Car, saces, l'amoureuse vie,
> Qui est deduisans et jolie,
> Voelt estre bellement menée,
> Et s'elle est en riens fourmenée,
> On pert son temps et sa saison. . . .
> (649–53)

> For, you know, the life of loving, which is so delightful and beautiful, needs to be very finely carried on, and if it is in any way mismanaged then all one's time is wasted.

The moral order of this world, as the dreamer recognizes, is invested in Plaisance and Esperance, whose function is to oversee "toute ordenance / De joie et consolacion" (everything that is necessary for joy and consolation, 840–41). Their instruction of the dreamer, like Love's admonition to serve him and the dreamer's lady, has to do with courtly behavior, and the object is gratification. Love promises reward: "Tu en auras tel guerredon / Que vrais amans doit prendre en don" (You shall have for it such a reward as a true lover ought to receive, 1361–62). The essence of this reward is pleasure, and when the dreamer finally addresses his lady and presents his ballade to her, she prepares a chaplet for him and proposes they go further into the forest to amuse themselves: "Alons, alons, / Esbanoyer d'une autre part" (Let us go, let us go to enjoy ourselves somewhere else, 1679–80). This is the structural climax of Froissart's dream. The poet has been comforted by his vision, and the world of desire he inhabits in the dream is precisely what he understands the Paradise of Love to mean: "Ensi fui je ravis jadis / Dedens l'Amourous Paradys" (Thus was I once ravished into the Paradise of Love, 1722–23).

By turning from Froissart's projection of his own desire to the stories of the clerks and poets, Chaucer redefines the role of poetic imagination in a different way from the literature of court entertainment. The book of romance is not didactic by design, nor does it follow the Augustinian dichotomy of use and enjoyment whereby aesthetic forms are directed toward divine ends through charity, nor yet does it approach the mathematical proportions of music, whose ratios were thought to evoke a corresponding order in the bodily humours.[4] The book is nonetheless beneficial because the tale it contains deflects "melancolye / And drede" (23–24) into structured forms of representation. Chaucer's follower Thomas Hoccleve adopts this method of displacement in the *Regement of Princes,* when "thought leyd on me full many an hevy loode" (42). Robert Burton likewise explains his writing *The Anatomy of Melancholy:* "I write of melancholy, by being busy to avoid melancholy." The book offers Chaucer's narrator a means for reorganizing subjectivity, for abandoning the circularity of purely internal images in favor of a richer source of imaginative power. The dialectic of images and "nothing" is resolved at the end of the first part of the poem in the "wonder thing" contained in another work, which is appropriated and reconstructed within the narrator's experience. Ovid's story is thus refashioned as an element of subjectivity. At the same time the story reshapes subjectivity by importing another set of images and an alternative structure into poetic consciousness.

Rewriting Ovid

The tale of Ceyx and Alcyone, which supplants the narrator's distracted imaginings, is remarkably fertile in its suggestions for the narrative and aesthetic dimensions of Chaucer's poem. Though the lines of Ovid's story do not offer exact parallels for either the narrator or the man in black, from a thematic viewpoint the tale describes a bond of love particularly suited to the rhetoric of elegy and the social occasion of Chaucer's writing. It is a story of faithful married love, and it dramatizes the need for comfort which brackets the *Book of the Duchess* in the figures of the narrator and the bereaved knight. Chaucer's version of the tale, like his borrowing from Froissart, also defines the intertextual situation of poetic composition. The story Chaucer tells is the product of a history of literary translations. Brooks Otis points out that in the *Metamorphoses* Ovid revised earlier versions of the myth which emphasized the pride and impiety of Ceyx and Alcyone and the divine vengeance against them. Ovid presents instead an ideal of conjugal love and the indifference of the gods; he creates "a tragedy of innocent, mutual love" that differs, too, from previous episodes in the *Metamorphoses* where love is pathological or criminal or where it effects a degeneration from the human to the animal. Love is no longer an "impersonal isolating force, but an element in the drama of *two* lovers" (268, 266).

Machaut's handling of the story in the *Dit de la Fonteinne amoureuse,* Chaucer's immediate source, subordinates this theme to what William Calin has rightly described as "a style of courtly living" (165). Ovid's tale of mutual love is resituated in a social environment that serves both as the imaginary world of the poem and the literary context of the poet. The first-person narrator of Machaut's poem overhears and transcribes the story, which is embedded in a complaint made by a chivalric lover standing for Machaut's patron, Jean, Duc de Berry, who is about to begin his exile in England. The story is doubly part of courtly discourse, since its function is not simply to exemplify an ideal love; Machaut's knight reads the tale primarily as a narrative model by which he might communicate his feelings to his lady: "qu'a briés mos / Le gentil corps qui n'a point de pareil / Sache mon cuer, ma tristece, mon dueil" (that in a few words my noble lady beyond compare may know my heart, my sadness, my grief, 710–12). His "propos" (699, 700) is determined by the contradiction inherent in courtly discourse: he wants to convey *sentiment* in a way that does not disclose private feeling through public language. The lady is to know his heart and emotions, and nevertheless she must preserve their opacity: "Et qu'il le tient par son dous riant vueil / Pris et enclos" (and that with kindly good will it be kept quite secret, 713–14).

Chaucer draws on the thematic developments of Ovid and Machaut to celebrate married love as a social and ethical norm with values of equality and stability and a notion of governance whose overtones are social and political as well as domestic. In the black knight's speeches married love is portrayed from the retrospect of elegy, but that portrayal is prepared for early in the poem by establishing a consistent tone that originates in the narrator's affective response to the story. Alcyone's reiterated "sorwe" (95, 98, 100, 203, 213) links the myth with the melancholic narrator (10, 21). Her "sorowful lif" is an example of what the narrator projects in his "sorwful ymagynacioun." The narrator and the heroine are "for sorwe ful nygh wood" (104), and both pray for sleep as a way of ending their distress. Furthermore, he establishes his "pitee" as the ethical center of the poem, for his capacity to identify with the story imbues imagination with a human and moral resonance.

Chaucer also goes beyond the thematic correspondence to explore still other possibilities contained in the classical and medieval texts. Ceyx changes from the carefully elaborated figure in Ovid who is oppressed by the monstrous sight of the sea-wolf and anxious for more prophetic knowledge. He resembles a chivalric knight like Arveragus in the Franklin's Tale, who also undertakes a foreign journey, but the main effort in Chaucer's version is to reduce the importance of Ceyx as a character with a complex and independent history. The effect is to focus the narrative on Alcyone. For her part Alcyone loses her initial foreboding of disaster, mentioned twice by Ovid (11.427–38; 547–60) and amplified in the *Ovide Moralisé* (11.3029–79), and becomes something close to the heroine of medieval romance who, like Dorigen, remains behind with worries that grow with her husband's absence.

In Machaut's version of the story the catastrophe occurs "par fortune" (544, 557), just as the mourning knight of Chaucer's poem will blame Fortune for the loss of his lady. Fortune emerges as a cause that replaces Ovid's "divine indifference," and it allows a rehabilitation of the pagan deities. Juno, irritated by Alcyone's insistent prayers in the *Metamorphoses,* becomes beneficent in Machaut's retelling: "Juno, la deesse, ot si grant / Pité de li" (565–66). Machaut's change in characterization may have been prompted by an ambiguous passage in the *Ovide Moralisé* (11.3423–24): "Ne pot Juno longues souffrir / Que cele perdist sa proiere."[5] Whatever the source, Chaucer develops Machaut's suggestion to the point of making Juno into Alcyone's patron, a role more fitting to her traditional duties as the goddess of marriage.

In Ovid geographical descriptions are integral to the meaning of the poem, and in Chaucer they serve both to represent action and comment on the terms of representation. Otis remarks that Ovid intends the cave of Somnus to contrast with the storm that drowns Ceyx. "The elaborately allegorical picture of the cave," he says, "seems carefully designed to take us away from Ceyx's tragedy and Alcyone's grief into a realm of pleasing paradox and unreality" (250). It is, in short, a realm of aesthetic perception. Chaucer's description of "the derke valeye" (155) inhabited by Morpheus presents a wasteland; it portrays the topography of distraction by containing "nothing." It recalls, too, the narrator's earlier equation of his melancholy and the darkness of night (49). Ovid has depicted a shaded space with luxurious flora and fragrances. Machaut shows Iris arriving in a valley between two mountains with a meandering stream and a "maison qui fu bele a merveille" (595). But Chaucer paints an intentionally sterile landscape.

Although Chaucer's portrayal of the underworld borrows partly from Statius's famous description of the Cave of Sleep (*Thebaid* 10.84–117), Chaucer seems specifically to be redeploying Ovid's description of the stillness encountered at the threshold of the cave ("ante fores antri").

> non vigil ales ibi cristati cantibus oris
> evocat Auroram, nec voce silentia rumpunt
> sollicitive canes canibusve sagacior anser;
> non fera, non pecudes, non moti flamine rami
> humanaeve sonum reddunt convicia linguae.
> muta quies habitat. . . .
>
> (11.597–602)

> There no wakeful, crested cock with his loud crowing summons the dawn; no careful watch-dog breaks the deep silence with his voice, or goose, still shrewder than the dog. There is no sound of wild beast or of cattle, of branches rustling in the breeze, no clamorous tongues of men. There mute silence dwells.

The landscape Chaucer reconceives is not an aesthetic counterpoint to the forces of natural destruction, as in Ovid, but an extension of devastating power: "Ther never yet grew corn ne gras, / Ne tre, ne [noght] that ought was, / Beste, ne man, ne noght elles" (157–59). Ovid depicts Somnus's house with a boundary that does not impede entry: "ianua . . . / nulla domo tota, custos in limine nullus" (there is no door in all the house, . . . no guardian on the threshold, 11.608–9). Chaucer offers a vision of barrenness such as recurs in the empty field of sand in the *House of Fame* (480–91). The opulent interior of the classical poem comes to resemble a "helle-pit" (171) in Chaucer's poem, the geographical analogue to distraction, the poetic emblem of self-enclosed imagination.

The most striking change Chaucer makes is the suppression of the final part of the Ovidian myth, in which Ceyx and Alcyone are transformed into seabirds. In Machaut this transformation symbolizes the Duc de Berry's hope to transcend his exile; in Gower's *Confessio Amantis* it will be a figure "for the trowthe of love" (4.3090) and Alceone will continue "to do the plesance of a wif" (4.3111) after she is reunited in changed form with Ceix. But Chaucer tells the story without this last episode and consequently gives it a different accent and meaning. In a transitional passage at the end of the tale, he makes it clear that the stress falls on "this dreynte Seys the kyng / And of the goddes of slepyng" (229–30). Chaucer's main interest evidently lies in the dream in which Morpheus appears as Ceyx. It is an interest that grows out of an astute reading of the earlier texts.

Morpheus's role as the titular deity of sleep in the *Book of the Duchess* marks a decisive change from Ovid's personification of Somnus. For Chaucer the change may owe to Machaut, who retains the "Dieus de sommeil" (569, 603, 652) in the narrative action of the *Fonteinne amoureuse* but originally entitled the whole poem *Morpheus* and sent it to Péronne d'Armentières under that title (Hoepffner 3:xxi, Poirion 203). In Ovid, Morpheus is the archetypal persona, the actor-orator among the thousand sons of Somnus, hence a figure of the poet's rhetorical and imaginative powers.

> ... artificem simulatoremque figurae
> Morphea: non illo quisquam sollertius alter
> exprimit incessus vultumque sonumque loquendi;
> adicit et vestes et consuetissima cuique
> verba; sed hic solos homines imitatur. . . .
> (11.634–38)

> ... a cunning imitator of the human form. No other is more skilled than he in representing the gait, the features, and the speech of men; the clothing also and the accustomed words of each he represents. His office is with men alone. . . .

Ovid's Morpheus recounts Ceyx's pathetic drowning by verbal description and the visual imitation of character. What is significant about his appearance in the dream is the way in which it makes claims for the powers of imaginative representation. Morpheus at first appears to define representation as a semiotic relation of sign and signified, image and reality. He tells Alcyone, "respice: nosces / inveniesque tuo pro coniuge coniugis umbram" (You will know me then and find in place of husband your husband's shade, 660). The shadow is the natural sign of the man, the simulacrum of his being and paradoxically the token of his absence; it operates as metaphor (a representation of the man) and metonym (the shadow connected to the man). Morpheus, however, complicates this already complex distinction between sign and referent: "non haec tibi nuntiat auctor / ambiguus, non ista vagis rumoribus audis: / ipse ego fata tibi praesens mea naufragus edo" (And this tale no uncertain messenger brings to you, nor do you hear it in the words of vague report; but I myself, wrecked as you see me, tell you of my fate, 666–68). Not just a shadow but a perceptual reality ("tibi praesens"), Morpheus becomes the image of Ceyx and thereby displaces him.

In this passage Ovid artfully exploits the various meanings of *auctor* as 'author' and 'narrator' in order to conflate resemblance and identity. By being the 'narrator' of the story Morpheus becomes its 'author.' He is not *ambiguus,* 'uncertain,' for his power to imitate speech, gesture, and appearance renders a true and compelling account of Ceyx's drowning. Nonetheless, he is pure illusion, *artificem simulatoremque figurae.* Further, his powers of representation are constrained by the species and not the individual. Morpheus imitates men but not other creatures ("hic solos homines imitatur"), but he imitates all men and not just one. In the figure of Morpheus, Ovid intentionally obscures the boundaries of fiction and reality. He offers a model of representation that locates poetic creation within the problematic grounds of imagination.

Medieval versions of Ovid's tale reject the implications of his portrayal of Morpheus by insisting on the illusory quality of dreams. In the *Ovide Moralisé* the God of Sleep is surrounded by a host of images that generate illusions beyond any comparison with things in the natural world. The movements of these dream images anticipate the flow of internal images that Chaucer associates with the narrator's distraction in the *Book of the Duchess* and with the transformations of speech into images in the *House of Fame*.

> Entour lui multiplietez
> De songes et de vanitez
> Plus qu'il n'a d'espis en moissons
> Et qu'il n'a fueilles en buissons
> Et plus qu'il n'a sable ou rivage.
>
> (11.3472–76)

> Dreams and empty images were multiplying around him more than corn at harvest-time or leaves in a bush or gravel on a river bank.

The physics of the dream world may simulate and even exceed the plenitude of Nature, but the images remain distinct from empirical reality. Morpheus is reduced to being a category in this nominal world. He has the ability to mimic speech and mannerisms, but he lacks substance in himself. The text is precise and revealing on this point: "Li peres cest songe apeloit / Morpheüs" (3529–30). Accordingly, the message to Alcyone stresses the truth of what Morpheus portrays rather than his being the "auctor."

> Je sui cil qui presentement
> Le te di, si le dois miex croire,
> Sans douter que ma mors soit voire,
> Que s'uns autres le te deïst,
> Qui menconge espoir i meïst.
>
> (3593–97)

I am the one who says this to you at this moment, and you ought to believe without doubt that my death is true, for if someone else should say otherwise, he would want to lie.

The *Ovide Moralisé* reinforces the distinction between illusion and reality by the author's comment after Morpheus appears to Alcyone: "En tel samblant, en tel ymage, / Ot fet Morpheus son message" (3602–3). The verb *sambler* appears twice in the passage (3604, 3611), as if to insist further on the distinction.

Machaut's treatment follows in these directions while serving the aims of courtly discourse. The knight in the *Fonteinne amoureuse* tells the tale of Ceyx and Alcyone against the background of his own erotic dilemma; his desire and frustration are the real referent of the mythological *fabula*. Morpheus is the means for conveying his emotions through images that both reproduce a human figure and stand for something beyond the mere figure. Morpheus appears before Alchioine as an image of Ceyx.

> Lors Morpheüs
> Prist la fourme que Ceïs avoit nus
> Et moult forment fu mouilliez et emplus;
> Plus tors avoit les cheveus et locus
> C'une cordelle.
>
> (658–62)

Then Morpheus took the naked shape of Ceyx, much drenched and filled with water, and with matted, dishevelled hair.

His appearance is a sign: "Voy mes cheveus, voy ma barbe grifaingne;

/ Voy mon habit / Qui de ma mort te moustre vraie enseingne!" (see my hair, see my wild beard, see my clothes, which show you a true token of my death, 677–79). The point of the knight's story ("mon propos") is that Morpheus should discharge a similar office for him. He asks that Morpheus transport himself five or six times before the dreaming lady "En ma fourme qui est a moitié morte" (in my form, which is half-dead, 717) and plead his case. In this way Morpheus will disable the social controls that impede the knight, whose exile compounds his fear that the lady might not know of his love for her. Morpheus will convey the message secretly to her heart ("en son cuer tient secretement close / De Morpheüs la parole et enclose," 756–57) where it becomes an object of memory and reading ("l'en souveigne et la glose / Et qu'elle dongne a chascun mot sa glose," 759–60).

Machaut's version of the story incorporates a measure of irony and comedy while it dramatizes the patron's dilemma as a lover. It takes only one appearance for Morpheus to deliver the message in Ovid, but half a dozen may be required to penetrate the defenses of social convention in Machaut. The knight sees himself in the situation of Ceyx but only by approximation; he is half dead, and the cause is love rather than a catastrophe at sea. Kevin Brownlee (*Machaut* 194–95) points out that the appeal to Morpheus depends on the *Roman de la rose* as a poetic subtext. The lover wants his lady to understand that "Songier souvent ne doit mie estre fable, / Einsois chose doit estre veritable" (often-thinking [lit. dreaming] should not be something fanciful, but rather it should be something substantial, 783–84). The line directly echoes Guillaume's opening defense of the reliability of dreams in the *Roman*. What is not at issue in Machaut is the poetic ambiguity that Ovid exploits. Morpheus is never more than a sign, a reproductive image from the external world circulating in the play of dreams and desire.

Against this intertextual background Chaucer's presentation of Morpheus focuses certain questions about the nature of poetic representation. Ovid employs a tale of faithful love to posit a theory of representation in a character whose name (Morpheus) is a variation of the poem's title (*Metamorphoses*) and its essential process of change (metamorphosis). Chaucer deals with problems of the imagination in an elegy about married love, whose reality is fixed, though the process of consolation remains fluid. In the *Metamorphoses,* Morpheus's ambitious claim to substitute the sign for the signified occurs as the climactic development in the demise of prophetic verse that began with the death of Orpheus at the start of Book 11: the vatic singer has devolved to the ventriloquist inhabiting a corpse, and the next step for Ovid is the beginning of human history with the story of the Trojan War. Robert W. Hanning suggests that "Chaucer would have found in Ovid not only an affecting tale of love and loss, but a sophisticated consideration of his own art" ("First Ovid" 129–30). Yet Chaucer, like other medieval writers, rejects the terms that permit Ovid to extend Morpheus's impersonation into a self-sustained representation. He observes the belief already expressed in the *Ovide Moralisé* (3536–48) and Machaut (536–50) that "fourmes," "figures," and "faintes illucions" comprise a discrete realm of imagination.

Chaucer's Morpheus follows Juno's bidding that he "crepe into the body / And doo hit goon to Alcione" (144–45). His address to her makes no claim about the truth of his representation but focuses instead on her welfare ("I praye God youre sorwe lysse," 210) and his need for burial. The language of address is at once courtly and domestic: Alcyone is by turns "my swete wyf" (201), "swete" (204, 209), and "goode swete herte" (206). By constraining Morpheus's ventriloquism Chaucer maintains the discrimination between illusion and reality, the sign and the thing signified. His Morpheus conspicuously remains within the bounds of aesthetic imagination so that the poet-narrator cannot substitute the imitation for the exemplar. In this respect Gower's version of the tale serves as a gloss on Chaucer's handling of his own sources. Gower restricts Morpheus to the limited function of imitating men and supplements this function with other figures; Ithecus imitates voices and Panthasas imitates "the rihte forme" of everything. These three together, he says, create "al thapparence" of dreams, "which otherwhile is evidence / And otherwhile bot a jape" (4.3053–55).

Chaucer's reading of Ovid and Machaut concentrates equally, then, on the question of imagination and the use of myth within courtly discourse. Though Chaucer rejects Ovid's conflation of the signifier and the signified here, he returns to something much like it in the *House of Fame,* where "tydinges" assume the shape of their speakers. Furthermore, Morpheus anticipates the role that the narrator will play later in the *Book of the Duchess* by leading the black knight to announce that his lady is dead. It is Morpheus, too, who presumably brings the dream that offers consolation. The narrator's dream explicitly diverges from biblical and classical traditions. Authorities like Joseph and Macrobius, he says, will be able to "rede" (279, 281, 289) the dream "no more than koude the lest of us" (283). The vision is separated from prophetic, oracular, and enigmatic dreams, hence from the authority that Guillaume invokes in the *Roman de la rose;* it contains no elaborately veiled meanings, no revelations which yield to interpretation. Morpheus represents the capacity to create an independent fiction within a social and literary language.

The Dialogue of Complaint and Comfort

Most questions of interpretation in the *Book of the Duchess* concern the encounter between the narrator-dreamer and the man in black. Their encounter takes place in an intentionally decentered landscape. In the *Roman de la rose,* the dreamer, unaware of being stalked by the God of Love, proceeds through the garden toward the fountain of Narcissus and the rose who is located at the central axis. Chaucer's narrator discovers the man in black in a parabolic landscape whose only landmark is the "long castel with walles white, / . . . on a ryche hil" (1318–19). The rose as object of desire is replaced in the *Book of the Duchess* by the architectural symbol of John of Gaunt and his duchess.

Critics generally divide the episode into three sections, corresponding to the points where the narrator interrupts the man's speeches.[6] The elegy progresses from the knight's complaint against Fortune to his account of himself as a young lover and finally to a description of his love affair with White. The major crux has to do with the supposedly obtuse narrator, who seems not to understand that White is dead until the knight tells him so explicitly after the three speeches. The narrator hears the knight's lament clearly enough in the first part to repeat some of the verses, yet he seems to miss the point. Consequently, he must be either naive and stupefied or tactfully pretending ignorance so as to lead the knight around to saying that his lady is dead.[7] Alternatively, the issue can be treated as a matter of divergent styles. The aureate language of the knight's lament, it has been argued, is too exalted for the narrator, who can respond feelingly to scenes from Ovid, the *Roman de la rose* and the Troy Book but is confused by the man in black's Boethian meter.[8] Accordingly, he either does not comprehend the fact of White's death or wrongly assumes that the verses are a courtly lament about a lady who has rejected the lover's suit. In either case, the nature of language and not the fictional consistency of the narrator—his obtuseness or therapeutic cunning—is at issue.

Whatever the confusions or outright contradictions in the fictional surface, it is clear that the exchanges between the narrator and the man in black proceed dialectically through a series of parallels and contrasts.[9] Furthermore, these exchanges combine the language of narrative description and aesthetic speculation. Like the narrator, the man in black is preoccupied with his own mental world: "he spak noght, / But argued with his owne thoght" (503–4). His inner discourse turns on "hevy thoght" (509) and sorrow, which is obsessively reiterated here as it is earlier with the narrator and Alcyone. The account of his "firste youthe" recalls the narrator's "ydelnesse," and he suffers the same condition— "al my thoght varyinge" (802). He arrives at the same leveling of perception that characterizes the narrator's melancholy: "Al were to me ylyche good / That I knew thoo" (803–4).

But unlike the narrator, the man in black cannot be diverted from his sorrow by the stories of the clerks and poets. The narrator attempts to discover the cause of sorrow in terms that recall his own shift from distraction to formal structures of imagination: "Anoon ryght I gan fynde a tale / To hym, to loke wher I myght ought / Have more knowynge of hys thought" (536–8). The discursive aim of probing his "thought" would presumably be translated into the "tale" that reveals something of the grief. The knight's unwillingness to continue the dreamer's metaphor of the "hert-huntyng" marks, however, a crucial difference in the two figures: "My thought ys theron never a del" (543). This refusal to displace sorrow through imaginative equations is directed specifically at the narrator's therapy. On the model of Lady Philosophy's driving off the Muses, the knight rejects the option of deflecting melancholy and denies the efficacy of artists and physicians alike: Ovid, Orpheus, and Daedalus and also Hippocrates and Galen. The image he offers of himself as a "wrecche, that deth hath mad al naked" (577) contrasts pointedly with the dreamer who lies "in my bed al naked" (293) amid a chamber filled with song and visual wonders. The knight's lament composed "withoute noote, withoute song" (472) is "the antithesis of the 'oon acord' of the harmonious chamber" (Peck "Theme" 81).

These parallels and contrasts have led readers to argue variously that the narrator and the man in black are both bereaved lovers, opposing figures, or even differing aspects of the same poet. More important, I think, is the way in which these patterns exemplify differing conceptions of language and poetry. Chaucer separates the narrator's concern with the formal aspects of imagination from the black knight's absorption in his grief. The separation is repeatedly asserted in the knight's comment to the narrator: "Thou wost ful lytel what thou menest; / I have lost more than thow wenest" (743–4; cf.1137–38; 1305–6). Their dialogue, as the man in black remarks, has to do with the relation of language to experience. It involves the power of received discourse to weigh against the reality of suffering and loss. The traditions of epideictic oratory, which Chaucer follows in his poem and his narrator follows in the dialogue with the knight, at once proclaim and defer consolation. They provide a vehicle of formalized expression but hold the speaker within the limits of a rhetorical system. Thus as the speakers enact a drama of complaint and comfort, the adequacy of discourse remains at issue throughout the poem.

The knight immediately impresses the narrator as "tretable, / Ryght wonder skylful and resonable" (533–34). All three of these terms deal with the aesthetic ordering of experience in a discursive form, which the knight finds inadequate. "Tretable," which the knight later applies to White (923), signifies one's being open to logical persuasion, argument, and discussion.[10] The knight is "wonder skylful" in his literary craft and "resonable" not only in a capacity for judgment but in his ability to discuss matters, to bring them into discourse (*OED*, s.v. "reasonable"). The description asserts that the knight is articulate and cultivated in speech, as the narrator surmises; and it connects him to a style of discourse that appeals to the intellect as surely as the narrator's appeals to the imagination. But it does so in a way that complicates the issue and finally leaves it for Chaucer to explore in other poems.

The knight's complaint reveals precisely the qualities he claims to have lost. Protesting that sorrow "hath myn understondynge lorn" (565), he nonetheless conducts a self-analysis and sets out a pattern of elaborate antithesis which expresses his conflict. "My lyf, my lustes, be me loothe" (581), he says, and this estrangement from sensation reduces him to the abstraction of an allegorical figure: "y am sorwe, and sorwe ys y" (597). A protracted list of antitheses (*contrastio*), in the style of Machaut's narrative *dits,* explains this change as the cumulative effect of more limited reversals. Behind them all is Fortune, who embodies the figure of antithesis. The "ydole of fals portrayture" (626), she is the apparent source of the reversal that the mourner has experienced and must resolve within his own understanding. Yet unlike Morpheus, whom the narrator has invoked "in my game" (238), "She ys pley of enchauntement" (648).

The difference between these two figures and the play they represent is a difference in kind, and Chaucer invokes it in order to distinguish the faculties at work within aesthetic creation. The narrator addresses Morpheus as a figure for imagination, while the man in black confronts Fortune as part of his own effort to discover reason. His real complaint, he finds, is directed not at Fortune but at his own limited knowledge. Fortune is indeed "the false thef" (650), but in the chess game that symbolizes the loss of White, Fortune merely presses an advantage that falls to her through the young lover's ignorance. As Philosophy instructs Boethius, Fortune cannot be reviled for being what she is, and the knight admits, "Myself I wolde have do the same, / Before God, hadde I ben as she" (676–77).

The portrayal of the man in black uncovers, then, a radical disparity that does not surface in the narrator's speeches. Despite his understanding of Fortune, the man in black is unable to achieve consolation. Knowing the truth does not free him from mutability and the sorrow of earthly loss but instead mires him deeper in grief. His response challenges the fundamental assumptions of the *Consolatio Philosophiae* and the courtly narratives built on the teachings of Boethius, for he both admits and resists Boethius's solution. The knight concedes, "ther lyeth in rekenyng, / In my sorwe, for nothyng" (699–700). The power of philosophy and reasoning is not in question so much as a failing in human terms.

An important part of that failing stems from difficulties inherent in language. The rhetoric of complaint allows the knight a posture instead of release because oratory weighs too heavily on experience. Martin Stevens has suggested, "In the final analysis, the suffering of the Knight is caused by the inefficacy of codified sentiments. He is a paragon of courtly manners. As such, he cannot grasp the truth which his rhetoric obscures and which the humbler person knows instinctively" (32).[11] This misapplication of language continues, in more modest dimensions, in the narrator's attempt to console the knight, for he construes the metaphor of the chess game literally and offers catalogues of strangely inapplicable examples of tragic suicide. The initial failure in both speakers, though in different degrees, has to do with courtly discourse.

Chaucer's source for the scene between the dreamer and the man in black is Machaut's *Le Jugement dou Roy de Behaingne,* the earlier of two narrative *dits* by Machaut in which a lady and knight debate whether the death or the betrayal of a lover constitutes the greater loss. The *Behaingne* is also the source for specific lines which Chaucer quotes and paraphrases. For example, Machaut's knight tells the bereaved lady (89–92):

> "Mais je vos jur et promet par may foy,
> S'a moy volez descouvrir vostre anoy,
> Que je feray tout le pooir de moy
>   De l'adrecier."

> But I swear to you and promise by my faith
> That, if you'd reveal your troubles to me,
> I would do everything in my power
>   To put them right.

Chaucer assigns the speech to the narrator (548–51) and translates it in a way that echoes the key phrase *descouvrir vostre anoy.*

> "But certes, sire, yif that yee
> Wolde ought discure me youre woo,
> I wolde, as wys God helpe me soo,
> Amende hyt, yif I kan or may."

The borrowing functions as both a source and a citation: Chaucer recreates the scene in Machaut and at the same time signals his appropriation of the original text. Within the context of his poem, however, the borrowing, like the earlier use of Froissart, points toward a strategy of intertextual revision. The narrator and the knight, like the noble speakers of Machaut's poem, are constrained by the language they use to express and examine their predicaments. Understanding lies beyond the narrator's absorption in imagination or the knight's rationalizing. It depends on sublimating sensitive to intellectual memory, on holding and keeping things "apprehendid and iknowe bi þe ymaginatif and *racio*" (Trevisa 2:98).

The need for such a development is apparent in the black knight's description of himself as a young man. He portrays his youth as a sensibility without direction. The indeterminate period from his first inclination to pursue love until the decisive encounter with White, like the narrator's more recent insomnia, is dominated by ethical concerns that are formulated as aesthetic questions. Love "cam first in my thoght" (789): "I ches love to my firste craft" (791) over "other art or letre" (788). But it is a governance in which service lacked an informing principle. He remembers himself as a *tabula rasa.*

> "Paraunter I was therto most able,
> As a whit wal or a table,
> For hit ys redy to cacche and take
> Al that men wil theryn make,
> Whethir so men wil portreye or peynte,
> Be the werkes never so queynte."
>
> (779–84)

In this retrospective self-portrait as earlier in the dreamer's chamber, writing is equated with the visual imagination. The knight draws on imagery that derives ultimately from Plato's *Thaeatetus* (140a) and refers specifically to problems of knowledge and cognition. The proximate source is Machaut's *Remede de Fortune,* which elaborates the conceit of the art of love by defining how one learns the art. For Machaut the first requisite, as with the man in black, is character and inclination: "La premiere est qu'il doit eslire / Celui ou ses cuers mieus se tire / Et on sa nature l'encline" (The first is that he should choose something to which his heart is most drawn, or to which his nature inclines, 3–5). As the knight in the *Behaingne* explains in a nearly parallel passage, this inclination soon finds its object in the lady; implicitly, she has been the object all along, and love guides the lover to her (*Remede* 71–94; *Behaingne* 261–80).

Chaucer, by contrast, dwells on the black knight's potential for love, his negative capability within an aesthetics of desire. Machaut's aim is to describe the general discipline needed to learn an art ("Armes, amours, autre art ou lettre," 40); he strikes a pose, as Kevin Brownlee points out (*Machaut* 38), of clerkly authority. Chaucer portrays a specific exercise of will and habit for which the objects of desire are arbitrary. The man in black presents himself as the blank space of writing, and unlike Machaut's lovers, who move, albeit with some anxiety, under Love's firm direction, he accepts the inscription of every image—"Be the werkes never so queynte" (784).

In this passage, the man in black duplicates the Stoic argument that Boethius had reproduced in the *Consolation:* "Ymages and sensibilities (*that is to seyn, sensible ymaginaciouns or ellis ymaginaciouns of sensible thingis*) weren enprientid into soules fro bodyes withoute-forth." Boethius had rejected the argument from an epistemological basis. He asks, "whennes comith thilke knowynge in our soule, that discernith and byholdith alle thinges?" (*Boece* 5.m4.28–30). Boethius's implication is that the shapes impressed from the exterior must correspond to what is already inscribed.[12] But the youth's conduct of love separates itself from what should be intrinsic, much as the rhetoric of his complaint diverges from the emotional core of lived experience.

The significance of Chaucer's rewriting portions of the *Remede* and *Behaingne* becomes evident in the portrayal of White. She embodies the inner qualities absent from the black knight's description of himself. Readers have long seen in her the personification of "all those virtues which courtly love prized" (Manning 99). But she represents more than the culmination of courtly virtues. Wimsatt ("Apotheosis") connects the Marian imagery of her description to a theological tradition in which the Virgin's physical beauty reflects inner perfection. John Fyler (65–81) contends that Blanche represents in a fallen world the Golden Age portrayed earlier in the poem by the tale of Ceyx and Alcyone.

White introduces moral substance to the knight's potential for love by adding the values of truth, perseverance, temperate governance, and reason. D. W. Robertson, Jr., rightly observes that "the virtues of Blanche belong to the realm of the intelligible," even though the man in black seems not to grasp the meaning of his own suggestion ("Setting" 186). As lover and poet, hence as the figure situated at the center of courtly discourse, he must appreciate both facets of love. White's "mesure," manifesting the proportions given her by Nature, is exemplified throughout the description of her that balances and completes the knight's self-portrait. It is nowhere more apparent than in the knight's remarks on her "goodly, softe speche" (919), which combines the substance and form of reason into natural eloquence. The "tretable" and "resonable" speaker of the complaint, as the narrator describes the knight, only adumbrates White's speech, which is "up al resoun so wel yfounded, / And so tretable to alle goode" (922–23) that it effects a synthesis of rhetoric and truth.

The knight calls his portrait of White "my firste song" (1182). Its most important sources, like those for his own self-portrait, are Machaut's *Behaingne* and *Remede*. Chaucer's deployment of Machaut's poems in the portrait of White significantly differentiates their functions, however. The *Behaingne* provides the description of White within courtly society (817–29, 848–58), the inventory of her physical features (859–74, 895–918, 939–47, 952–60), a language of address borrowed from the courtly lyric (1035–41), and the outline of the black knight's suit to win her love (1183–1297). The *Remede* furnishes most of the language of ethical description. It provides a way of speaking about White's social virtues (833–43), her capacity to fuse language and truth (919–37), her power to transform the lover's erotic inclinations into worship and purposive service (1088–1111), and his acceptance of love without disclosing it to the lady (1146–51). The portrait is combinative, but it is to the same extent compensatory. The world of subjective perception and social action set forth in the borrowings from the *Behaingne* needs to be complemented by the moral discriminations that Chaucer imports from the *Remede*. The source for White's portrait is, after all, the description of a woman who betrays her love in the *Behaingne*. Thus the *Remede* is the conceptual and thematic corrective to the description over which the black knight sketches his portrait of White.

The differentiation of these sources into separate functions reveals at the level of poetic composition the aesthetic problem that the black knight embodies as a character. How is the poem to advance from imagination and sensitive memory toward understanding? And how is the grieving knight to find comfort through the process of complaint? Chaucer's response to the first question, as I have indicated, is finally disjunctive; he fabricates a composite in which the ethical stature of White presumably cancels out the betrayal recorded in the original text. The knight's response to the question facing him is, according to most readers, simply inadequate; it is, as the dreamer suggests, "shryfte wyth-oute repentaunce" (1114). The aesthetic issues involved here can be seen perhaps most clearly when Chaucer's poem is viewed against another work which has the twin purposes of memorial recollection and poetic beginning. The work I have in mind is Dante's *Vita Nuova,* the lyrico-narrative book of memory that celebrates Dante's love for Beatrice. My point is not that Dante served as a source for Chaucer's elegy (Chaucer's borrowings certainly mark his debt to Machaut) but that Dante provides a way of reading Chaucer's text in its full possibilities and of gauging its poetic achievement.

Both Chaucer and Dante begin their careers as narrative poets by con-verting the retrospective impulse of elegy to the anticipation of new po-etry. Their works share a number of common topics and operate within the same conventions of epideictic rhetoric. Each preserves the poems of lovers and records their fretful service to the ladies. White's first ap-pearance has the same effect as Beatrice on Dante's spirits: "Apparuit iam beautitudo vestra" (Now your bliss has appeared). White is "lady / Of the body; she had the herte" (1152–53), whereas Beatrice eats the poet's heart in his first vision. The knight sees White framed in "the fayrest companye / Of ladyes" (807–8); Dante receives Beatrice's first greeting as she walks between two "gentili donne" (noble ladies, chap. 3). Names hold a con-spicuous place as signs of an informing order of values in each poem. The knight believes in the appropriateness of White's name: "She was bothe fair and bryght; / She hadde not hir name wrong" (950–51). He thus shares Dante's cardinal assumption: "Nomina sunt consequentia re-rum" (Names are the consequences of things, chap. 13).

In their separate accounts Chaucer and Dante examine the power of memory to recreate experience. Both accounts go past commemoration and mere aesthetic formulations to probe the inherent significance of experience. In so doing they portray a complex interaction of choice and necessity and of sense and reason. While describing his youth, for instance, the man in black presents a subtle balance of amorous incli-nation and will. The origin of his rational powers ("any maner wyt" and "kyndely understondyng") is coterminous with his inclination toward love. He emphasizes that he becomes Love's servant "hooly with good entente, / And throgh plesaunce . . . / With good wille, body, hert, and al" (766–68). Will and reason are joined in love, and the role of Love's "tributarye" is undertaken in awareness and consent. Yet the formulation stands incomplete. Full knowledge requires the addition of rational memory, and this carries with it the universals that render categories of human experience intelligible.[13]

In Dante the details of the earlier life are missing from the prose, having been omitted from the poet's Book of Memory and therefore irrelevant to the new life. The poet recognizes that from the first meeting Love dominates him through imagination, and imagination concedes the power of volition: "D'allora innanzi dico che Amore segnoreggiò la mia anima, la quale fu sì tosto a lui disponsata, e cominciò a prendere sopra me tanta sicurtade e tanta signoria per la vertù che li dava la mia immaginazione, che me convenia fare tutti li suoi piaceri compiutamente" (From that time forward I say Love reigned over my soul, which was so quickly pledged to him, and he began to take such assurance and mastery over me through the power that my imagination gave him that it was proper for me to do all his pleasures completely, chap. 2). The effects of Beatrice's appearance on the senses similarly permit Love to move the body, "lo quale era tutto allora sotto lo suo reggimento" (which was then wholly under his governance, chap. 11).

This way of explaining Love's power broadens the scope of the knight's aesthetic notion of love. Imagination, operating through sight in Dante and through portraiture in the young man, impedes the will and transmutes the affinities of reason. The image of Beatrice, inscribed in the mind and reigning over the senses, guarantees Love's continuing influence on the faculties. Dante stresses that the image contains such qualities that Love partakes of its rationality: "[la sua imagine] era di sì nobilissima vertù, che nulla volta sofferse che Amore mi reggesse sanza lo fedele consiglio de la ragione" (Her image was of such most noble power that it never allowed Love to govern me without the faithful counsel of reason, chap. 2). For Chaucer's knight the first sight of White also fixes her image "in my thoght" (837). He describes a process that differs essentially from his early conduct of love: "I ne tok / No maner counseyl but at hir lok / And at myn herte" (839–41). The conjunction of inner and outer vision imparts a rational unity to both experience and the stages of recollection. The harmonizing of image and heart regains for imagination the status that Dante ascribes in the *Convivio* (3.vi.88–105), where he explains that the intellect rises to perception through imagination.

The *Vita Nuova* provides an equally important contrast, however, to the elegiac materials of Chaucer's poem. Although both works end before their narrators reconcile themselves to loss, they conceive different possibilities and levels of meaning for the women. Dante projects beyond the present to a link with Beatrice that continues unfolding in time. The future of his own work is a new project of writing and an eventual reunion with the lady. Memory leads to new invention: "Io spero di dicer di lei quello che mai non fue detto d'alcuna" (I hope to say of her what never before was said of any woman). And invention leads to reintegration: "E poi piaccia a colui che è sire de la cortesia, che la mia anima se ne possa gire a vedere la gloria de la sua donna, cioè di quella benedetta Beatrice" (And then may it please him who is King of Courtesy that my soul might rise to see the glory of its lady, that is of that blessed Beatrice, chap. 42). Chaucer's character remains in the present, constrained rather than animated by the realization of death. John Lawlor has emphasized the knight's "attainment of the highest earthly good" and a requited, faithful love ("Pattern" 633). The only prospect he allows himself, though, is a persistent view toward the past. If a pattern of consolation shapes the narrative action, its fulfillment becomes problematic. As in the complaint against Fortune, the understanding of good is unable to redress the loss.

In some measure, the knight's emotional and moral stasis derives from the very ethical quality that White embodies. She is a paragon of social virtue and conduct, but by defining her through the resources of Machaut's *dits* Chaucer inevitably leaves her bound by human contingency. Beatrice transcends to a realm in which the "sire de la cortesia" is a figure for divine love and in which she participates fully in the perfection of the Virgin. White remains within the limits of an earthly court.

At these limits the poem's social and artistic purposes converge. Chaucer's efforts to console John of Gaunt, if consolation was indeed the purpose, follow from terms that are predictable and limited from the outset. To the extent that the knight's speeches bring a grieving nobleman around to affirming these conventional values, the logic of consolation is circular. The poem resolves itself not in a climax of the fictional dialogue but in the creation of the art work. While the man in black holds a steady gaze backwards, Chaucer brings his project of defining a narrative structure into general accord with Dante's. The narrator's awakening in bed with book in hand purposely returns the poem to its first scene. He promises a work which, like the tale from Ovid, will impose a formal order on imagination: "I wol, be processe of tyme, / Fonde to put this sweven in ryme / As I kan best, and that anoon" (1331–33). Its moralized, secular history will be consistent with the noble lives recorded in the book of romance, though less ambitious than Dante's intention of saying something never said before. The poem thus converts retrospect to anticipation, and the groundwork of elegy supports an evolving view of poetic art. It is, however, a groundwork that has been only sketched out, mapped only in the large dimensions. In the narrative poems that follow the *Book of the Duchess,* the concerns with sense, imagination, and intellect develop into more subtle and complicated questions about the poet's craft.

Imagination and Memory (II): The *House of Fame*

We have seen that Chaucer represents the beginnings of his narrative art in the play of imagination and memory. The *Book of the Duchess* dramatizes the movement of the imagination from distraction to aesthetic order and then from the order of literary texts to a retrospective account of subjective experience founded on literary convention. In this trajectory psychological terms become poetic terms; imagination and memory appear first as elements of subject experience but quickly become categories of aesthetic speculation. Chaucer's first narrative poem defines and reflects on aspects of its narrative art in the very process of creating it.

In the practice of his poetic theory Chaucer, like Dante, seems to be suggesting from the outset that sense and imagination must lead toward a form of rational memory, memory which preserves the impressions of imagination and subjective experience according to ontological categories and ethical qualities. But Chaucer's first narrative poem does not make a complete shift from sense to intellect. Despite her virtues, the "goode faire White," who is the ethical locus of the *Book of the Duchess,* remains situated imaginatively in society, and her portrayal is constrained artistically by the limits of courtly language. Chaucer's beginning as a narrative poet claims a certain theoretical and social ground as its artistic domain but does not promise a more ambitious poetic enterprise or "a still greater work to come" such as Dante envisions at the end of the *Vita Nuova*. Chaucer's objective at the end of the poem is that of the courtly maker—"to put this sweven in ryme" (1332).

Within the limits of the material, Chaucer has nonetheless set himself the formidable task of reflecting on the nature of language and imagination, the relation of subjectivity and formal order, the conventionality of language, the ethical facets of representation. He has also linked the themes of love and poetry in an equation that will remain central, though varied in its permutations, throughout his career. This is a major part of Chaucer's legacy to English poetry. As A. C. Spearing points out, "To be a poet, in the courtly circle for which Chaucer wrote, was the same as to be a love-poet" (83). Conversely, the way Chaucer knows about love is to rely on the written authority of his predecessors. The relation between love and poetry is reciprocal, and to treat one necessarily entails the other.

All these issues emerge powerfully but indirectly in the *Book of the Duchess*. By contrast, in the *House of Fame* (written about 1380, and again in the context of a social occasion) the strategy of indirection is largely abandoned. Whatever the occasion of the poem (probably Richard II's planned marriage to Caterina Visconti), Chaucer brings the poetic issues into the foreground. His concern is to explore the nature of language, the relation of signs to truth, the functions of memory and authority as determinants of aesthetic representation.

It is by now a commonplace of modern Chaucer criticism that the *House of Fame* addresses the subject of poetry itself. Lawrence Shook has called the poem an *ars poetica,* and other readers treat it variously as a satire of literary conventions or as a serious philosophical statement encompassing several levels of medieval thought.[1] The position I want to argue in this chapter is that the poetic speculations of the *House of Fame* are not discrete but rather are contextualized by the earlier poem. Whereas the *Book of the Duchess* emphasizes the role of imagination in the narrator and the man in black and subordinates the function of memory, the *House of Fame* gives a relatively greater weight to memory both as a category of aesthetic speculation and a formal system of representation. Poetic emblems and mnemonic techniques dominate the poem, and poetry itself emerges as an act of memory.

Second, I intend to show that the hypotheses about language and poetry that Chaucer develops in his second dream vision are irresolvably problematic. However much they may depend on complex and sophisticated philosophical sources, each with elaborate rationales and systematized principles, they amount to a poetic dead end. The poem's incompletion, despite the endings added by Caxton, Lydgate, Skelton, Douglas, and Pope, literally depicts the abandoning of one line of thinking about poetry. The lesson of this failure has much to tell us about the direction that Chaucer's poetics subsequently takes.

"Be avisions or be figures"

The *House of Fame,* like the *Book of the Duchess,* begins with a discussion of its narrator's mental life and implicitly develops the analogy between dreams and poetry. It differs, however, by substituting the general problem of knowledge for the narrower emphasis on sensation. Where "ydel thoght" and "sorwful ymagynacioun" define the opening condition of the *Book of the Duchess,* Chaucer dramatizes a negative doctrine of imagination and memory in the *House of Fame.* In his long and justly famous Proem, the narrator explains that he does not know the cause of his dreams: "For hyt is wonder, be the roode, / To my wyt, what causeth swevenes / Eyther on morwes or on evenes" (2–4). To the extent that causes cannot be found, dreams are not intelligible species or proper objects of knowledge; they are not part of the rational knowledge of *scientia* as scholastic and Aristotelian thinkers conceived it. Knowledge through causes depends on the abstraction of form or species to acquire a knowledge of entities or kinds of things. Dreams, the narrator tells us, belong instead to the realm of the particular, to experience (*experimentum*) and opinion from which no reliable inference can be made. Unable to identify the sources of dreams, the narrator cannot determine their status as true or false representations, and he consequently ponders a curiously neutral ground on which language and reasoning confront the ambiguity of dream life.

The contrast with Guillaume de Lorris's opening of the *Roman de la rose* is particularly significant, and we might read the Proem to the *House of Fame* as a continuation of the critique that Chaucer makes in translating Guillaume's argument. Guillaume argues "That dremes signifiaunce be / Of good and harm to many wightes" (*Romaunt* 16–17) because many, though not all, of the things seen figuratively later occur literally. As we have seen earlier (chapter 1), Chaucer's translation of the *Rose* differs from the original at the point where Guillaume's argument proves logically invalid and false. Here in the Proem Chaucer offers the opposite formulation of Guillaume's claim for meaning and advances a position closer to Jean de Meun's skepticism in the later part of the *Rose.* He confronts the discontinuity between formal orders of human reflection ("my wyt") and the objects and events they are supposed to give accounts of. It is worth noting, though, that he, unlike Jean, does not reject dreaming as a means of perception any more than he relies on its enigmatic figures. The issue is focused instead on discrepancies and discontinuities within perception, hence on the truth value of aesthetic representation.

The problem with dreams—as with mental images at the start of the *Book of the Duchess*—can be formulated alternatively as a problem of sequence: "why th'effect folweth of somme, / And of somme hit shal never come" (HF, 5–6). Given that dreams are supposed to be prophetic, the narrator wants to know why some are predictive and others not. He is faced with inconsistency that nonetheless differs from the radically arbitrary projections of the imagination that form the starting point of the *Book of the Duchess* and define the initial conditions of the narrator's ethical and aesthetic paralysis. Here he can assert his own ignorance (not his psychic disorganization) and so is able to displace the contradictions of perception into his own discourse. In short, he finds a way to put them in language. The categories of dreams that had been elaborated by classical and medieval authorities thus offer no remedy for the seemingly disjunct nature of dreaming or for the separation of signs and truth which also lies at the center of language and poetry. Spearing says of these systems of dream taxonomy, "they had one fundamental drawback: there was almost never any way of telling from a dream itself which category it belonged to" (74). This is the same drawback that Chaucer's narrator will discover presently about linguistic representation.

The categories that Chaucer's narrator enumerates at the start of the poem derive almost certainly from Macrobius's commentary on the *Somnium Scipionis* and from medieval dream lore.[2] The narrator speaks of six kinds of dream—*avisioun, revelacioun, drem, sweven, fantome, oracles.* But his listing differs from the usual sources on several counts: the terms designating them are inexact translations of a technical vocabulary, their number increases from five to six, and the meaning of even the categories remains obscure (Newman, Giaccherini). The narrator insists that he "kan hem noght" (15), and does not know "hir signifiaunce / The gendres, neyther the distaunce / Of tymes of hem, ne the causes" (17–19). Nor can he deduce an order of probability among the categories—"why this more then that cause is" (20).

The Proem raises these questions only to leave them unanswered. But in another sense it raises them precisely in order to leave them unanswered. The narrator does not know the cause of dreams and cannot assess the reliability of dream categories, yet his claim of ignorance converts the two questions into one assertion by seeming to progress naturally from the first to the second. For we expect that if the cause of dreams can be determined, their reliability will necessarily be demonstrated. On reflection, however, it becomes clear that the first gesture of the poem is to redirect language so as to bridge discrete aspects of a problem that has not yet even been posed. The essential question is, what do dreams mean, what is their status as representations? But Chaucer comes at it by focusing on the secondary issues (the origins and typology of dreams). In doing so he establishes in the poem the aesthetic tension between the rational order of inquiry and the irrationality of his subject matter.

The poet's opening move is part of a strategy of displacement that develops as the narrator amplifies the theme of causality. Dreams, he tells us, are occasioned by a variety of factors—from physiology, psychology, life experiences, and spiritual influence (21–52). His elaborations in a long passage of rhetorical amplification represent a principle of addition that will figure prominently later in the discussions of Fame and Rumor. They also represent a principle of approximation, which is even more crucial to the poet's theme. The narrator cites these additional causes "as yf" (21) they might explain the sources of dreaming. At a conceptual level, then, the indicative edges into the subjunctive. At a stylistic level, the strategy of displacement takes the concrete form of metrical irregularity, run-on lines, a syntax whose complexity disguises redundance and compounding as if they were all part of an elaborate and sustained subordination. Despite all its amplification, however, the narrator's account doubles back to the initial difficulty: "But why the cause is, noght wot I" (52).

This proliferation of causes and categories reveals something essential about the poem as a literary text and about the poetic concerns it broaches. Laurence Eldredge finds in the discussion of dreams an "implicit epistemology" ("Via Moderna" 110). Certainly the discussion of dream categories is an instance of what Eugene Vance has termed a "poetics of inflation." The narrator's list of causes could, in fact, be amplified beyond its already multiple explanations. Since the causes and categories are only *possible* (all are "as if" and none is really any more likely than the others), adding to them would guarantee the identical effect; more becomes the same. It is this logic that governs the repeated locutions when the narrator attempts to argue difference: "why th'effect folweth of somme, / And of somme hit shal never come" (5–6). At base the narrator's explanations comprise a realm of discourse around an absent center. Not knowing what causes dreams, the narrator is free to hypothesize any number of reasons, each already conceived as a distant account, leveled by compounding and removed by approximation, for something that he cannot define positively. Like his counterpart in the *Book of the Duchess,* who exists between images and "nothing," the narrator finds an economy of signs without implicit purpose or term. He discovers an area of invention without constraints.

The narrator's inability to discriminate causes and categories, hence the conditions of a dream's being true or false, leads some critics to see a general connection with the problem of future contingency in three-value logic and with nominalist thinking. William Wilson argues that Fame violates the laws of noncontradiction, identity, and the excluded middle: "Fame's logic is an illogic, or a mock-logic, for she violates the law of contradiction by giving one group the opposite of what she gives an identical group; she flaunts the law of identity by being sometimes short, sometimes tall, sometimes fame, sometimes ill fame; and she ignores the law of the excluded middle, *tertium non datur,* when she offers a *tertium quid,* no reputation at all" ("Scholastic Logic" 183). Eldredge finds in the Proem and in the narrator's later journey to the heavens the influence of the fourteenth-century Via Moderna, which granted more power to human reason than earlier philosophical positions had ("Via Moderna" 115). Sheila Delany points to a "skeptical fideism" that allows one to preserve, if not reconcile, faith and reason.[3] The historical context of Chaucer's themes indicates the complexity and seriousness of his reflection on the problem of knowledge and poetry. Equally important, though, is the network of verbal links with the *Book of the Duchess.* Chaucer's evocation of the *Book of the Duchess* draws our attention to the poetic treatment of the materials and not just the philosophical sources. As in the *Duchess,* his emphasis falls not on whether dreams about the future prove true or false but on what one can say about them in the here and now.

It is in this framework, I think, that we must read the narrator's plea, which brackets the Proem in two slightly different forms. "God turne us every drem to goode" (1), he asks at the beginning. At the end, leaving the question of causality to "grete clerkys," he implores "oonly that the holy roode/ Turne us every drem to goode!" (57–58).[4] His plea takes on a function similar to that of the "goode faire White" in the *Book of the Duchess,* for it posits a direction for imagination and a final cause for visionary experiences that have hidden origins and indeterminate status. The "goode" that he articulates now in spiritual rather than social terms allows the narrator to predicate an outcome and effect of dreaming. He proposes, by shifting to the optative, that some kind of intention ought to be at work. Delany sees the repeated plea as a fideistic appeal to resolve contradictions. It does not, however, solve the problem of cause. The origin of dreams, like the cause of distraction in the *Book of the Duchess,* remains hidden, and the narrator comes no closer than before to locating their source. So, too, the problem of interpreting the phenomena continues unchanged. The "avisions" and "figures" surpass understanding: "For hyt is warned to derkly" (51).

What the narrator seeks in his prayer is an ultimate reference, a moral index that does not solve the immediate confusions so much as guarantee that they will finally be superseded. The "goode" originating in God and made material by Christ's "holy roode" promises to transform the aesthetic constructions of mental life. It offers a way to escape the circularity of imagination by insisting that, although dreams are not in themselves objects of knowledge, they stand, like other natural "wonders," as signs of divine power. But this rationale, though implied by the reiterated appeal to a "goode," is the "signifiaunce" toward which the poem only ostensibly moves. In point of fact, it never attains this sublimation of sense to intellect, for this kind of spiritual meaning is a condition outside of language that the poem does not allow.

The Glass Temple

The narrator's dream of Venus's temple, the palace of Fame, and the House of Rumor builds on the themes developed in the Proem. For his dream the narrator claims a uniqueness partly based on the topos of poetic uniqueness, Horace's "carmina non prius / audita" (*Odes* 3.1).

> For never sith that I was born,
> Ne no man elles me beforn,
> Mette, I trowe stedfastly,
> So wonderful a drem as I
> The tenthe day now of Decembre, ...
> (59–63)

The uniqueness is also implied in the poem's treatment of dreams as dislocated signs. To the extent that categories reveal nothing about the nature and cause of dreams, the narrator's "wonderful" dream shares the general and singular property of being unlike any other. The claim to uniqueness depends not on a special vision so much as on the common state of all dreams' being different, or at least of no dreams' being similar. Chaucer thereby establishes the ground of the poem by arriving at the logical inference that there can be no firm ground at all.

The narrator's account of his "wonderful" dream enforces this paradoxical and argumentative singularity. There is little foregrounding in the action of the imagination; the narrator, like a weary pilgrim, falls asleep quickly. Whatever may constitute the dream as a structure of imagination, it exists poetically as a structure of memory. The narrator, like the dreamer in the *Roman de la rose,* proposes to reconstruct it under the limits of his own temporality—"as I kan now remembre, / I wol yow tellen everydel" (64–65). His ostensibly unique dream finds expression in a telling constrained from the outset by partiality and the contingencies of the moment. Further, he invokes the god of sleep "that he wol me spede / My sweven for to telle arygħt" (78–79). He thereby turns from a tradition that seeks inspiration from the Muses to one that defines divine aid as a power of recollection. The prayer is directed not up to the heavens but down to the underworld where Morpheus resides. When the narrator finally addresses Apollo at the beginning of Book III, it is to ask the god to complement an art that again recognizes its contingencies: "Nat that I wilne, for maistrye, / Here art poetical be shewed" (1094–95). He seeks formal refinement because "the rym ys lygħt and lewed" (1096), but more important, he seeks the inspiration to remember: "helpe me to shewe now / That in myn hed ymarked ys" (1102–3).

The glass temple which the narrator describes in the first part of his dream (Book I) narrows the general concern with memory to a form of theater. Dedicated to Venus, as the dreamer rightly surmises from her imposing portrait, the temple appeals first and foremost to the visual imagination. The narrator insists on what he has seen, and his language is preeminently the language of the eye—"ymages, portreytures, [and] figures," iconographical attributes and colors. J. A. W. Bennett has argued that the structure is more a Gothic church than a classical temple and suggests that Chaucer had seen contemporary murals that might have inspired the *ekphrasis* (*Fame* 12–15). Perhaps the most revealing evidence of visual appeal in the poem is the adroit conversion of song into picture. Vergil's epic proposition ("Arma virumque cano") stipulates that the poet intends to present his work as song, but in the narrator's recollection this intention becomes a caption inscribed on a brass placard.

> But as I romed up and doun,
> I fond that on a wall ther was
> Thus writen on a table of bras:
> "I wol now singen, yif I kan,
> The armes and also the man
> That first cam, thurgh his destinee,
> Fugityf of Troy contree,
> In Itayle, with ful moche pyne
> Unto the strondes of Lavyne."
>
> (140–48)

In one gesture, then, the public and vocal quality of the classical epic transforms to a private, intimate show of figures.

These figures play within a theater of the mind brought to life by dreaming. The narrator wanders among "sondry stages" (122) as if Vergil's poem had been set out as a group of historiated (narrative) scenes in a miniature cycle or as multiple mansion stages in the drama. Just as church architecture from the early Middle Ages onwards sought to reproduce Biblical actions and locales, the temple of Venus recreates the classical poem in a kind of imaginative space that the narrator experiences by moving from one part to another—"as I romed up and doun." In the late Middle Ages such movement would approach the dramatic forms of staging drama and stylized events such as royal entries in which the honored personage advanced from one allegorical or descriptive tableau to another (Wickham 1:51–111). Arranged sequentially, the poem's dramatic images have the effect of concentrating Vergil's narrative into a memory system of tokens and loci which can later serve as catalysts for retelling. And in such recollection retelling implies translation. One instance of this translation appears in the treatment of Dido and Aeneas, which is substantially changed from Vergil's portrayal of tragic necessity. The narrator recounts the early books of the *Aeneid* and the poem's second half as a rapid series of images. But when he recounts the love of Dido and Aeneas, he chooses to reshape his version with asides, invented quotation, and examples of other tragic love affairs. The effect, as it had been for other medieval readers, is to give a new emphasis to the classical poem, to reconceive epic as romance, and perhaps, as E. K. Rand once suggested (146), to see the episode as if it had been written by Ovid. Whatever the analogy, the narrator demonstrates to his readers and himself that an act of memory, even one founded on the apparent determinacy of painted images and engraved texts, is a drama of recollection and that bringing the past into the present involves some measure of transformation.

This theater of images does not completely banish sound, however, and in the artful counterpoint of seeing and hearing Chaucer sets out themes that the poem will develop later. Throughout the *ekphrasis* of the narrator's dream Chaucer subtly interweaves sound and speech. The narrator's reports of what "I sawgh" are balanced by his hearing the lament for Creusa and her final words to Aeneas and by the "lowde" winds that Eolus frees. Synon's "fals forswerynge" (153) not only overturns Troy in the beginning but intimates that betrayal through language is the mechanism that dominates Vergil's poem and Chaucer's own work. The interplay of visual and aural elements becomes still more evident when the narrator leaves the fixed images of the temple and enters a large field which, like the dark valley of the *Book of the Duchess,* is completely barren. Most interpreters believe that this desert stands for sterility, but the function is more complex and reflexive.[5] For it is here that the narrator discovers the extent to which vision and sound are convertible. The sand (*sonde*) of the field, minute and as seemingly infinite as in the Libyan desert, represents what he is about to uncover in a realm of ever increasing sound, where more discord and falsehood are made "then greynes be of sondes" (691). And as the pun takes shape before him, the narrator prays to escape what the imagination has created: "Fro fantome and illusion / Me save" (493–94).

Thus far I have been suggesting that Book i of the *House of Fame* returns to the same formal problems treated in the *Book of the Duchess.* There are tonal and thematic differences, of course, such as the absence of melancholy in the second poem's narrator and a shift in focus from tragic but faithful love in the *Book of the Duchess* (Ceyx-Alcyone, White and the man in black) to tragic and betrayed love in the *House of Fame* (Dido and Aeneas with the exempla added to their case). Nonetheless, the terms that define poetic representation remain generally constant. Chaucer's aesthetic concern is with the experience of mental life through images and sound. His art consists in giving mental impressions form, and he knows that in some measure it will always prove inadequate. But this is not wholly or merely a process of misrepresentation; it is also the life of poetry and the poet's experience of his art. The continual struggle, as the narrator asserts, is "to tellen al my drem aryght" (527).

At the end of Book i the *House of Fame* reenacts and adds a new dimension to Chaucer's poetic reflections. In the desert of *sonde* Chaucer has created a figure for the poetics of imagination and sensitive memory. But rather than promise, as he had in the *Book of the Duchess,* that he will "fonde to put this sweven in ryme / As I kan best, and that anoon" (BD 1332–33), the narrator discovers what lies behind the aesthetic terms themselves. In other words, he begins a vertical movement—literally in the grasp of the eagle who carries him from the desert and figuratively in his approach to knowing the actual conditions of language and memory. The means for escaping the aesthetic impasse expressed symbolically by the desert are given by two figures borrowed from Dante's *Commedia,* the eagle and the apostrophe to "Thought."

The eagle who carries "Geffrey" off represents a kind of vision beyond the narrator's trackless dreaming, though one finally not removed from the problems Chaucer has identified earlier in the poem. Chaucer's main source is *Purgatorio* 9 where Dante falls asleep in the valley of the negligent princes and dreams that he looks up to see an eagle with golden feathers poised in the sky, who then swoops down on him and carries him upward.[6] As the eagle and pilgrim rise, both catch fire, burning in an imagined flame.

> in sogno mi parea veder sospesa
> un'aguglia nel ciel con penne d'oro,
> con ali aperte ed a calare intesa;
> ed esser mi parea là dove fuoro
> abbandonati i suoi da Ganimede,
> quando fu ratto al sommo consistoro.
> Fra me pensava: "Forse questa fiede
> pur qui per uso, e forse d'altro loco
> disdegna di portarne suso in piede."
> Poi mi parea che, poi rotata un poco,
> terribil come folgor discendesse,
> e me rapisse suso infino al foco.
> Ivi parea che ella e io ardesse;
> e sì lo 'ncendio imaginato cosse,
> che convenne che 'l sonno si rompesse.
> (19–33)

I seemed to see, in a dream, an eagle poised in the sky, with feathers of gold, its wings outspread, and prepared to swoop. And I seemed to be in the place where Ganymede abandoned his own company, when he was caught up to the supreme consistory; and I thought within myself, "Perhaps it is wont to strike only here, and perhaps disdains to carry anyone upward in its claws from any other place." Then it seemed to me that, having wheeled a while, it descended terrible as a thunderbolt and snatched me upwards as far as the fire: there it seemed that it and I burned; and the imagined fire so scorched me that perforce my sleep was broken.

The pilgrim's dream ends here, and Vergil, who is evidently unaware of the dream's content, then tells Dante that during his dream St. Lucy has arrived to carry him to the gate of Purgatory. The dream has been a veil that covers the real action, which is an act of grace that marks a point where human reason must walk behind faith.

Chaucer's poem is connected to Dante's by shared motifs—the eagle's gold plumage, the thunderbolt, the image of burning—and by a focus on the narrator's state of consciousness. At the same time the connection serves to point up crucial differences. Chaucer's response, as in the *Book of the Duchess,* is to "the beaute and the wonder" (533) of the eagle rather than its terrible power ("terribil come folgor"). The eagle remains as a symbol and character in the fictional economy of Chaucer's poem, whereas in Dante he symbolizes something else that occurs simultaneously in the pilgrim's dream. Indeed, the gap between symbol and event in the *Commedia* marks an absence and mystery that art can never fill. Dante points insistently to that gap by repeating the verb *parea,* 'it seemed,' four times. Chaucer's adaptation reflects a different poetic orientation, at least at this point. Instead of imitating Dante's subtle masking of the chief action by a symbolic vision, he narrows his focus to the dream structure. It is as if he understood Dante's repeated assertions of mere appearance as claims made on behalf of subjectivity. He turns away from Dante's art, which is always careful to distinguish illusion and reality, and concentrates instead on the forms of perception that operate within consciousness. In short, Chaucer reads the eagle back into a conventional dream structure. Consequently, his treatment of Geffrey's vision is necessarily framed within the experience it presumes to explain. Dream and reality occupy the same ground for him; the fictional and the discursive are convertible.

At an artistic level, Chaucer fully understands the craft of Dante's description. The eagle is seemingly suspended in the sky ("sospesa / un'aguglia nel ciel") and ready to swoop down ("a calare intesa"), and in the interval between seeing the eagle and seeing him descend, Dante has time to muse on Ganymede's fate, a motif that Chaucer will later use comically. Chaucer achieves the same effect of suspension by ending Book I with the eagle starting to descend and delaying the continuation of action in Book II with a Proem that contains the second major borrowing from the *Commedia,* an adaptation of the invocation that Dante makes at the start of his journey proper.

In the Proem to Book II Chaucer calls on Venus and the Muses, and then turns to the power that animates Dante's vision.

> O Thought, that wrot al that I mette,
> And in the tresorye hyt shette
> Of my brayn, now shal men se
> Yf any vertu in the be
> To tellen al my drem aryght.
> Now kythe thyn engyn and myght!
> (523–28)

Chaucer's source for the passage, *Inferno* 2.7–9, marks the beginning of Dante's journey with Vergil: "O Muse, o alto ingegno, or m'aiutate; o mente che scrivisti ciò ch'io vidi, / qui si parrà la tua nobilitate" (O Muse, o high genius, help me now. O memory that wrote down what I saw, here shall your worthiness appear). *Mente* is usually glossed as memory, and *ingegno* refers to the poet's own *virtù,* as distinct from the power of the Muses to lend inspiration (Singleton 2:22–24). Chaucer translates *mente* as "Thought," and shifts from Dante's immediate sense of the vision he has seen ("ciò ch'io vidi") to the more distant structure of the dream he seeks to recount: "al that I mette, / And in the tresorye hyt shette / Of my brayn" (523–25). Howard Schless points out that Chaucer's adaptation of the passage has a limited conception of narrative powers: "Dante, unlike Chaucer, worries not about the powers of his memory but rather about the nobility, the stature, and the heights, that it can attain" (50).

In the Proem to Book II, then, memory remains a formal operation for Chaucer. It is defined as a capacity for description. Chaucer also links it to imagination by adding, "Now kythe thyn engyn and myght!" (528). The line may owe to the prayer Dante makes in the *Paradiso* when he asks Pegasus's aid to describe the luminous script that transforms into the eagle: "paia tua possa in questi versi brevi" (*Paradiso* 18.87). The addition makes it unclear whether Chaucer conceives imagination ("engyn") as an independent faculty or, as the passage suggests here, a part of memory. Piero Boitani, arguing for the latter, proposes, "Chaucer is here underlining not so much the 'remembrance' on which he will rely later (in the *Legend*) as the importance of 'thought' in poetic activity, while considering native talent and inventiveness ('ingengo'— 'engyn') as slightly less central than Dante does—and in this he is characteristically more humble, and perhaps paying an indirect compliment to Dante himself, the poet of Thought and 'engyn' *par excellence*" ("Dante" 123). The essential point, though, is that his adaptation of Dante treats memory as the source of poetic invention. Visual impressions stand behind art, shut up "in the tresorye . . . / Of my brayn" (HF 524–25) like the earlier fantasies in the *Book of the Duchess* that "ben in myn hede" (BD 28).

Dante offers a way to transcend the limits of the kind of dream vision that initially defines Chaucer's poetry. That Chaucer recognized those limits is clear from the action of Book I and from his prayer at the end of it: "Fro fantome and illusion / Me save" (493–94). But Chaucer's response to Dante here and elsewhere in the *House of Fame* is constrained by his governing assumption that poetry is located in the play of imagination and memory and not in the spiritual meaning that lies beyond representation. Chaucer's adaptations of the *Commedia* are predominantly secular. As the eagle carries him off, he protests to himself, "I neyther am Ennok, ne Elye, / Ne Romulus, ne Ganymede" (588–89). The lines echo against Dante's own claim to Vergil of his unfitness for the journey, "Io non Enëa, io non Paolo sono" (*Inferno*

2.32), and they are examples of what Boitani rightly calls Chaucer's "continuous counterpoint to Dante's text" ("Dante" 117). But they are consistent, too, with the rejection of prophetic dreams in the Proem to the *House of Fame* and with the explicit statement in the *Book of the Duchess* that the poet's dream stands apart from biblical and classical dreams. When Geffrey asks himself, "what thing may this sygnifye?" (587), his question is not about the spiritual significance of the eagle's seizing him but about how it can have meaning within a world constructed on "wonders."

The corollary to this secular interest is that Chaucer's adaptations of Dante are concerned with description. Chaucer's apostrophe to Thought in Book II treats memory as a storehouse of images to be called forth. The Proem to Book III, which invokes Apollo in a way that recalls Dante's invocation in *Paradiso* 1, continues along these lines. Too modest to ask to be shown "art poetical" (1095), the narrator petitions that his verse be made "sumwhat agreable" (1097). "I do no diligence / To shewe craft," he says, "but o sentence" (1099–1100). What he means by sentence, however, is notably limited. The narrator invokes "devyne vertu" in order "to shewe now / That in myn hed ymarked ys" (1102–3). Dante, by contrast, conceives the materials of memory as an adumbration of a spiritual realm that lies beyond description: "O divina virtù, se mi ti presti / tanto che l'ombra del beato regno / segnata nel mio capo io manifesti" (*Paradiso* 1.22–24). In the same canto Dante will make the point again in a passage that could not escape the notice of a later poet writing about a journey toward the heavens: "Trasumanar significar *per verba* / non si poria; però l'essemplo basti / a cui esperïenza grazia serba" (The passing beyond humanity may not be set forth in words: therefore let the example suffice any for whom grace reserves that experience, 1.70–72). Chaucer, as Boitani insists ("Dante" 129, *Fame* 186), turns from the *trasumanar*. If he shares Dante's conviction that language fails to express meaning adequately, it is because he has a more limited conception than Dante of what meaning might include. In *Troilus and Criseyde,* Dante will provide a way of discovering moral significance, but in the *House of Fame* he is a source that Chaucer assimilates to his own poetic notions.

Poetry and Physics: The Eagle's Sermon

Chaucer's poetics operates within the imaginative economy of the dream world, and this circularity conditions whatever knowledge Geffrey is supposed to gain from his flight. The eagle announces that the goal of their journey is didactic: "And this caas that betyd the is, / Is for thy lore and for thy prow" (578–79). Jupiter "thorgh hys grace" has decided to recompense Geffrey's futile "labour and devocion" to Cupid by transporting the bookish servant of love to the House of Fame "to do the som disport and game" and to gather "of Loves folk moo tydynges." As a preparation for the experience, the eagle intends to teach his passenger about the construction of the house and the properties of the sounds entering it. The ostensible goal of the journey—to learn more about love—gives way, then, to the prior task of examining how one comes to learn about love. Like the earlier discussion of dream categories, this teaching concerns itself with the conditions of knowing, and poetic discourse is both the instrument and object of inquiry.

The eagle's dissertation seeks to explain discourse empirically by outlining a physics of speech. Like Vergil (*Aeneid* 4.173–94) and Ovid (*Metamorphoses* 12.39–64), the eagle places Fame between earth and heaven.

> "Hir paleys stant, as I shal seye,
> Ryght even in myddes of the weye
> Betwixen hevene and erthe and see,
> That what so ever in al these three
> Is spoken, either privy or apert,
> The way therto ys so overt,
> And stant eke in so juste a place
> That every soun mot to hyt pace; ..."
>
> (713–20)

The key terms of the eagle's account are Nature, habit, and multiplication. Citing Aristotle and Plato as his authorities but probably relying on Boethius and possibly on Dante, the eagle proposes that the design of Nature governs language.[7] Everything in the world is drawn toward "a kyndely stede ther he / May best in hyt conserved be" (731–32). Language, because it is a phenomenon of nature, must necessarily follow the same laws. Rhetorically, the iteration of *kynde* ("kyndely thyng," "kyndely enclynyng," "by kynde," "kyndelyche stede," "kynde place," "kyndely to pace") suggests that language indeed conforms to the workings of a properly ordered universe whose principle of operation is motion directed toward a necessary goal. Understood in its elements, "soun ys noght but eyr ybroken" (765), and its motions include all forms of discourse—"rouned, red, or songe." This reduction, as Martin Irvine has shown (862–67), closely follows the commonplaces of medieval grammatical theory.

But language differs from other physical entities in the eagle's materialistic reduction because it works through paradox. The law of Nature is conservation: "every thing, by thys reson, / Hath his propre mansyon / To which hit seketh to repaire" (753–55). And yet the conservation of language depends on increase. Unlike the "propre mansyon" of physical objects, which simply preserves and contains, the House of Fame seeks to multiply.

> ... every speche, or noyse, or soun,
> Thurgh hys multiplicacioun,
> Thogh hyt were piped of a mous,
> Mot nede come to Fames Hous."
>   (783–86)

Chaucer thus elaborates two kinds of equilibrium, one a material economy in which a physical object returns to its natural place "ther-as hit shulde not apaire" (756), the other a flow or dispersion in which language outruns its source. The mechanism of multiplication at work in the second kind reaches its furthest extent when sound appears to recreate the original speakers. The eagle explains that speech arriving at Fame's palace assumes the shape of "the same wight / Which that the word in erthe spak" (1076–77).[8] This "wonder thyng" of generating "so verray hys lykenesse" tropes the *ekphrasis* of Book I, where the images of Venus's temple are converted into speech, and recalls the scene in the *Book of the Duchess* where Morpheus takes on the appearance of Ceyx to deliver his speech. But it also marks the radical separation of signs from what they signify. Speech does not reestablish the *res-verba* connections assumed by medieval theorists; it does not run backward to its source. Rather, it escapes further into a realm of autonomous discourse.

Although the eagle's dissertation relies on classical and medieval authorities, as Koonce and others have shown, its theory of language remains problematic in Chaucer's poem. The initial premise—that love is to be understood by examining speech about love—displaces the narrator's account from its actual subject and makes all understanding dependent on self-reflexivity. Geffrey is continually enmeshed in details and preparation for a topic that remains inaccessible. Meanwhile, the terms of poetic reflection themselves reveal other complications. Like the dream categories analyzed in the Proem, they offer contradiction and uncertainty; their sequence confuses type and cause, chance and result. And while the dreamer can presumably escape the paradoxes of dream in a waking state, there is no similar disengagement from language. Chaucer makes just this point at the beginning of Geffrey's flight, when the eagle utters a sound "in mannes vois" suitable to bird or man" "Awak!" (556). As a linguistic sign, the sound (*vox*) disrupts the settled distinction between articulate and inarticulate speech. Furthermore, the eagle's dissertation about language becomes part of the phenomenon that it would recount. As he carries the dreamer toward the House of Fame, expounding on physical wonders and metaphysics along the way, he coevally approaches the condition of everything else that enters the palace. His efforts to define "thynges" slip into *simulacra,* and language loses its power of representation. After all, the movement of sound occurs without regard to content or intention—"spoke in suerte or in drede" (723), "lowd or pryvee, foul or fair" (767), "in ernest or in game" (822). Reduced to its "substaunce" (768), language seems hardly capable of saying anything at all.

While Chaucer reveals the internal contradictions of these terms, we are made aware that the account of language is a consciously rhetorical gesture. The eagle labels his speech "a propre skille / And a worthy demonstracion / In myn ymagynacion" (726–28). Joseph Grennen (42) has shown that "demonstracion" and "ymaginacion" are two distinct forms of proof in the fourteenth century. In equating them, however, the eagle nullifies the distinction between "thynges" and "tydynges" (634–44) that his teaching presupposes. Reasoning ("propre skille") and the process of deliberation ("demonstracion") collapse into a mode of imaginative discourse where natural philosophy supplies the materials of poetic invention. As a logical demonstration, the speech is founded on a confusion of part and whole, what rhetoricians as capable as the eagle would (or should) recognize as an undistributed middle. The eagle forgets that, although speech is sound, all sound is not speech. The distinction was a common dictum in the grammatical treatises (Irvine 856–57); nonetheless, the eagle equates "voys, or noyse, or word, or soun" (819).

The eagle also confuses levels of argument by mixing analogy and proof. He takes from Boethius's *De musica* (1.14) the comparison of multiplying sound and the advancing concentric circles made by a stone thrown into a pool of water. But he treats similarity as if it were proof by induction, reducing metaphor to a physical literalism. Further, the iterations of *kynde* at the beginning and end of the speech (729–49, 823–52) have the effect of begging the question. When at last the eagle asks confirmation that he has proved his point without "subtilite / Of speche" or "figures of poetrie, / Or colours of rethorike" (855–59), the dreamer carefully avoids a direct answer. The eagle seeks acceptance of his "conclusyon," but Geffrey grants only that it is "a good persuasion" (872). In the discourse of imagination, then, logic and rhetoric assume a false equivalence, and the attempt to define language objectively and materially succeeds only in discovering the subjective motives that prompt speech in the first place.

Throughout the celestial journey of Book II Chaucer emphasizes the dialectical nature of the narrator's understanding, which remains at base an act of critical interpretation. Experience and authority, the antinomy Chaucer develops in even greater detail in the *Canterbury Tales,* are the modes for Geffrey's learning the design of the universe. Neither of them, he finds, can be followed without language. If the eagle tries to "preve / Be reson" (707–8) or offer "a preve by experience" (878), he must still in each case propose a "sentence" (710, 877)—an idea expressed and formed in language. The authorities he invokes likewise connect understanding to language and so eventually to literature. Plato, Aristotle, Boethius, Macrobius, Martianus Capella, Alan of Lille—all the philosophical commentators return the description of the world to a world of books. So, too, do the textual references to Alexander's adventures, to Enoch and Elijah, and to classical mythology. Indeed, when Geffrey finally decides to stem the eagle's lecture on the placement of the stars and "al the hevenes sygnes" (998), he has only to indicate that the poetic accounts are adequate for his modest purposes: "I leve as wel, so God me spede, / Hem that write of this matere" (1012–13). By so doing he suggests that empirical knowledge—the "hard mateere" to be discovered—is embedded in imagination and texts.

Several mythologies lie behind the theme of the celestial journey in Western literary tradition, and Chaucer creates a subtle balance among them, as earlier he balanced competing views of dreams and prophecy. Unlike Dante, who calls up the models of St. Paul and Aeneas (albeit in contrast), Geffrey and the eagle identify a variety of analogues for their flight toward the House of Fame. Their variety reflects, as it must, the multiple possibilities of space filled with increasing sound, of signs detached from referents. The mention of astronomical data, the minuteness of the earth, and the sudden impact of sound on the dreamer's consciousness indicate that the *Somnium Scipionis* remains a central paradigm, again as in the discussion of dreams. Bennett (*Fame* 86) points out, however, that Chaucer despiritualizes Cicero's creed, and a group of cautionary examples undermines any ready acceptance of a single model of knowledge and discovery in the journey.

The warning begins comically, as Geffrey fears he has been carried off like Ganymede, but it turns more ominous with mention of Icarus's catastrophic end. In the extended treatment of Phaeton (935–59) Chaucer goes directly to the dark implications of discovering the nature of things in the soul's flight toward heaven. Phaeton symbolizes the intellect destroyed by the experience of confronting knowledge. The anonymous *Ovide Moralisé* had viewed him historically as an astronomer who wished to publish books on the heavens but was thwarted by Jupiter, who erased the text ("Si fist ses livres effacier / Et sa sentence metre arier," 2.681–82); morally, he exemplified pride and could be compared to Lucifer. Chaucer's treatment replaces these allegorical accounts with a psychological explanation. Seeing the Scorpion, whose "sygne" remains in the heavens, Phaeton "for ferde loste hys wyt" (950) and all sense of "governaunce." In other words, Chaucer constructs a myth of the intellect thrown into terror by the experience of knowledge. His emphasis falls on the perils of knowledge and the mind's destruction at the moment when it is fully engaged with understanding and discovery.

This warning combines with another reworking of myth to define the governing conditions of Geffrey's journey. In Cicero and Macrobius, Scipio stands dumbfounded after his grandfather's account of astronomy, and when he recovers his senses he hears "a great and pleasing sound." The sound is the *musica mundana*—the music of the spheres, whose harmony manifests the mathematical proportions and reason (*ratio*) of a providential universe. Chaucer presents the equivalent scene when Geffrey is able to end the eagle's tedious instruction and the attention of both figures shifts to the House of Fame and its "grete soun." The crucial difference is, of course, the substitution: celestial music finds its counterpart here in "the grete swogh" "full of tydynges, / Bothe of feir speche and chidynges, / And of fals and soth compouned" (1027–31). By thus moving from music to *tydynges,* from mathematical proportions which reflect God's shaping of nature to multiplying rumor which is a source of man's confusion, Chaucer replaces Cicero's ethical concerns with his own interest in the formal construction of imagination. At the same time he lays the conditions of discovery in this imaginative world. The mind, he suggests, will function in the tensions between known and knower, object and subject. The eagle makes it clear that there is no determining shape to Geffrey's discovery, only "aventure or cas" (1052). What the mind comes to learn will be inseparable from what it knows by and about language.

Geffrey's destination, reached at the end of Book II, turns out to be both a recursion and a point of arrival. His journey upwards into the heavens beyond his limited social experience succeeds in again framing questions about knowledge and reality and their interrelation in language. The construction and geography of Fame's palace, its "hous and site" (1114), express these questions in a rich and evocative poetic emblem of memory and image-making. As imaginative space, the palace is that region where abstract concerns about the truth value of language and poetry take literal shape, and the fact of such conversion gives some measure of the intellectual complexity that Chaucer weaves into the poem. The "aventure" which the eagle leaves Geffrey to find returns him to what he has managed to escape before in the *Book of the Duchess* and the temple of Venus—previous authors, interiors adorned with figures and sound, ideal poems with exhaustive commentaries. It returns him as well to the predicament of defining values for what the senses and imagination perceive. But now he faces the questions unable to disengage himself from the experience of perception and driven to self-conscious reflection of his own mind and language. At length he comes to imagine a world that the mind cannot inhabit. Moreover, in this process the poetics that Chaucer hypothesizes in Book III of the *House of Fame* advances from considering the nature of poetry as a problematic form of knowledge to the far riskier speculation that poetry might be the only form of knowledge—or stated conversely, the diminished possibility that something besides poetry can stand as a form of knowledge.

Memory obviously has a crucial function in a world so conceived. Geffrey has signaled its importance earlier by giving his account of the glass temple with its theater of images, each fixed in its place and preserving the key events of Vergil's epic. As he climbs toward Fame's palace, memory now emerges through a consciously developed symbolism in which names, the minimum conditions of linguistic designation, stand for language and poetry. The rock he scales recalls Venus's temple by being "lyk alum de glas" (1124). He soon discovers that it is "a roche of yse, and not of stel" (1130), and concludes, "This were a feble fundament / To bilden on a place hye" (1132–33). Covered with names, half of them melting away under the sun, the rock is a symbol of Fame's transience and the erasure of the names a foreshadowing of the caprice that the narrator will witness later in Fame's palace. Geffrey's reference to the "feble fundament" amplifies the theme by echoing the biblical parable which compares a man who hears Christ's words but does not act on them to a man who builds his house over sand (Matthew 7:26–27). The parable asserts the permanence and reliability of divine speech, but Chaucer emphasizes mutability instead. The chiseled names show what will happen to language moved from being to becoming, moved into time and made part of nature. By substituting ice for the sand mentioned in the parable Chaucer obliquely calls up the sand that represents a distraction at the end of Book I, and he prepares for a more elaborate symbolism that represents the status of poetic discourse.

The ice foundation contains a text that exists physically within a world of change, an objective entity inseparable in kind from other "thynges."

Unlike the interior of the glass temple, though, the rock does not fix a text absolutely in memory. The "famous folkes names fele" (1137) inscribed on the rock are literally governed by natural laws and not by the private associations of mental life or the aesthetic order of an anterior text, as in the *Book of the Duchess*. Heat and cold control the rhythms of change and permanence under the orbit of the sun. The scarcely legible letters, Geffrey conjectures, "were molte awey with hete" (1149), while the names written on the northern side, "fressh as men had writen hem here / The selve day ryght, or that houre" (1156–57), were "conserved with the shade / Of a castel that stood on high" (1160–61).

In this juxtaposition of cold and heat as properties of language, Chaucer may be drawing on a mythographic tradition in which writers like Bernardus Silvestris relate physical and psychological properties, connecting heat with imagination and cold with memory. Glossing Aeneas's approach to the Sybil in *Aeneid* 6, Bernardus describes the threefold division of the mind into imagination, reason, and memory, and proposes that imagination and memory have different origins: "Ingenium namque ex ignea natura, memoria vero ex frigore oritur" (Jones 48). Chaucer's interest here is less in elaborating analogies to psychological faculties than in positing an account of language as a product of Nature. The image of names and reputations melting away under the sun is the pendant to the earlier image of sound multiplying like a stone thrown in a pool. Nature's internal economy requires increase to offset the loss depicted here. Much as heat "defaces" (1164) writing, cold preserves traces of the past craft, and it is in this dialectic that Chaucer works to define a notion of poetic memory that accounts for both the survival and transformation of texts.

Geffrey says clearly that his inspection of the rock's properties has to do essentially with knowledge. Viewing the record of Fame requires of him a particular attention and concern with detail.

> ... I ententyf was to see,
> And for to powren wonder lowe,
> Yf I koude any weyes knowe
> What maner stoon this roche was.
>
> (1120–23)

He acts within the dialectic of the knower and the known, for the means of his inspection ("yf I koude any weyes knowe") is as problematic as the object of inquiry ("what maner stoon this roche was"). And from the outset knowledge of the thing is an aesthetic perception. The rock impresses Geffrey with its clarity, and the names preserved in the shade of the castle are fully recognizable as "writynge" (1162).

Geffrey's inspection consciously takes over the metaphors of poetic invention from Geoffrey of Vinsauf's *Poetria Nova*. Following the rhetorician's admonition to measure the dimensions of a work with the heart's compass before turning to construct it, he reckons (*caste*) the qualities of heat and ice "in myn herte" (1148) and contemplates the castle, for which no one "ne coude casten no compace / Swich another for to make" (1170–71). In echoing the vocabulary of medieval poetics, however, he also shifts the categories that were presumed to underlie artistic creation. Geoffrey of Vinsauf treats a writer's conceptual knowledge of his work under the rubric of rhetorical invention and aligns it with the power of imagination. Chaucer's Geffrey displaces this knowledge to memory as both a rhetorical and a psychological category. His capacity to write depends on memory, just as the edifice of Fame depends on the "fundament" of a literary text subject to transformation.

Fame's Palace and the House of Rumor

The castle, whose "substance / I have yit in my remembrance" (1181–82), overtly connects memory and poetry. Modeled on a cathedral, it presents a seamless web of construction ("wythouten peces or joynynges," 1187) that enshrines poetry.[9] But unlike the Gothic cathedral, which embodies the metaphor of musical harmony in its architectural proportions and organization of space, this structure contains poetry and song directly; it is a space of literary preservation, a treasury of authors and their stories. "Ymageries and tabernacles," windows and pinnacles house a statuary of "alle maner of mynstralles / And gestiours" (1197–98). These players represent the classical and native traditions of tragedy and comedy, "al that longeth unto Fame" (1200). Seated beneath them "smale harpers with her gleës" (1209) play in avowed imitation, "as craft countrefeteth kynde" (1213); behind and in the distance still others take up lyric, festive, and epic matter.

Geffrey's catalogue of the poetic figures contained in the structure includes classical, biblical, and modern characters whom he presumably recognizes from the shapes their sounds take. Numberless as the stars, they show the literal form that all language assumes in Fame's palace—hence, the materialization of love dances before the narrator's eyes and the "blody soun" of military trumpets appears before him. The last group he mentions is composed of "jugelours, / Magiciens, and tregetours" (1259–60) and clerks, all of whom work by incantation. Their "magik naturel" represents a powerful analogy to poetry as Chaucer has discussed it before. Like poetry and the imagination in the *Book of the Duchess,* natural magic can affect a man's health: "thrugh which magik

/ To make a man ben hool or syk" (1269–70). More important, it represents the absolute accord of language, will, and objective conditions in the world. "Al this magik naturel," Geffrey says, "craftely doon her ententes / To make, in certeyn ascendentes, / Ymages" (1266–69), and it is this "magik" that affects man's physical and moral being.

The conservation of poetry in this scene, like the earlier conservation of sound, depends on multiplication. Inspecting the beryl walls as intently as he viewed the ice foundation, Geoffrey notices that the physical properties tend to magnify: the brightness "made wel more than hit was / To semen every thing" (1290–91). Bennett argues that the magnification "embodies that *multiplex sermo* by which in *Aeneid,* iv. 189, *Fama* magnifies Dido's fault—a detail Chaucer had withheld from his adaptation of Virgil's passage in Book One" (115). The gate through which Geffrey passes adds to this empirical process of expansion by producing carved images "be aventure / Iwrought, as often as be cure" (1297–98). The "lusty and ryche place" that he finds within then multiplies language yet again in cries and names and the blazoning from coats of arms. The attending nobles wear their language of images.

> For certeyn, whoso koude iknowe
> Myghte ther alle the armes seen
> Of famous folk that han ybeen
> In Auffrike, Europe, and Asye,
> Syth first began the chevalrie.
>   (1336–40)

Fame, when she arrives trailing their shouts and anthems of praise, appears as a creature with myriad eyes, ears, and tongues—the objectification of the primary senses associated with language.

Throughout the palace scene Geffrey balances the literary and physical sources of perception. The blazons worn by the personnel would comprise "a bible / Twenty foot thykke" (1334–35). The stones adorning the hall can be recognized from a lapidary (1352), and Calliope and the other Muses add "the hevenyssh melodye / Of songes ful of armonye" (1395–96). Fame herself, "a femynyne creature, / That never [was] formed by Nature" (1365–66), is a literary composite—the "monstrum horrendum" that Vergil portrays as Rumor, Ovid's *Fama loquax* who grows as she adds false news to true reports, and the earthly glory that Lady Philosophy denigrates (Hanning "Ovid" 142–44). Her changing size is a perverse combination of Ovid's expanding goddess and Boethius's Philosophy whose size varies from the human to the divine: "somtyme sche constreyned and schronk hirselven lik to the comune mesure of men, and somtyme it semede that sche touchede the hevene with the heghte of here heved" (*Boece* 1.pr1.13–17).

Chaucer describes the architecture of Fame's palace along the lines of a formal memory system. The pillars which extend from Fame's throne to the doorway support capitals representing the epic and historical writers. The chief authors writing about Troy and Rome—Josephus, Statius, Homer, Dares, Dictys, Lollius, Guido delle Colonne, Geoffrey of Monmouth, Vergil, Ovid, Lucan, and Claudian—flank the hall of the palace. Beryl Rowland rightly identifies this arrangement as an artificial memory house, which classical rhetoricians had proposed as a technique for recall, using a system of loci and catalytic tokens to mark the major sections of a speech. Medieval authors, including Chaucer's contemporaries, had adopted the memory house as a metaphor for artistic composition. "The interior of Fame's Palace is a typical memory hall," Rowland says, where important writers "are tied together by various mnemonic devices, in which the focal aid to memory is the pillar" and the different metals lend associations and transitions ("Bradwardine" 49).

Chaucer seems, however, to distinguish the operation of memory from Cicero's mnemotechnics and from rote memorization, which Quintilian had championed in antiquity and which persisted as an alternative to artificial memory. Geffrey makes a point of saying that he will not recite the contents of the pillars in exact order: "I hem noght be ordre telle" (1453). Therefore he consciously chooses not to use the sequential, contiguous structure of an artificial memory system with its adjacent places and tokens. At the end of his description he repeats the point: "But hit a ful confus matere / Were alle the gestes for to here / That they of write, or how they highte" (1517–19). This refusal obviates a direct identification of poetics with artificial memory and reveals something about what Chaucer intends when he appropriates memory as an aesthetic category. By purposely diverging from the artificial order of the loci and tokens, Chaucer draws attention to the slippage that inevitably occurs in a narrative account, even one based on an extrinsic system; he enacts the transformation that Geffrey has already seen at work in other emblems of the poetic text. Geffrey focuses on the immediacy of recollection, on the dim metal preserving the texts rather than on determined forms. He turns away from shapes fixed absolutely by memory, much as his verse turns away from a reductive, technical conception of craft and his understanding always hovers somewhere short of knowledge.

This theme of flux within memory connects, in turn, with the reputations bestowed by Fame, which Chaucer earlier associates with poetry. In a scene parallel to Juno's sending for Morpheus in the *Book of the Duchess,* Fame summons Eolus to bring two trumpets, Clere Laude and Sklaundre, which broadcast praise and shame respectively to the world. The nine groups of petitioners who successively come before her throne are assigned reputations that the trumpets magnify and, in most cases, distort. The similes Geffrey appends to their reputations describe how fame spreads through the world according to the principles of multiplication: "the ferther that hit ran, / The gretter wexen hit bigan" (1651–52). Here as elsewhere language and story are amplified by the physics of speech, but this distortion only magnifies a prior and essential disjunction between words and things.

One group of petitioners approaches Fame to ask only the "name" of noble deeds, and she grants their request in an appropriately ironic phrase, "be my trouthe" (1763). Like mankind's dreams, her judgments have no determinate cause. Geffrey admits, "What her cause was, y nyste" (1543), and ascribes the caprice of Fame's rulings to her being a sister of Fortune. She is pressed by other supplicants to explain her motives ("Telle us what may your cause be" 1563), but she avoids the question: "For me lyst hyt noght" (1564). As the figure of arbitrary designation and naming, Fame denies a connection between merit and reward, being and reputation. "Good werkes shal yow noght availle" (1616), she tells one group of petitioners. Instead, she offers a perversion of grace, forcing renown on contemplatives who want to avoid it, granting rightful claimants even more than they deserve, but commanding for others "a sory grace" (1790). But if Fame is not moved by justice, she is not responsive to evil, either. The distinction is crucial, for it shows Fame's naming of reputations as capricious, not malicious. When she faces a company of traitors she withholds good reputation, claiming, "hyt were a vice. / Al be ther in me no justice, / Me lyste not to doo hyt now" (1819–21). She is withal indifferent to good and evil, and her true nature becomes clear at last to the final petitioner, who concedes that he will accept ill fame if he can have none other.

Chaucer's portrayal of Fame connects and intensifies two propositions about language and poetry: first, language, including poetry, operates under a law of transformation; and second, there is a radical separation of words from things. These principles are argued even more forcefully in what must be the poem's most evocative symbol—the wicker House of Rumor lying in the valley below the castle. Constructed of twigs and shaped like a cage sixty miles long, the "Domus Dedaly" is filled with tidings, and it whirls about so quickly that Geffrey dare not risk entering it alone. The eagle reappears and, eager to resume his role as guide and teacher, carries Geffrey inside, where in the jammed, whispering mass of figures each tiding grows on every tongue: "Were the tydynge soth or fals, / Yit wolde he telle hyt natheles, / And evermo with more encres" (2072–74). As he watches the arbitrary tidings meet at a single exit from the House of Rumor and "medle ... ech with other" (2102), Geffrey realizes, "Thus saugh I fals and soth compouned / Togeder fle for oo tydynge" (2108–9).

These two poetic emblems are the final expression of a line of aesthetic speculation that has built cumulatively through the poem. The glass temple in Book i and the journey toward Fame's palace in Book ii have given an account of how language creates and preserves texts within an economy regulated by natural law. Imagination and memory, the dialectical poles of aesthetic creation, operate through transformation and arbitrary designation. Thus Chaucer arrives at an elaborately articulated formal definition of poetry. But near the end of Book iii he also reaches the limit inherent in a strictly formal conception. For the definition, consciously or not, has been working all along within an incomplete model. Imagination and memory are inadequate by themselves; their power extends to images and sensation, and they require a third element—namely, the intellect, which provides an access to ontological categories and ethical values and thereby offers a way of connecting words and things. Boitani suggests that the palace of Fame "can be seen as a sort of gigantic intellect" (*Fame* 214), but its distortion of signs is an infernal and parodic version of the capacity to abstract an intelligible species from the particulars of perception; it is closer to sensitive than rational memory. Working within the limits of a formal conception, Chaucer discovers that if language and poetry are to foster a knowledge of things, they must embody the same faculties as the mind itself—imagination, memory, and intellect. In other words, he learns the need for a symmetry between the mind and poetry, between the locus and instrument of knowledge.

By omitting intellect as the middle term of a poetics, then, Chaucer has been following an alternate hypothesis to traditional faculty psychology. The style and sources of the hypothesis may lie in a tradition of skepticism and nominalism, but the important point is the aesthetic questions posed by this line of speculation: can the mind invent something different from itself as a tool for understanding? If so, what does it learn? If not, what might this inability reflect? By placing Geffrey in the House of Rumor as a witness to the birth of tidings, Chaucer discovers that he can indeed devise an alternative to conventional notions of language, but only through a deficient model. He can create poetry (we might call it in modern terms an absolute or pure poetry) by suppressing a notion of categories and values, hence the hierarchical relation of language to things. In this way the poetics of Geffrey's dream gives a necessary but not a sufficient account of aesthetic creation. Privative and formalistic, it reduces poetry and language to physical properties and thereby allows an extensive set of analogies between texts and other kinds of signs; but it has no differential of exclusion. In other words, it can tell what poetry is like but not how it differs from other objects and means of knowledge. Still less can it establish the truth value of signs, language, and poetry. Absent a poetic equivalent to the intellect, linguistic representation must at one level remain arbitrary and problematic.

It is this suppression of predication, dramatized for the narrator and made part of his recounting, that gives us the proper context for reading the ending to the *House of Fame*. As Geffrey watches the images of truth and falsehood join at the openings of the wicker house, he hears a noise in the corner, where the men who exchange love tidings leap into a growing pile. A "man of gret auctorite" (2158) approaches him, but before the man speaks the poem breaks off. Chaucer's early editors supplied an ending for the poem that resembles the ending of the *Book of the Duchess:* the dreamer awakes and resolves to begin writing. Caxton writes the following conclusion (*Riverside Chaucer* 1142):

And wyth the noyse of them wo
I sodeynly awoke anon tho
And remembryd what I had seen
And how hye and ferre I had been
In my ghoost and had grete wonder
Of that the god of thonder
Had lete me knowen and began to wryte
Lyke as ye have heard me endyte
Wherfor to studye and rede alway
I purpose to doo day by day
Thus in dremyng and in game
Endeth thys lytl book of Fame.

Despite its irregularities of meter and style, Caxton's addition accurately registers a sense of the poem's having reached an impasse. The poem doubtless ends in dreaming and game; that is where it begins and has remained all along. Later readers have tried, however, to supply a different sense of ending by identifying the man of great authority with topical or literary figures (Richard II, John of Gaunt, Boethius, Cupid). But as Paull F. Baum (255) and subsequent critics observe, the climax achieves a good effect.

The logic of the ending follows directly from the hypothesis that

Chaucer has been developing through Geffrey's visionary journey. Donald Fry contends that the sudden break at the end is deliberate and that "there is no authority, much less great authority, possible in secular human affairs" (38).[10] His argument gives a rationale for the poem's incompletion, but at the same time it restricts the scope of Chaucer's conception. The issue, I think, is not secular human affairs but the wider possibility of imagination and knowledge. The man of great authority is an ironic figure not just because he represents earthly concerns but because anything he might say within the system of discourse that Chaucer has conceived would necessarily be subverted. He stands within the wicker house where true and false images become interwoven, yet his placement there is an accident of location rather than the substance of Chaucer's idea. Were he outside this "Laboryntus," the same conditions would hold. No authority is possible because the faculty that allows discriminations is absent. Given that absence, it is impossible to make any statement outside the circuit of devalued language. Discursive speech comes to be, and indeed has been all along, a part of what it explains, and any authoritative statement would be indistinguishable from a poetic fabrication.

I argued earlier that the *House of Fame* leads Chaucer to a philosophical dead end and want to conclude by returning briefly to that point. Now it should be obvious from the definitions of language and poetry set out in the poem that no linguistic utterance, discursive or poetic, can claim a truth value; linguistic representation has no ontological status in Geffrey's dream. The proposition that leads Chaucer to this impasse is the speculative thesis that language, including poetry, can be reduced to a physical property and that as a thing it is equivalent to other sounds—noise, tidings, inscriptions. But in another sense this proposition leads past the impasse. By that I mean that Chaucer's locating poetry within nature provides a different kind of access to knowledge from the representational epistemology of signs.

Implied in the reduction of poetry to sound that the eagle argues in his instruction of Geffrey is a tacit recognition that language is not just *about* the world but *of* the world. It is one of the "wonder thynges" that it seeks to describe. In addition, language is a social medium, created as Augustine and Dante say, in order to allow men to know each others' minds. If our knowledge of experience through language is mediated and problematic, as it surely is, it is nonetheless founded on a direct perceptual acquaintance. In the scheme that Chaucer hypothesizes in Geffrey's dream, how we know experience is continuous with what we know as experience. This is the conceptual symmetry that develops from the aesthetic speculations in the *House of Fame* and allows finally some connection between words and things. More important, this intuition that poetry has an authentic existence in the world—as a physical property and a social product—is what prepares Chaucer to address the aesthetic problem that informs his last early narrative, the *Parliament of Fowls.* For in the *Parliament* he turns from a formal to a substantive definition of poetry; he locates the topic that defines his subject matter and informs his understanding of poetic craft and its process.

Intellect: The "Certeyn Thing" in the *Parliament of Fowls*

The *Parliament of Fowls* represents the first consolidation of Chaucer's narrative art and poetics. At the level of technique, the rime royal stanzas show his advance beyond seeking a "sumwhat agreable" rhyme (HF 1097). Chaucer has mastered complex versification and applied it to narrative poetry with a skill as great as Machaut's or Boccaccio's. No less secure is his control over the form of the dream vision and the conventions of courtly poetry. Chaucer has learned to modulate a structure of progressively expanding narrative episodes; though his poem ends with a sense of indeterminacy in the formel eagle's refusal to choose among her suitors, it avoids the effects of anticlimax, as in the *Book of the Duchess,* and of narrative and thematic impasse, as in the *House of Fame.* The *Parliament* assimilates a variety of literary antecedents (Dante, Cicero, Boccaccio, and Alan of Lille) without losing coherence. The poet's persona, which makes possible the decentered narrative of the earlier dream visions, appears now as a given, an element within the narrative code; although his uncertainties remain, he is playing a familiar role. As he will later in the *Legend of Good Women,* Chaucer seems to count on his audience's recognizing this fictive person as someone of their acquaintance.

At a conceptual level the *Parliament* brings to completion a sustained movement within Chaucer's speculations about the nature of poetic creation. We have seen that in the *Book of the Duchess* and the *House of Fame* Chaucer uses the categories of imagination and memory as the topoi for his speculations. These categories reflect the emphasis on poetic subjectivity in writers like Machaut and Froissart. Moreover, they impose a decidedly formalistic cast on the theorizing in Chaucer's two poems. Chaucer wants to explore the ways in which imagination and memory create images that operate as mimetic equivalents to experience. His poetics consequently operates within a representational epistemology. This line of aesthetic speculation proves self-defeating, however.

In his early formulations of poetic theory, Chaucer commits the fallacy of reaching for the limit: he tries to establish an absolutely sure ground of knowing, as if anything less could not yield a valid understanding of reality and the truths of human experience. He also discovers that the difference between poetry and the world is by no means absolute. The reduction of language to sound in the *House of Fame* succeeds in showing, among other things, that poetry has some real status in nature. Poetry is part of the world it describes, a metonym and not just a metaphor, and participation in the world gives access to knowledge about the world. Furthermore, language is by nature social, and it constructs a kind of reality based on Fame that mimics poetic fiction and undermines any naive claim to full representation. Hence the predicament of the man of great authority situated in the labyrinthine House of Rumor.

From a critical perspective, the formalistic approach of Chaucer's first two narratives amounts to a poetic thought-experiment conducted within the resources of subjective, courtly narrative. The poems take imagination and memory as their essential terms, and Chaucer tries to see whether two of man's "sapiences three" can carry the burden of the whole. Translated from cognition to the domain of poetic creation, imagination and memory complicate and intensify aesthetic perception, but they do not determine its status as an act of knowing or establish images as reliable modes of representation. Chaucer's experiment, in other words, is to try to define poetic creation through an intentionally defective model of cognition. What is suppressed in the first two poems is something equivalent to the intellect. Chaucer's formulation has nothing to operate as what John Trevisa calls the "vertu estimatiue" (2:98), the power to abstract intelligible species and kinds of things from the particulars of the senses, imaginative experience, and the reconstructions of memory.

I want to suggest that the *Parliament* addresses the problem of the intellect on two related levels. Within the poem's narrative action, the narrator's search to discover a "certeyn thing" in his reading of literary authorities symbolizes and makes concrete Chaucer's effort to define the thematic substance of his poetry. Most readers of the poem believe the "certeyn thing" that the narrator seeks is the meaning of love. Robert Worth Frank, Jr., points out that the three major parts of the poem are unified thematically by their attitude toward love: "They differ sharply in their points of view, but these differences of opinion about love are the source of the poem's over-all comic view and of its final unity of theme" ("Structure" 532). Laurence Eldredge has argued that the views of love expressed through Cicero, Boccaccio, and Alan of Lille represent the philosophical positions of idealism, nominalism, and realism, respectively ("Poetry").

But the significance of the narrator's search goes beyond a definition of poetic matter and formal unity. Aristotle observes that the intellect, when it is in act, is identical to the objects of thought (*De anima* III.8). It follows, then, that Chaucer's poetic art changes in consequence of his defining the central concern of his poetic matter. As he works through the doctrines represented by Cicero, Boccaccio, and Alan and approaches some general understanding of the substance of love, Chaucer discovers the relationship between poetic creation and erotic desire. The intellect is a topos for poetic matter and critical reflection alike. Chaucer's pressing need, evidenced by the indeterminacy of the earlier narrative poems, is for a pragmatic middle term on which to ground poetry as a form of knowledge. We can gauge the poetic significance of the intellect for Chaucer by briefly examining the ways in which one of his near contemporaries uses it to artistic effect.

Juan Ruiz and the Intellect

The issue addressed in the *Parliament* has an interesting analogy in the strategy used by Juan Ruiz, the Archpriest of Hita, to defend the multifaceted treatment of love in his *Libro de buen amor.* The *Libro* is a pseudo-autobiographical collection of stories and songs about the Archpriest's effort to secure *buen amor,* a term whose ambiguity is central to the subtle inversions of didactic and artistic aims in the work. The Archpriest's book exists in two versions. The earlier 1330 version of the *Libro* celebrated a "good love" that ranged over courtly love, Ovidian comedy, the erotic adventures of the *pastorela,* love with a nun, and finally an abortive attempt to approach a Moorish girl. The subject matter and theme are largely secular (Willis xxviii–xxxvi). The 1343 version added such material as a new opening, a prose prologue defending the author's intentions, and still more amorous adventures, all of which depict the Archpriest's frustration as a lover.

The prose prologue of the 1343 version complicates the theme of the *Libro* by extending the notion of *buen amor* to the love of God and opposing it to the *loco amor del mundo*. At the same time it introduces a justification, based on the notion of the intellect, for the *Libro*'s treatment of love. The reason for adding the prologue remains unknown (Juan Ruiz refers to a prison that may be literal or figurative). The effect is subtle and ironic, yet the prologue succeeds in connecting the varieties of love as parts of a comprehensible unity of experience. Juan Ruiz takes as his text the passage from the Psalms (32:8), "Intellectum tibi dabo et instruam te in via hac qua gradieris, firmabo super te oculos meos" (I will give thee understanding, and I will instruct thee in this way in which thou shalt go; I will fix my eyes upon thee). Pierre L. Ullman and Janet A. Chapman have shown that the structure of the prologue derives from the medieval learned sermon, which builds an extended interpretation from an opening *thema*. The poet's glossing of the text is consciously homiletic, employing a rhetorical *divisio:* "En el qual verso entiendo yo tres cosas, las quales dizen algunos dotores filósofos que son en el alma e propiamente suyas" (In this verse I understand three things, which certain men schooled in philosophy say are in the soul and pertain particularly to it, Willis 4–5). These three things, he explains, are understanding, will, and memory—the three powers which Augustine examines in the *De Trinitate*.

Understanding is the first power Juan Ruiz discusses, and it prepares for the other two; the three together confer spiritual and bodily health, honor, and knowledge of the good. The last point is the particular province of the understanding. Juan Ruiz gives it a formulation that is at once correct in doctrine and self-consciously ironic in its tautology: "Ca por el buen entendimiento entiende ombre el bien, e sabe d'ello el mal" (For with good understanding, man understands the good, and from this he knows the bad). He goes on, in exegetical and homiletic fashion, to cite David and Solomon as authorities who confirm that, knowing the good, man will fear God, which is the beginning of all wisdom. From understanding comes love of God (will); understanding and will are then stored in memory—"en la cela de la memoria porque se acuerde d'ello e trae al cuerpo a fazer buenas obras, por las quales se salva el omne" (in the bin of the memory in order to keep it in mind and it leads the body to do good works, by which man is saved).

On a moral and spiritual plane the soul's power of understanding allows man to distinguish good and evil. Ullman insists (158) that Juan Ruiz follows Augustine's doctrine of voluntarism (human free will aided by divine grace) rather than the Aristotelian-Thomistic tradition, which tends to subordinate the will within the intellect. Juan Ruiz's poetic use of the scriptural passage emphasizes, however, the play between understanding and the multiple experiences associated with it.[1] The poet recognizes that man is sinful ("umanal cosa el pecar"), and although he wrote his book mindful of the good ("fiz' esta chica escritura en memoria de bien"), he admits that it contains the tricks, subtleties, and deceptions of the *loco amor del mundo* which can be used for sin. His intention, he says, is different from the uses to which the materials can be put: "E Dios sabe que la mi intención non fue de lo fazer por dar manera de pecar nin por mal dezir" (And God knows my intention was not to compose the book in order to provide ways to commit sin or speak evil). His aim was thus to lead back to the memory of good works and good conduct and to warn people against the deceits of *loco amor* so that they can defend themselves. The moral action of the will depends on knowledge abstracted from the contrary forces of experience.

The didactic purpose adduced in defense of the *Libro* is subverted by Juan Ruiz's artistic intentions. The Archpriest wants to write about the diversity of love, chiefly about erotic desire, to a lesser extent about the spiritual exemplars of love. His tone is comic and his approach elegiac—that is, like Ovid, he finally celebrates rather than judges human conduct. The artistic achievement of the prologue is that he manipulates didacticism to elegiac ends. His means for doing so lies in the way he glosses the term *intellectum*. Alan D. Deyermond points out, "The *intellectum* which provided the sermon's *thema,* or opening quotation, and which consequently underlies its whole structure, turns out to be a true understanding of God, or a skilful technique for seduction; the reader may please himself" (56). Although the intellect is formulated as understanding (*entendimiento*) and human volition determines the spiritual outcome of understanding, the reader is left to abstract a species from particulars. And it is in the plenitude of the specific that Juan Ruiz is interested. Good understanding (*buen entendimiento*), he argues, involves good and bad love. Yet the semantic manipulation of the scriptural passage, as Dayle Seidenspinner-Nuñez observes, is such that "its didactic connotation has been neutralized into ambiguity" (27). By a kind of reading back from the universal to the particulars, the abstractive and moral qualities of the intellect are made to justify the diversity of erotic experience.

The use Juan Ruiz makes of the *intellectum,* like the one I propose for Chaucer, is topical rather than systematic or allegorical. The "dotores filósofos" who interpret Scripture provide a schema within which the Archpriest can define his artistic intentions, even as he parodies the schema. In his case the intentions are announced in retrospect as an apologetic, and they impose still another framework of reading (*buen amor* as love of God) on what may have originally been a narrative of worldly, if sometimes elevated, love. In Chaucer's case the topos of the intellect is written into the narrative from the beginning; it is both part of the textual economy of narrative and a means for critical reflection.

The "Certeyn Thing"

The "certeyn thing" for which Chaucer's narrator searches in his habitual reading adapts a phrasing that appears at several junctures in Boethius's *Consolation of Philosophy* (Mehl 39). At the end of Book I, Philosophy asks Boethius whether he thinks the world is governed by chance and accident or by reason. He answers, "I ne trowe nat in no manere that so certeyn thynges schulden be moeved by fortunows [folie]" because God, "makere and maister, is governour of his werk" (*Boece* 1.pr6.11–15). Later, in the discussion of divine foreknowledge and free will, the phrase is the object of rhetorical iteration and dialectical scrutiny. Boethius asks, "In whiche manere knoweth God byforn the thinges to comen, yif thei ne ben nat certein?" (*Boece* 5.pr3.118–20). He sets out the case for God's prescience by distinguishing between the opinions of mankind, which deem "thinges uncertayn," and divine knowledge: "But yif so be that noon uncertein thing ne mai ben in hym that is right certeyn welle of alle thingis, than is the betydinge certein of thilke thingis whiche he hath wist byforn fermely to comen" (5.pr3.141–45). Boethius then turns to the antithetical problem of free will, and reasons that virtue and vice would be indistinguishable and God would have to assume the authorship of evil, if man had no free will.

Chaucer's adaptation of the term removes it from the questions of divine providence and omniscience to the human problem of knowledge. In the third stanza of the poem he describes his habit ("usage") of reading old books "a certeyn thing to lerne" (PF 20), and he makes it clear that this search has been both repetitive and absorbing. Like the eight-year illness in the *Book of the Duchess* but to a different end, it has engaged his energies over time and taken his powers of concentration: "The longe day ful faste I redde and yerne" (PF 21). The shift from "sorwful ymagynacioun" to reading in the *Book of the Duchess* and the celestial journey to learn tidings in the *House of Fame* are troped here as a symbolic and reflective search for a precise referent, an order of knowledge outside the observer, "a certeyn thing."

The quest for knowledge is the narrative trajectory that links the discrete sections of the *Parliament*. J. A. W. Bennett believes that by the end of the poem "there emerges a view of the place of love in human life which is balanced, harmonious, and satisfying, yet which does not ignore the paradoxes and dilemmas that are as old as human society" (*Parlement* 186). A. C. Spearing likewise contends, "what the narrator is seeking is presumably the meaning of that love which is the major subject of medieval courtly poetry, but which he sees chiefly as a cause of suffering; what he finds in the dream is a subtle placing of love in the larger context of the social order and of the relationship between the natural and the human, nature and culture" (90). The poem brings into a coherent relation several disparate conceptions of love—love as social virtue, desire, cupidity, a natural drive, an expression of Nature's plenitude and divine order. Yet there is sharp disagreement on the organization of the "certeyn thing," on the thematic coherence and ideological structure of the traditions.[2]

The point of departure for most contemporary readings of the *Parliament* is Bennett's analysis of structure and meaning, which conceives the structure of the poem along the lines of Hegelian dialectic. According to Bennett, after the narrator's introduction, which sounds the twin themes of love and literature, the poem's thesis is stated in a summary of Cicero's *Somnium Scipionis* and the account of Africanus's appearance to the narrator in a dream vision. Bennett holds that Chaucer uses Cicero and Macrobius to formulate the initial doctrine that love of the common weal is the only earthly good. The antithesis emerges as Africanus leads the narrator to the gates of "a park walled with grene ston" (122) where contradictory inscriptions celebrate "that blysful place" as "the welle of grace" and "the wey to al good aventure" (127–31) but warn at the same time that "Disdayn and Daunger," barrenness and entrapment lie within. Inside the park, which evokes the garden from the *Roman de la rose,* the operation of love as natural appetite and sexual passion is depicted by Cupid, Priapus, and the temple of Venus. As the dreamer finishes his inspection of the temple and turns his attention from its depiction of love's misfortunes, synthesis appears in the figure of Nature, "the vicaire of the almyghty Lord" (379) who governs appetite as part of divine creation according to principles of harmony and measure. Love and mating, the chief points of the debate among the royal eagles which ensues under Nature's direction, are, Bennett argues, related to the poem's initial concern with the common weal. Although the specific question of the debate remains undecided and the formel eagle defers choosing a mate, Nature gives the other birds their mates "by evene acord" (668), and the final roundel sung "to don Nature honour and plesaunce" (676) marks a point of synthesis and an expression of harmony.

If Bennett's analysis is correct, Chaucer has succeeded in defining love in a way that connects ethical and social considerations to the workings of appetite and passion and then subsumes those drives within a providential creation administered by God's regent. This synthesis depends, however, on a strategy of interpretation which, in the first place, renders Cicero accessible to Christian ethics and metaphysics and, in the second, subordinates Venus to Nature. It is essentially on these two points that a reading of the poem depends. (To the extent that the theory of love represented in the poem is a mosaic of sources rather than a discursive structure, Chaucer's "certeyn thing" remains, of course, problematic.) I want to take up these two points as they relate to Chaucer's attempt to define love as a substance knowable in human terms. Since both points depend on antecedent literary sources, we must examine Chaucer's intertextual handling of the materials.

Three Doctrines of Love

It is generally thought that Chaucer's treatment of the *Somnium* is informed by a direct and close reading of the text rather than a reliance on intermediaries, as it had been in the *Book of the Duchess*. As in the *House of Fame,* Chaucer reproduces the description of the *Roman de la rose* that has Scipio see the divisions of a Christian cosmos ("Si con fist Scipio jadis / veit enfer et paradis," 18367–68), but he gives a full account here of the subject matter in the *Somnium*. What is significant in this account is the pattern of omission and emphasis. Chaucer's retelling creates a version of the narrative with a marked shift in theme. "The point of the story of Scipio's dream," George Economou remarks, "is that man must win salvation through service to 'commune profit' ('patriam' or 'rem publicam' in Cicero's words)" (127). Although it asserts stable values, Cicero's theme does not allow much scope for discovering the substance of the experiences Chaucer writes about. "The trouble with the Dream of Scipio," Derek Brewer writes, "is that it takes no account of the value of the world as God's creation, a creation which, according to medieval thought, sprang from, and was continuously maintained by, God's regulating love. To put it briefly, there is nothing about Nature or love in the Dream of Scipio."[3] Nonetheless, the pattern that unfolds in Chaucer's summarizing of Cicero's meaning indicates a thoughtful revision of the original. The narrator promises, "Of his sentence I wol yow seyn the greete," (35), so his retelling offers a guide to the poetic possibilities Chaucer saw in the *Somnium*.

In his seven-stanza précis of the *Somnium*, Chaucer omits elements that would readily offer motifs and themes to connect Cicero's text to later sections of the *Parliament*. The narrator sees a contradictory message of joy and sorrow carved on the gate to the love garden. The lines are taken from the words inscribed over the portal of Hell in Dante's

Inferno, and in Dante's poem Vergil pierces their obscurity by telling Dante, "tu vedrai le genti dolorose / c'hanno perduto il ben de l'intelletto" (3.17–18). In Chaucer's poem the ambivalence of the message is anticipated by the joyful tears with which Masinissa greets Scipio as the effigy of the elder Africanus (6.9); later Scipio greets his father Paulus with the same conflicted gesture: "Quem ut vidi, equidem vim lacrimarum profudi" (When I saw him I poured forth a flood of tears, 6.14). Though it heightens the thematic resonance, Chaucer does not report the latter scene.

Africanus prophesies that at the end of his life Scipio will become a beneficent dictator charged with the moral imperative of restoring order to the commonwealth: "dictator rem publicam constituas oportet" (it will be your duty as dictator to restore order in the commonwealth, 6.12). His obligation clearly parallels the role of Nature, who ministers the sublunary world as God's vicar, but Chaucer does not draw the parallel. In Cicero's text it is precisely this need to administer human affairs that prompts the elder Africanus to begin the discussion of cosmology: "Sed quo sis, Africane, alacrior ad tutandam rem publicam, sic habeto" (But, Africanus, be assured of this, so that you may be even more eager to defend the commonwealth, 6.13). He goes on to explain that justice and statecraft are most pleasing to God, who prepares a special place (*definitum locum*) whence the "rectores et conservatores" (rulers and preservers) come and to which they return in the afterlife. Paulus, who does not appear at all in Chaucer's retelling, confirms the civic foundation, urging Scipio to cultivate justice and piety ("iustitiam cole et pietatem," 6.16), for they are owed to parents, kinsmen, and most of all the fatherland.

The omission of these elements is pointed. Chaucer tells how Masinissa joyfully embraces Scipio ("hym for joie in armes hath inome," 38), but he suppresses mention of the tears that lend poignancy to Cicero's version. The silence is particularly notable when we recall the affective identification the narrator makes with Alcyone and Dido in earlier poems. Chaucer also suppresses the familial and genealogical aspects of political morality in Cicero, so that the souls in question are no longer those of rulers and preservers of the state who migrate from and return to a special place appointed for them in heaven. Divine reward becomes, as Economou says, "salvation," but the theological formulation of redemption gained by works is Chaucer's.

> ... what man, lered other lewed,
> That lovede commune profyt, wel ithewed,

> He shulde into a blysful place wende
> There as joye is that last withouten ende.
>
> (PF 46–49)

The effect of these omissions is, in the first case, to mute the sense of ambivalence that might otherwise surround the narrator's vision and, in the second, to set out an ethics and cosmology independent of the political morality that Cicero believes subtends human action. Chaucer reshapes the *Somnium*'s morality to make it apply not to the citizen but to the soul in general.

By contrast, Chaucer accents the elements of the *Somnium* that confer a providential outlook. Cicero's specific location of a place where the blessed enjoy an eternal life ("ubi beati aevo sempiterno fruantur," 6.13) provides the clue for the spiritual conditions of "blysse" and "grace" that Chaucer will repeat throughout the poem, rhetorically linking the authorial text of Scipio's dream to his own vision of the love garden. Cicero's *patriam* and *rem publicam* are reformulated, through Boethius, as the "commune profyt" that governs biological, moral, and social life (Bennett *Parlement* 33). Whereas Africanus dismisses ordinary life as being death and bondage ("vita mors est," 6.14) and remarks that the earth is too small to support glory and fame (6.20), Chaucer gives an Augustinian and Boethian version of *contemptus mundi,* which balances an acceptance of "harde grace" in this world with an insistence on man's moral choices and his proper understanding of the significance of worldly experience: "he ne shulde hym in the world delyte" (66).

Certainly the most difficult and potentially controversial adaptation of the *Somnium* involves Africanus's climactic assertion to Scipio, "Know, then, that you are a god" ("deum te igitur scito esse," 6.24). Bennett (*Parlement* 40) points out that Cicero's text is mediated by Macrobius's commentary, which explains the passage, "haec sit praesentis operis consummatio ut animam non solum immortalem, sed deum esse clarescat" (This is also the consummation of the present treatise: to make it clear that the soul is not only immortal but is a god, 1.12.5, Stahl 223). Chaucer recombines two of these elements (*immortalem* and *clarescat*) in order to purge the line of its pagan associations.

> "Know thyself first immortal,
> And loke ay besyly thow werche and wysse
> To commune profit, and thow shalt not mysse
> To comen swiftly to that place deere
> That ful of blysse is and of soules cleere."
>
> (73–77)

In rewriting his source, though, Chaucer would inevitably have discovered more from the rest of the passage. For Cicero goes on to qualify Africanus's assertion that man is a god in such a way as again to anticipate the thematic insistence on governance under Nature: "siquidem est deus, qui viget, qui sentit, qui meminit, qui providet, qui tam regit et moderatur et movet id corpus, cui praepositus est, quam hunc mundum ille princeps deus" (if a god is that which lives, feels, remembers, and foresees, and which rules, governs, and moves the body over which it is set, just as the supreme God above us rules this universe, 6.24). Man's sentient and intellectual qualities equate him with divinity, Africanus explains, and his control over his body exists in proportion to God's control over the universe.

It is this multileveled theme of government, moreover, that underlies Cicero's final image of libidinous souls freed from their bodies but condemned to whirl about the earth for many ages. Chaucer invests Cicero's image with a reminiscence of the wind that propels Paolo and Francesca: "La bufera infernal, che mai non resta, / mena li spirti con la sua rapina; / voltando e percotendo li molesta" (The hellish hurricane, never resting, sweeps along the spirits with its rapine; whirling and smiting, it torments them, *Inferno* 5.31–33). Relying again on Macrobius (Bennett *Parlement* 43), Chaucer makes this torment purgatorial: "And than, foryeven al hir wikked dede, / Than shul they come into that blysful place, / To which to comen God the sende his grace" (PF 82–84). These souls are "brekers of the lawe" and "likerous folk," but Cicero had made it explicit that their sensuality (*voluptas*) not only transgressed divine and human laws but subverted the very order which rightfully governs pleasure.

The narrator's summary of Cicero's large themes shows that Chaucer revised his source so as to address the broad ethical issues facing man's soul (Bennett "Second" 133–37). He reformulates morality within a tradition that diminishes worldly achievements while asserting spiritual resolutions for human dilemmas. At the same time, his summary suggests an inclusive notion of government and divine ordering. Chaucer cannot, however, follow these suggestions within the frame offered by the *Somnium*. At the end of his reading, he is, as at the start of the *Book of the Duchess,* "fulfyld of thought and busy hevynesse" (PF 89). He describes his state as a paradox of loss and possession: "For bothe I hadde thyng which that I nolde, / And ek I ne hadde that thyng that I wolde" (PF 90–91). The phrasing is borrowed from Lady Philosophy's discussion of true and false felicity: " 'And was nat that,' quod sche, 'for that the lakkide somwhat that thow noldest nat han lakkid, or elles thou haddest that thow noldest nat han had?' " (*Boece* 3.pr3.33–36). Chaucer uses the locution, too, in his lyrics. In "The Complaint unto Pity" the phrasing describes the experience of *Desir*: "My peyne is this, that what so I desire / That have I not, ne nothing lyk therto" (99–100). In "A Complaint to His Lady" desire has produced an ironic fulfillment: "For al that thyng which I desyre I mis / And al that ever I wolde not ywis, / That finde I redy to me evermore" (43–45). But if the structure of desire is the same in the *Parliament,* the meaning is not. The narrator's object of desire, constituted by his reading, is knowledge, "a certeyn thing to lerne" (20).[4] Although the *Somnium* allows some intuition of Chaucer's subject matter, it does not contain the "certeyn thing" he seeks to grasp.

Chaucer's effort to abstract the intelligible species of love turns to a second source in the tradition of the love garden. Africanus takes the dreamer by the hand through the gates of the garden, much as Vergil leads Dante among the "segrete cose" (*Inferno* 3.21) inside the gate of hell. Within the park filled with "blosmy bowes" (PF 183) and birds singing "with voys of aungel in here armonye" (191), the narrator encounters the principal figures of sexual passion: Cupid beside a well, Priapus "withinne the temple in sovereyn place" (254), and, "in a prive corner in disport" (260), Venus and Richesse.[5] The scene is taken from Boccaccio's *Teseida* (7.51–66), but the debts to the *Roman de la rose* are evident, too. Howard Schless points out that Chaucer "joins the solemn rhythms of the lines that Dante inscribes above the entrance to the Inferno and the poetic diction that typifies the love poetry of the French school of courtly writing" (89).

The central icon of the scene is the voluptuous description of Venus. Piero Boitani observes, "Boccaccio's Venus is a stratification of courtly love (represented by the personifications found in the *Roman*), sensual love (Priapus, the naked goddess), tragic love (the stories painted in the temple), and of the planet (the copper columns)" ("Style" 191). Boccaccio's own gloss (*chiosa*) sets forth the doctrine of the heavenly and earthly Venuses, but makes it clear that the figure of Venus represented here is "quella per la quale ogni lascivia è disiderata, e che volgarmente è chiamata dea d'amore" (Limentani 463).

The description of Venus that Chaucer borrows from Boccaccio is intentionally sensuous, appealing to sight, smell ("a thousand savours sote," PF 274), and taste (Bacchus and Ceres). The senses represent the properties of appetite, but Boccaccio's commentary stresses their moral significance. Boccaccio says of Bacchus and Ceres, "through these two he [the author] portrays gluttony which is much indulged in by pleasure-lovers." The enticement of smell he explains as follows: "The perfuming of the place is essential for those who indulge in such pursuits. For since the activity itself is so malodorous, if the sense of smell were not soothed by perfumes the stomach and the mind would easily be put off, and so would all the other functions" (Havely 132–33).

Venus herself is an object of spectatorial desire in Boccaccio. The description of her blond hair, face, arms, bosom, and breasts ends with mention of a garment so fine that it hides almost nothing of the rest of her: "e l'altra parte d'una / veste tanto sottil si ricopria, / che quasi nulla appena nascondia" (7.65.6–8). Boccaccio's commentary argues the need to see through the figure, just as one can see through the garment covering Venus.

> Next he describes the beauty of Venus whom he portrays reclining, partly naked and partly draped with a rich purple cloth so fine that it conceals hardly anything of those parts it covers. Through this reclining he represents the languour characteristic of pleasure-lovers and the life of ease. Through Venus's beauty, which we know to be a frail and transient thing, he represents that false judgment of pleasure-lovers which through true reason [*verissime ragioni*] we can very easily recognize and prove to be baseless. Through the partial nakedness of Venus he represents the appearance of things, which holds the attention of those whose understandings [*estimazione*] cannot grasp the truth about them [*non può passare all'essistenzia*]. Through the part of her that is visible under the fine garment he seeks to portray the secret belief [*l'occulta estimazione*] of those who judge by appearances.
>
> (Havely 132)

Chaucer's treatment brings the figure of Venus from the realm of appearances to a domain of knowledge. It foregrounds the erotic description in a common viewpoint of human experience. Venus is "naked from the brest unto the hed / Men myghte hire sen" (269–70), the narrator reports, translating the sensuous inventory of Boccaccio's lines, "le braccia e 'l petto e' pomi rilevati / si vedean tutti" (7.65.5–6). The "veste sottil" covering the rest of her (the euphemistic "altra parte") in Boccaccio becomes a "subtyl coverchef of Valence" (PF 272), and Chaucer adds to the scene two suppliants crying to Venus on their knees "to ben here helpe" (279).

Chaucer does not offer the overt moralizing that we find in Boccaccio's commentary, which is itself a cancellation of the erotic pleasure created by the poetic description. The iconographical tableau of Venus's temple is an object of inquiry for Chaucer. The narrator's sight and hearing serve the purpose of determining the substance of what he experiences in the temple. When the narrator finally locates Venus in the darkness, it is discovery ("Fond I Venus and hire porter Richesse," 261) rather than pleasure. If Chaucer makes a moral judgment, he does so implicitly by juxtaposition and the manipulation of poetic structure. Scholars have long remarked that Chaucer rearranges the order of stanzas in Boccaccio's poem so as to present the imagery of Diana's broken bows and the stories of catastrophic love affairs painted on the temple wall in the final and most emphatic position. The *ekphrasis* of classical and chivalric lovers is a commentary on the portrait of Venus. The lesson drawn from it gives a precise understanding of Venus's love: "Alle these were peynted on that other syde, / And al here love, and in what plyt they dyde" (293–94).

Boccaccio says explicitly that the Venus depicted in the *Teseida* is not the *Venus caelestis*. Chaucer finds a version of the heavenly Venus, however, in a third source. Walking forth alone from the temple to solace himself, the narrator encounters the goddess Nature sitting on a hill. The narrator's rhetoric in the passage brings Nature into the courtly, erotic domain of the love garden. She surpasses every creature as the light of the summer sun surpasses starlight. Her beauty is "over mesure" (300), and "here cast and here mesure" (305) construct out of branches an equivalent to the man-made halls and chambers of Venus's temple. As in the portrait of Venus, the source for the goddess is textual, but Chaucer consciously marks his borrowing this time (Boccaccio is nowhere mentioned in Chaucer's writing): "And right as Aleyn, in the Pleynt of Kynde, / Devyseth Nature of aray and face, / In swich aray men myghte hire there fynde" (316–18). Though the acknowledgment of authority differs, the figures of Venus and Nature are treated through the same narrative technique. Like Venus, Nature is seen from a common viewpoint—the rhetorical description (*effictio*) men can find in Alan of Lille's *De planctu naturae*. She is a figure from the narrator's obsessive reading. And again like Venus, Nature is the object of knowledge and not a simple projection of desire.[6]

There are two conventional interpretations of the thematic and narrative significance of these emblems. The majority opinion is Bennett's belief that the poem makes Venus subordinate to Nature: "The outskirts of the temple merge on the one side with the park and on the other with Nature's 'launde': as if to show that courtoisie is meet and commendable if regarded not as an end in itself but as part of the preparation of Youth for adult life and marriage" (*Parlement* 118). Dorothy Everett connects Venus to courtly love and Nature to a love of creature with creature ("Visions" 110). "The 'scale of Nature,' " Brewer remarks, "represents the graded perfection of the universe" (*Parlement* 29) in which procreation has a lawful place, and Economou points out that Alan restricts lawful coition to marriage and so places sexual passion under control and moderation (87). The alternate view holds that sexuality and procreation are juxtaposed rather than governed by reason. Conceding that Venus is subordinate to Nature, Dorothy Bethurum nonetheless contends, "Nature and Priapus are the presiding deities in the Garden." ("Center" 45). Elizabeth Salter finds a strain of elegiac observation and moral neutrality in Boccacio and "very little evidence that Chaucer felt the necessity to remould the Italian in any very important way": "nothing in the English poem hints at the unsuitability of Cupid, Venus, and their court for such a [paradisiacal] setting" (135).[7]

The basis for both these approaches—and for the intermediary positions between them—lies, I think, in the issue of Chaucer's intertextual practice. For the concept of love expressed in the poem emerges not simply as a theme extracted from antecedent texts (*Venus impudica* or *Natura ministrans*) but as part of a literary discourse. Chaucer turns to Boccaccio and Alan as sources for description and thematic expression, yet the sources come to him already implicated in structures of textual meaning.[8] We have seen in the treatment of the *Somnium* that the passages suppressed in Chaucer's summary no less than those rendered directly bear on the meaning of the *Parliament.* So, too, Boccaccio's description of the garden and temple expounds meaning by separating aesthetic observation from moral significance. Chaucer's portrayal of Nature as the presiding emblem in the final section of the poem is similarly the product of textual sources and not merely an isolated borrowing. Chaucer discovers in Alan's presentation of Nature a framework for grasping the nature of love. Though he stops short of the spiritual transcendence Alan finally proposes, he nonetheless finds a substantial unity that contains and makes intelligible the diversity of erotic experience.[9]

Reading Nature

The medieval conception of Nature owes much to Macrobius's image of Nature as *artifex,* participating in the biology of reproduction by helping to coin man from a mint (Economou 19). Alan uses the imagery of coining throughout the *De planctu naturae* and in the *Anticlaudianus* (7.34–36). Jean de Meun gives it surely the most popular medieval expression in the *Roman de la rose* (16005–17): "But when Nature, sweet and compassionate, sees that envious Death and Corruption come together to put to destruction whatever they find within her forge, she continues always to hammer and forge and always to renew the individuals by means of new generation. When she can bring no other counsel to her work, she cuts copies in such letters that she gives them true forms in coins of different monies" (Dahlberg 271).

Although they share this central image, Alan and Jean differ radically in their conception of Nature's role in love. Alan places lawful sexuality within the structure of marriage, while Jean treats the impulse toward procreation as a general characteristic of man and does not limit its legitimacy to marriage. La Vielle advises earlier in the *Rose,* "never doubt that she [Nature] has made all us women for all men and all men for all women, each woman common to every man and every man common to each woman" (13855–58). Alan views sexual passion within the dialectic of lust and reason, whereas Jean's moral neutrality leads him to emphasize the separation of Reason and Nature. In the *Parliament,* Nature formally separates herself from the figure of Reason ("if I were Resoun," 632), but she elsewhere asserts the mechanisms of divine *ratio* essentially as Alan describes them, and it seems evident that of the two figures presented by literary tradition Chaucer adapts the one depicted so forcefully in the *De planctu naturae.*

Chaucer's epithet "Nature, the vicaire of the almyghty Lord" (PF 379) borrows the terms with which Nature discloses herself to the dreamer in Alan's allegory: "dei auctoris uicaria rata dispensatione, legitimum tue uite ordinaui curriculum" ([I,] acting by an established covenant as the deputy of God, the creator, have from your earliest years established the appointed course of your life, VI.21–22). Chaucer tropes Boethius to express Nature's power to join opposing elements "by evene noumbres of acord" (PF 381): "Thow byndest the elementis by nombres proporcionables" (*Boece* 3.m9.18–19). But it is Alan who gives Nature specific scope and discrimination. Nature orders the rational arrangement of the body and effects a marriage of body and soul. Shaping man according to the pattern of the world's structure ("ad exemplarem mundane machine similitudinem hominis exemplaui naturam," VI.44–45), she employs the permutations of *concors discordia* to establish the microcosm of mankind. Lust and reason, the antinomies of moral existence, countercirculate in man in imitation of the planets and stars.

Alan attributes reason and proportion to Nature not only by the delegation of divine exemplars but also by dramatizing the effects of her works. Her first appearance prompts a festival of renewal, in which the licit desire of Juno and Jupiter and of Nereus and Thetis are the most powerful icons. Their lawful copulation looks forward structurally to the restoration of mankind made possible by the banishing of vice at the end of Alan's poem.[10] Elsewhere Nature affirms the need for moderation by contrasting rational and ecstatic art: "Solus homo, mee modulationis citharam aspernatus, sub delirantis Orphei lira delirat"

(Man alone turns with scorn from the modulated strains of my cithern and runs deranged to the notes of mad Orpheus' lyre, viii.54–55). Nature is not equated with reason, and Jean's Nature will say explicitly that she cannot create man's rational faculties or make him eternal (*Rose* 19055–76), but Nature's work still proceeds from reason.

The figure Chaucer encountered in Alan's poem is situated within a precisely defined hierarchy. God has established a harmony of lawful orders, conferred laws, and bound the universe with ordinances: "legitimi ordinis congruentia temperauit, leges indidit, sanctionibus alligauit" (viii.209–10). Nature acts as deputy and vicar ("tanquam prodeam, tanquam sui uicariam"), forging and stamping the proper seal on created life under divine guidance. Nature's relation to the *universalis artifex* nonetheless involves distance and multiplicity. As a humble disciple ("humilem discipulam"), Nature can only contemplate God from a distance, and she recognizes in an extended figure of rhetorical contrast the abiding difference between divine simplicity and the multiplicity of creation.

> Eius enim operatio simplex, mea operatio multiplex. Eius opus sufficiens, meum opus deficiens. Eius opus mirabile, meum opus mutabile. Ille innascibilis, ego nata. Ille faciens, ego facta. Ille mei opifex operis, ego opus opificis. Ille operatur ex nichilo, ego mendico opus ex aliquo. Ille suo operatur in numine, ego operor illius sub nomine. Ille rem solo nutu iubet existere, mea uero operatio operationis est nota diuine. Et respectu diuine potentie meam potentiam impotentiam esse cognoscas. Meum effectum scias esse defectum, meum uigorem uilitatem esse perpendas.

> His operation is simple, mine is multiple; His work is complete, mine is defective; His work is the object of admiration, mine is subject to alteration. He is ungeneratable, I was generated; He is the creator, I was created; He is the creator of my work, I am the work of the Creator; He creates from nothing, I beg the material for my work from someone; He works by His own divinity, I work in His name; He, by His will alone, bids things come into existence, my work is but a sign of the work of God. You can realise that in comparison with God's power, my power is powerless; you can know that my efficiency is deficiency; you can decide that my activity is worthless.

> (vi.131–39)

This hierarchical connection is recreated and extended in Nature's relation to Venus, though the metaphors that register their difference change from vertical to horizontal and from multiplicity to specialization and eventually perversion. Wishing to remain above change in the ethereal palace, Nature delegates Venus as her subvicar and charges her with assuring the continuation of human life. The location given Venus to carry out her tasks anticipates the relative placement of Venus's temple and Nature's "launde" in the *Parliament*: "Venerem in fabrili scientia conpertam meeque operationis subuicariam in mundiali suburbio collocaui" (I stationed Venus, learned in the artisan's skill, on the outskirts of the Universe to be the subdelegate in charge of my work, VIII.240–41).

With Hymen and Cupid, Venus is to carry out the labor of forging mankind. In a later section Alan clarifies this hierarchy of production. Nature says, "terrestrium animantium materiande propagini Venerem destinaui" (I selected Venus to be in charge of the work of propagation of earth's living things, x.21–22). At the same time she defines her own function by analogy to God's supervision of her. Venus shapes the rough materials of mankind with the hammers and anvils made available to her, and Nature applies the polishing hand in the manifold formation of human nature. Nature is thus at the beginning and end of creation: an intermediary of the universal artisan and the final shaper of mankind.[11]

In describing Nature's governance of man's biological and moral condition, Alan's poem offers Chaucer a ground for relating the discrete emphases of earlier portions of the *Parliament*. Nature's idea of procreation and her reproving of vices speak to the issue of true and false felicity, government, and divine ordering in Chaucer's poem; the points are addressed, much as Chaucer appropriates them from Cicero, to the individual soul as a moral being. Alan's subordination of Venus to Nature legitimizes sexuality and finally provides what Jean and Boccaccio do not furnish—a principle for distinguishing the reasons behind rewarding and disastrous love. The perspectives afforded by the *Somnium* and the *Teseida* enforce a univocal and deterministic outlook on love. Nature's multiplicity, as Alan articulates it, responds to the lesson that the *Parliament*'s narrator learns through observation and reading—namely, that human behavior is diverse yet intelligible. To be sure, Venus's adultery and the subsequent subversion of lawful coition amount to spiritual disaffection in Alan's poem. The key point, however, is that the framework of providential creation which Alan describes provides a source for poetic invention.

It is thus that Alan's Nature, capping Cicero's allegory of the common weal and Boccaccio's tableau of sensual pleasure, offers a way to define the "certeyn thing" that Chaucer's narrator seeks. Alan's doctrine of love is not a metaphor or a diffuse theme, nor yet is it a mere product of perception, like the figures projected by the imagination and sensitive memory. Rather, it is a category of experience that both informs and resides in creation; like language in the *House of Fame,* it is in the world, not just in the mind, and it is the universal that renders the particulars of appetite and desire intelligible.

This substantive definition of love governs the remainder of the *Parliament* and provides the rationale for its multi-level comic perspective. Chaucer presents an icon of naturalized social order in the tableau of birds arranged by degrees around Nature and anatomized in the narrator's catalogue. The pairing of mates occurs, as Nature says, "By my statut and thorgh my governaunce" (387), but it also depends on "plesaunce" (389) and mutual "acord" (371, 668). In this way the abstract principle represented by Alan's Nature returns to the particulars of experience. The refusal of the formel eagle to choose among the three tercels, the competing rhetorical styles of her suitors, the tumult of the lower birds frustrated by the delay—all these comprise the accidents of natural desire. Chaucer displays them as parts of Nature's regulation of erotic conduct, but he refuses to reduce them to a single ideal form. When the birds at last sing the French roundel honoring Nature, they celebrate the fundamental coherence of love, which remains despite its discrepancies—"Wel han they cause for to gladen ofte, / Sith ech of hem recovered hath hys make" (687–88). Chaucer's artistic and conceptual achievement consists in defining a unified poetic substance without refining away the singularities and discordant individualism of the particulars.

Creation and Writing

Much as Alan furnishes a means for grasping an intelligible structure within the multiform particulars of love, he also contributes something toward defining the other aesthetic question of the *Parliament,* the nature of the writer's craft. Donald C. Baker rightly contends that Chaucer "is a Poet of love, and his concern for the 'philosophy' in the poem, the philosophical problems revolving about love, is his concern for the materials of his craft" ("Poet" 85). A major theme complementing Alan's portrayal of Nature as God's vicar over mankind is the equivalence of procreation and writing. In the *De planctu naturae,* Nature's generative power operates by analogy and often by the instrumentality of composing images and texts. The rational order of natural production is identical to grammatical order. Alan gives both negative and positive formulations of this equation, counterposing sodomy and lawful coition.

The most noted expression of this equation comes at the beginning of the poem, where Alan's narrator complains that Venus has unmanned men. He sees sexual perversion in the metaphor of grammar.

> Actiui generis sexus se turpiter horret
> Sic in passiuum degenerare genus.
> Femina uir factus sexus denigrat honorem,
> Ars magice Veneris hermafroditat eum.
> Predicat et subicit, fit duplex terminus idem.
> Gramatice leges ampliat ille nimis.

> The active sex shudders in disgrace as it sees itself degenerate into the passive sex. A man turned woman blackens the fair name of his sex. The witchcraft of Venus turns him into a hermaphrodite. He is subject and predicate: one and the same term is given a double application. Man here extends too far the laws of grammar.

(i.15–20)

Rightful intercourse, the narrator contends, follows the same laws of declension and conjugation as right grammar. In her long denunciation of man's defection from divine order and his inversion of Venus's rules, Nature asserts that man's sexual perversion shows in the deformities of writing, grammar, and logic (viii.57–94). Later, Cupid's grammar is shown to be built around oxymoron (xi), and Venus's adultery with Antigenius is related again to grammatical and logical irregularity ("se gramaticis constructionibus destruens, dialeticis conuersionibus inuertens," x.142–43). The negative examples testify, however, to a defection from the normal rules of biological and linguistic order, and the forcefulness of the complaint against wrongful writing is an index of the importance of writing as a metaphor for creation.

Alan hints at the positive importance that writing will assume in the poem by sketching a scene of birth and reformation on the tunic of Nature, which the narrator describes early in the poem. A bear gives birth through her nostrils to ill-formed offspring, but gradually reshapes them into a better figure by using the stylus of her tongue: "ipsos stilo lingue crebrius delambenti monetans, meliorem deducebat in formam" (ii.252–53). The images pictured on Nature's garment appear and disappear in imitation of life and death, unable to persist in her plan of writing ("in scripture proposito imagines perseuerare non poterant," iv.7–8). The full significance of writing emerges later when Nature describes her duties of coining man and bestowing on him the proper insignia. This labor of coinage and inscription has to take place under divine guidance because Nature's pen ("mee scripture calamus") would deviate unless it were guided by God's direction ("nisi supremi Dispensatoris digito regeretur," viii.234–35). In her subsequent supervision of Venus, Nature furnishes a pen and oversees the correct orthography and the grammar of mankind's creation. The latter requires the proper joining of masculine and feminine genders, the agreement of nouns and adjectives, conjugation, and the proper ordering of logical syllogisms (x.30–57). When Genius is summoned at the end of the poem, his appearance recalls Nature's tunic, for he writes "ymagines momentanee uiuentes" (xviii.64–74) on an animal hide, and his sketch brings the images to life and lets them quickly expire. In Jean de Meun's version of Genius's anathema, writing, forging, and agriculture are analogous (*Rose* 19543–82).

The equivalence of ordered procreation and writing in Alan's poem provides Chaucer a model for connecting erotics and poetics. Alan suggests that to participate in the workings of love is to be a writer and especially one whose hand is guided by an author. As in his lyrics, Chaucer reverses the conventional equation: to write is to participate in love. Within the *Parliament,* Chaucer's permutation informs several key references to texts and production. The correlative of writing is the narrator's habitual reading, and it reflects the twin motives of desire and knowledge. The narrator, in fact, makes these aspects of procreation and composition convertible, when he describes his "usage" of reading: "what for lust and what for lore" (15). The equation between creation and textuality is given even greater articulation, however, in the agricultural image of textual production.

> For out of olde feldes, as men seyth,
> Cometh al this newe corn from yer to yere,
> And out of olde bokes, in good feyth,
> Cometh al this newe science that men lere.
>
> (22–25)

Commentators usually remark on the "proverbial flavor" of this passage and its echo in the *Legend of Good Women* (F 73–76), where Chaucer comically portrays himself sifting through the remnants left by lover-poets like a man gleaning grain after the reapers have picked the field. But the imagery more properly sustains the equation Alan makes in his learned poem, and the repetition of the word "lere" indicates that the "newe science" brought forth from reading must be the "certeyn thing" that the narrator seeks.

In retrospect we can see that the equation between love's creative power and the act of poetic composition is made from the very outset of the poem—that is, from the transposition of art and love in the first stanza.[12] Chaucer's rhetorical transposition thereby signals an equivalence between the object and mode of representation.

> The lyf so short, the craft so long to lerne,
> Th'assay so hard, so sharp the conquerynge,
> The dredful joye alwey that slit so yerne:
> Al this mene I by Love. . . .

Chaucer begins his poem by following one of several compositional strategies outlined in medieval poetic theory—the use of a proverb to open a composition (Everett 153–54). The proverb he adapts (*ars longa, vita brevis*) is derived from Hippocrates and promulgated as a moral apothegm by writers like Cicero, Horace, and Seneca (Burlin 259n). Amplifying the figure of *contentio* (contrast) within the original proverb, Chaucer redirects the meaning of the *sententia* away from its original designation of art as an object of labor and hard-won learning; he turns the reference instead toward love, and suggests by this conversion that love, too, is an art not unlike poetry and medicine: a skill with rules of operation and an intelligible structure behind it.[13]

The warrant for this conversion is given within medieval poetics, which provides the strongest context for reading the passage. Geoffrey of Vinsauf (Faral 201) advises that the use of proverbs requires the writer to maintain a special kind of aesthetic distance. The proverb, he says, should remain above the particular ("sententia sumpta / Ad speciale nihil declinet"); it should raise its head to some general truth ("caput edat / Altius ad quoddam generale"). The proverb acts as if disdainful ("quasi dedignata") of the contingency of particular meaning. Standing above the poem's material, it should predicate a meaning between the general and the particular in the manner of the intelligible species and its accidents: "Supra thema datum sistat, sed spectet ad illud / Recta fronte; nihil dicat, sed cogitet inde" (Let it take a stand above the given subject, but look with direct glance toward it. Let it say nothing directly about the subject, but derive its inspiration therefrom).

At a verbal level Chaucer's subtle and witty transposition of art and love teases our expectations about the proverb's meaning. It takes on still deeper significance, however, within the context of medieval poetics. Geoffrey of Vinsauf frames his own comments on the use of proverbs within a larger discussion of narrative disposition, the part of rhetoric which establishes the structure of choices within which a poet could begin his work. His discussion attaches a figurative meaning to the distinction between natural and artificial order. In natural order words and things follow the same path and the expository arrangement maintains the original sequence of events ("ubi res et verba sequuntur eumdem / Cursum nec sermo declinat ab ordine rerum," Faral 200). But natural order is sterile ("sterilis"). Artificial order, which rearranges time sequences in the service of narration, is not only more urbane ("civilior") but also fecund ("fertilis"). Continuing the organic metaphor, Geoffrey observes that the stock branches into many boughs ("solus in plures, unus in octo"), for the initial choice to follow artificial order yields additional possibilities. Extending the imagery to the use of proverbs, he says:

> Hoc genus est triplex, surgens de triplice planta.
> Plantae sunt partes in themate prima, secunda,
> Ultima. De quarum trunco quasi surculus exit
> Sicque solet gigni tanquam de matre triformi;
> Sed manet in latebris et, quando vocatur, obaudit. . . .

> This kind of beginning is threefold, springing up from three shoots. The shoots are the first, middle, and last parts of the subject matter. From their stem a spring, as it were, bursts forth, and is thus wont to be born, one might say, of three mothers. It remains in hiding, however, and when summoned it refuses to hear.
>
> (Faral 201)

When he discusses beginning in artificial order with an exemplum, Geoffrey again describes the blossoming of branches: "this one, too, like the one before it, rises up in three shoots" (Nims 21). Thus even as Chaucer begins to invent and arrange his material within the poem, the pragmatic choices he makes are already couched in a language of creation and fertility that anticipates his subject matter, particularly the representation of Nature's plenitude. The procedures by which the poet composes his work, codified within the framework of poetics, are seen as part of the same organic process that the poem will describe in its account of "engendrure" (PF 306).

It is this intuition of congruence and continuity that marks the conceptual breakthrough of Chaucer's early narrative poems. Chaucer has been able to formulate a general theme for his narratives out of the particulars of subjective experience and antecedent texts. In the theme of love his poetry locates an object of knowledge that remains intelligible despite the variety of its formations.[14] The man in black's courtly retrospect and the "love-tidings" promised by the eagle, Venus's cupidity and Nature's rationalized appetite are the particulars contained within a category of human experience governed by reason and providence and inscribed objectively in the world. Equally important, Chaucer has discovered the powerful analogy between this subject matter and his own art. Love and poetry function under the same principle of operation. If the *House of Fame* shows that poetry is part of the world it seeks to represent, the *Parliament* carries the discovery a step further and shows that the same process joins aesthetic creation and natural production.

By the end of the first phase of his career as a narrative poet, Chaucer has thus moved toward a heightened appreciation of the place of his craft and away from the terms that most courtly writers used to theorize about poetry. His speculations in the dream visions have gone beyond mere elaborations of poetic indeterminacy and demonstrations of the slippage and failure of language. He has realized in a fundamental way how poetry is part of the world it represents and thus that its claims, though always problematic, have real authority.

A Chaucerian Prospect: From "wonder thynges" to "olde appreved stories"

By the early 1380s Chaucer had essentially succeeded in creating a sophisticated English courtly narrative. His three early dream visions, like his lyric poems, stand as counterparts to those poetic forms and genres, already developed in continental literature, which found their chief audience in the late medieval court. Chaucer's contemporaries recognized the great artistic achievement of these early narrative poems. Jehan de Froissart and Oton de Grandson, poets who exemplify the cultural interchange between the English and continental courts in the late Middle Ages, were inspired to imitate the *Book of the Duchess* in two of their own poems, the *Dit dou chevalier bleu* and the "Complainte de l'an nouvel," respectively (Wimsatt *"Dit"*). Sir John Clanvowe reproduced a version of the *Parliament of Fowls* in *The Boke of Cupide*. Equally important, however, are the implications of the theorizing about his art that Chaucer makes part of the poetic meaning of these narratives. By way of conclusion, I want to examine the critical position Chaucer consolidates at this phase of his career and then trace its impact on later works.

We have seen that Chaucer's narrative poems form a body of writing unified by formal devices, literary conventions, shared themes, and a cohesive pattern of intertextual citation. They are also works that combine the domains of artistic representation and critical reflection. The early narratives depict an imaginary, fictional world at the same time they examine the conceptual basis for representing that world. Their concern with poetics, embedded as it is in the narrative action, is thus more than stylized self-consciousness or narratorial self-dramatization. The poems chart the philosophical terrain of the poet's art—its often troubled claims to authority, its problematic standing as a mode and object of knowledge—from inside the artifice.

The most significant theoretical development in Chaucer's early narrative is the evolution from a poetry based on radical subjectivity toward one founded on what can be described as a modified, pragmatic realism. The trajectory of Chaucer's aesthetic theorizing proceeds, as we have seen, through the topoi of imagination, memory, and intellect. Chaucer begins by associating poetry with imagination and the sensuous images contained in memory; his initial interest is to explore how language can establish an order of meaning by itself, and he discovers the radical extension of this possibility in "the grete swogh," the figure of "fals and soth compouned" in one tiding (HF 1029, 2108) that dominates the Palace of Fame and the House of Rumor. This figure offers a brilliant critique of language and signification, of the indeterminacy and slippage of meaning that in some respect must underlie all poetic representation; but it also marks a conceptual impasse, leaving poetry either to repudiate or compromise its powers of depiction. Chaucer turns consequently to a more productive line of aesthetic speculation, which I have proposed is the problem of the intellect. He makes the search for knowledge, the "certeyn thing" that reveals the intelligible species of love, his central theme in the *Parliament of Fowls*. Without reducing his poetic materials to a single abstractive formulation, he focuses on the relation of a universal principle to the particulars of experience.

We can follow the development of Chaucer's views perhaps most clearly in one example taken from the *Parliament*. Chaucer, in fact, amends his intentions during the course of the poem, and this redirection mirrors the development of his poetics. At the outset, the narrator says that his habit of reading is guided by the aim of discovery and knowledge: "a certeyn thing to lerne, / The longe day ful faste I redde and yerne" (20–21). This aim leads him to Cicero's "Dream of Scipio" in his waking life and to the tableaux of the paradisiacal park, Venus, and Nature in his dream vision. Much as in the notion of the two Venuses which Boccaccio announces in the *Teseida,* one of Chaucer's sources for the *Parliament,* Venus is the monitory example of what the narrator seeks, and Nature represents the positive doctrine. But the narrator makes his authentic, if less certain, discovery in the welter of contradictions and particulars that surface in the gathering over which Nature presides.

Nature embodies the rational principle of generation; the birds assembled under her enact that principle by choosing their mates on Saint Valentine's Day. They do not, however, simply or programmatically flesh out the sketch of the principle; they are not like the figures mutely cycling through life and death which Alan of Lille had originally depicted on Nature's gown. The scandal of the poem is that the formel eagle decides not to choose a mate from her three royal suitors. Her decision only delays the event, though; it does not overturn the fundamental process, nor does it subvert Nature's authority. Rather, it marks the point where the abstract principles of Nature—and of Cicero and Venus, too—take substantial form through agents in a social context. The essential principle Chaucer establishes for love, Nature's regulation of creaturely appetites according to a divine plan, becomes empirical, pragmatic, and down to earth.

The artistic tension is between the universal and concrete individuals, and one effect is the boisterous comedy of the birds' debate, a rhetorical tapestry of conflicting styles animated as much by class differences as by sheer impatience and thwarted appetites. Another and more subtle consequence is a shift in the narrator's objective. He has sought the "certeyn thing," but what he discovers and makes his new objective is qualified and provisional. After the birds choose their mates and sing the roundel to honor Nature, the narrator wakens, determined to continue reading so as to dream "som thyng for to fare / The bet" (698–99). The revision of intention signals a decisive, though highly nuanced, shift in outlook. While the narrator, like the poet, remains a diligent reader, the object of his search changes from absolute knowledge and universal principles to practical, ethical action rooted in particulars. Chaucer gives up the "certeyn thing" for a kind of partial knowledge ("som thyng") with moral consequences lived in experience ("to fare / The bet").

This shift establishes the ground of Chaucer's poetry as a pragmatic, philosophical realism. Chaucer has achieved a substantive understanding of his subject matter, an intuition of its essence and accidents. He has gone beyond exploring what is given by perception and sensibility in order to grasp his poetic material as an object of knowledge in its own right, hence something that cannot merely be read back into subjective experience. The universal, he discovers, is embodied in particulars; particulars make sense, if they make sense at all, because they belong to classes that have some real place in the world. Although

Chaucer is at times fascinated with the imaginative possibilities that nominalism allows and tends to speak of Platonizing idealism to the detriment of scholastic thought (Howard *Chaucer* 29), the modified realism expressed in the *Parliament* determines the aesthetic basis of his later work.

In some measure, what occurs in the *Parliament* is anticipated by the other poems. The man in black's complaint in the *Book of the Duchess* turns, for instance, on the disparity between the human reality of White and the courtly language that tries to describe her idealized virtue, and the knight's predicament has to do with his inability to negotiate the disparity. The eagle in the *House of Fame* chastises Geffrey for knowing nothing "of thy verray neyghebores, / That duellen almost at thy dores" (649–50). Chaucer's praise of love, he says, has been abstract and derivative, impoverished by the absence of concrete, lived reality. On the other hand, there is almost too much of the particular and concrete in Fame's palace and the House of Rumor, a phantasmagoria of detail that reduces truth and falsehood to indistinct "tydynges." What the *Parliament* does, then, is to establish a relation between species and genera, the general and the particular; it posits a principle of erotic governance yet situates that principle within the diversity of the phenomenal world. Chaucer arrives at a position that is more tolerant of contradiction than in the *Duchess* yet more confident of its own coherence than in the *House of Fame*.

The kind of realism I have been describing gives us a critical perspective on the later directions of Chaucer's poetry and allows us to grasp some of the powerful continuities within the whole body of his work. From the perspective of the early narrative, the poetry of the middle and late phases represents a closely integrated structure of transitions. These transitions have to do externally with matters of form, theme, and characterization, but they carry deeper resonances in Chaucer's practice and his conception of poetic art. In addition, Chaucer returns to some of the early positions he has abandoned, casting his initial formulations about language and poetry into the light of his mature artistry.

The most apparent yet far-reaching development is the formal shift from the dream vision to a third-person serial narrative. Unlike many of his predecessors and contemporaries, Chaucer employs the vision for exclusively secular purposes. He follows the tradition of the *Roman de la rose* and of Machaut and Froissart in locating his poetry within the narrator's consciousness; there is no objectification such as Langland's or Gower's social vision or the mystical truth revealed in *Pearl*. The dream narrative is not, however, modern point-of-view narrative (though the narrator retains a point of view) but a comparatively de-centered narrative in which the first-person speaker plays against other voices. The subsequent movement of the narrator from the center to the periphery of his poems reminds us that Chaucer's art is rhetorical as well as mimetic; he is interested in the truth and drama of his speakers as much as in fashioning a comprehensive structure to contain them.

In this respect, Chaucer's return to the dream vision at mid-career in the *Legend of Good Women* is a special case in his artistic development, for the F and G Prologues to the *Legend* in effect reenact the transition from the dream vision to serial narrative. In the F Prologue, Cupid commands the narrator to write the lives of women martyred for love, and the narrator turns immediately to his task: "And with that word my bokes gan I take, / And ryght thus on my Legende gan I make" (F 578–79). The impression is clearly that the stories are contained within the dream vision. The G Prologue changes that impression. Echoing the end of the *Parliament,* the narrator says, "And with that word, of slep I gan awake, / And ryght thus on my Legende gan I make" (G 544–45).

All the narratives of Chaucer's middle phase, except the Prologue to the *Legend,* are stories that operate outside the narrative framework of the dream vision. *Anelida and Arcite,* though dated by many scholars before the *Parliament,* is in any event a transitional piece which combines a new-found historical focus with the structures of subjectivity that Chaucer has been elaborating in his dream visions. Chaucer invokes Mars, Bellona, and Athena (apparently confusing the last two) to preside over a story supposedly taken from Statius and Corinna. The epic machinery of the Theban cycle is all in place as Theseus returns under the banner of Mars, leading Hippolyta and Emily as his captives. The poem situates itself at a moment of historical and dynastic change: Thebes stands ready to suffer its fate, "the blood roial was broght a-doun" (65), and Creon has installed a city-based tyranny over the traditional nobility of the region. The main action is centered, however, on Arcite's betrayal of Anelida. As later in *Troilus and Criseyde,* the weight of historical determinism bears on the intimate and private, for the collapse of personal bonds mirrors the imminent destruction of a pagan society.

The language that describes personal collapse in the poem borrows noticeably from the diction of the lyrics and early narratives. Anelida's lament is an ostensibly feminine voice translated to the stylized complaints Chaucer wrote throughout his career; she speaks the woman's part that is left unsaid in such divergent complaints as "Lady," "Pity," and "Mars." Her love is driven by the same mechanism—"thoghte"—

that drives the narrator and characters of the dream visions. While Arcite plays out the socioerotic dramaturgy of "sleght and flaterie" (125), Anelida constructs her view of him out of the projections of her own desire. In her lament, she recognizes correctly, "Myself I mordre with my privy thoght" (291). But unlike the narrator of the *Duchess,* she finds no remedy, not even in ancient stories. (She occupies, in a sense, a mythological ground zero, for Thebes is the subtext of the Trojan story, the limit of earlier possible worlds to medieval historians and mythographers.)

Chaucer reveals the illusory, subjective nature of Anelida's desire by associating it with the figure of Morpheus as he is portrayed in the *Duchess.* Anelida says in her complaint:

> And yf I slepe a furlong wey or tweye,
> Then thynketh me that your figure
> Before me stont, clad in asure,
> To profren eft and newe assure
> For to be trewe, and merci me to preye.
>
> (328–32)

The passage resonates with ironies. Anelida is a distorted version of Alcyone, and she does not realize that the separation that makes possible her desire is also a necessary condition of Arcite's betrayal. Arcite's image, dressed in the symbolic color of constancy, may fulfill her wish for him to be faithful, but the phrase *newe assure* (oxymoronic because *newe* connotes instability) discloses the impossibility of what she wants. Her desires are products of erotic and aesthetic imagination rather than realistic perception.

The most arresting irony, of course, is that Anelida evokes an image portraying Ceyx, the faithful husband as revenant, in order to express her wish that a faithless lover should reform and conform to her ambitions for him. We have seen that in the *Duchess* Chaucer carefully suppresses those dimensions of Morpheus which suggest he can represent an order of linguistic meaning independent of external referents. The poem cancels out the possibility, given by Ovid, that Morpheus's poetic and rhetorical impersonation can comprise an order of meaning in itself. But here Chaucer turns the suggestion against Anelida. In her speech, Arcite appears like Morpheus precisely because she projects an image that is counterfactual and removed from reality. Anelida's Arcite inhabits the realm of absolute imagination that Chaucer's dream narrators have escaped. This kind of defining irony is dependent in no small way on the formal change from the dream vision to another mode of narrative. Chaucer has transformed his narrative technique and divided the stress between a first-person speaker and the heroine. The narrative "I" enters chiefly to make transitions; the heroine's complaint is the thematic focus. Though the stylistic ambition is to imitate the epic ornamentation of Boccaccio's *Teseida,* the basic dynamic is between an empathetic narrator and a character who speaks her predicament in a way she cannot fully grasp. The full exploitation of this formal development will come later in the rhetorical display of the Canterbury pilgrims, but the juxtaposition here of the narrator and Anelida is a forerunner of the play of voices in the narratives of the middle and late phases of Chaucer's writing.

If the generally accepted chronology of Chaucer's poems is correct, the poems written after the early narratives divide into two broad classes of subject matter—chivalric epics and moral stories based on legends and exempla. *Anelida and Arcite* inaugurates a group concentrating on the Theban and Trojan stories, which serve as a nexus for the complicated mythology that Chaucer associates with pagan antiquity. The "love of Palamon and Arcite / Of Thebes," which Alceste mentions in her defense of Chaucer (*Legend* F 420–21), is usually taken as an early version of the Knight's Tale, and *Troilus and Criseyde* is surely Chaucer's crowning statement about love in a violent, fallen world. Despite their differing emphases, all these poems reflect the synthesis of the martial and erotic material which Chaucer earlier places in the decorated chamber of the *Duchess*—"hooly al the story of Troye" (BD 326), of which Thebes is the dark prefiguration, and the *Rose*. They also reflect, far more directly than the portrayal of Venus in the *Parliament,* Chaucer's confrontation with Italian literature, particularly Boccaccio's blend of classical epic and medieval romance. The second group is somewhat more diffuse, partly because of the mix of secular and religious materials, partly because its place in the chronology is less precise. The Second Nun's Tale, also mentioned by Alceste (*Legend* F 426), is in the same rhyme royal stanza as the *Parliament* and *Troilus,* and the tragedies recounted in the Monk's Tale show a debt to Boccaccio's *De casibus virorum illustrium.*

The importance of Chaucer's shift from the dream vision to a mode of sequential narrative does not lie in just the formal development. It has to do, rather, with what the subject matter comes to mean. Chaucer moves from a poetics of interiority toward an understanding of social context and a grounding in historical experience. In the Theban materials and the story of Troy, Chaucer confronts the pastness of the past. Unlike the Ovidian story retold by way of Machaut in the *Duchess* or the pillars bearing up ancient poetry in the *House of Fame,* the subject matter of *Anelida,* the Knight's Tale, and *Troilus* hovers at a distance that Chaucer cannot recover; certainly he cannot reinscribe it within subjectivity. The image of devouring time that Chaucer places at the opening of *Anelida* is one formulation of historical distance: "elde, which that al can frete and bite, / As hit hath freten mony a noble storie, / Hath nygh devoured out of oure memorie" (12–14). The narrator of *Troilus* gives another formulation when he addresses Clio, "Ye knowe ek that in forme of speche is chaunge / Withinne a thousand yeer" (2.22–23). There are, to be sure, approximations of the past and present in the dazzling rhetorical texture of Chaucer's anachronisms: Anelida's lament is couched in the discourse of the court; the Knight reads himself and his values into Theseus and the pageant of courtly life; Troilus's world has an allure that the narrator must resist. But if these materials suggest analogies to Chaucer's contemporary experience, as in some way they must, they nonetheless remain apart from his world, for they are situated irrevocably in pagan culture.

The alterity of the past, despite the anachronisms that embellish Chaucer's narration, finally resists the appropriations of imagination and sensitive memory, and requires, as in the *Parliament,* the *sensibilis ratio* or "vertu estimatiue" (Trevisa) of the intellect. The past, unlike "wonder thynges," is an object of practical reasoning, and Chaucer seeks to know it in the same way that he has endeavored to know the nature of love. That is, he understands it through categories and particulars. An informing typology is evident in the life of Saint Cecilia, for example, and in the lives mentioned at greater or lesser length in the Monk's tragedies, but the details of Chaucer's narrative show at the same time that the stories are rooted in specific moments and locales (early Christian Rome for Cecilia, particular countries and regions for the others). The artistry of the Knight's Tale and *Troilus* similarly depends on elaborating the particulars of their fictional worlds. Morton W. Bloomfield remarks that Chaucer has "a sense of cultural diversity between the past and the present" ("History" 309). Those worlds are intelligible structures that remain apart from Chaucer's historical position. Each represents a facet of the pagan past that carries a social and political significance for Chaucer's age—the amalgamation of Thebes and the Amazons under Theseus and Athens, the Trojan origins of England. Such meaning arises from an inquiry into the nature and not just the expressive possibilities of the past; it goes beyond the imagination's work of apprehending and composing impressions.

Chaucer, like Shakespeare, uses this sense of historical difference in order to establish a dialectic of representation. Although medieval writers found in pagan culture an immense treasury of spiritual, moral, and political exempla (Minnis), Chaucer avoids their penchant for collapsing history to a single paradigm of human behavior. When the narrator admonishes the "yonge, fresshe folkes" (5.1835) at the end of *Troilus* to retreat from worldly vanity, he claims the power of Troilus's example while asserting it is an example unalterably rooted in the past ("payens corsed olde rites," 5.1849) and so removed from the divine love of Christ who "nyl falsen no wight" (5.1845). The contrast with Gower is also informative, for Genius's strategy (and much of Gower's) in the *Confessio Amantis* is to show the properties of love by organizing pagan myths as examples of the vices that oppose love. When Chaucer turns to this kind of allegorizing, it is notable that his only systematic effort, The Tale of Melibee, is a story without historical or social grounding; the allegorical personnel are as deracinated there as Gower's moralized pagan figures.

Chaucer's customary approach is to stipulate the differences that separate his stories from his audience. A characteristic set of locutions ("whilom," "as I writen fynde," "this olde storie") marks the difference, so that the historical and cultural distance of the subject matter serves to define a space of artistic representation. The narrators, especially the Knight and the narrator of the *Troilus,* may empathize with their characters, but Chaucer's narration does not lose sight of the fact that the story it tells remains somehow unassimilable. For the narrators the danger lies specifically in collapsing the distance. This is a key distinction between the early and later narratives. Where the narrators of the dream visions can bring stories from a remote past directly into the circuit of their imagination, the narrators of later works struggle to mediate the alterity of their subject matter. They are less given to the aestheticizing of the *Duchess* or the *House of Fame*; less able, for instance, to trace their own emotional arc, as the narrator of the *Duchess* does, within a character like Alcyone.

In *Troilus,* where the narrator confronts the blandishments of the past most intensely, Chaucer returns to some of the abandoned hypotheses of the early poems, and his ironic treatment of them offers a way of seeing how he controls historical and aesthetic distance. Pandarus seems to echo the narrator's determination to "drive the night away" in the *Book of the Duchess* (49) when he exhorts the despondent Troilus, "Ris, lat us speke of lusty lif in Troie / That we han led, and forth the tyme dryve" (5.393–94). Criseyde's letters, which Troilus rereads in her absence (5.470–76), serve the same purpose of displacing melancholy with determinate images that the "romaunce" serves in the *Duchess.* Even more remarkable, Pandarus's repudiation of dreams in Book 5 restates the argument made at the beginning of the *House of Fame.* Troilus has dreamed of a boar with large tusks who holds Criseyde in his arms while she lies kissing him. The dream, modified from the original version in Boccaccio's *Filostrato,* warns of Criseyde's betrayal of Troilus for Diomede, and Cassandra will later interpret it correctly, supplying as well a full mythological gloss on Diomede's genealogy.

Pandarus argues, however, that "dremes many a maner man bigile," because "folk expounden hem amys" (5.1277–78). He tells Troilus, "thow kanst no dremes rede" (5.1281), and then proposes that the boar may signify Calkas, Criseyde's father, at the point of his death. He concludes with phrasing that will be echoed in Cassandra's interpretation, "Thus sholdestow thi drem aright expounde" (5.1288). As in the Proem to the *House of Fame,* Pandarus initially contends that dreams are indeterminate and men impose arbitrary interpretations on them. His own interpretation is a case in point, for the cause of Troilus's dream is as uncertain as the categories Chaucer parodies in *Fame.* Moreover, though Pandarus does not see the irony of reasoning from his premise of indeterminacy to a conclusion that triumphantly proclaims meaning, we can see it clearly. As readers, we know that he is the most manipulative figure in doomed Troy; he has played his role in the middle distance between history and the intimate lives of the other two principal characters. Thus we can appreciate Chaucer's subtle displacement of what his narrative persona says in the *House of Fame* to a character whose fabrications and stratagems most closely approximate the poet's own role. He has consciously located an earlier version of his narrative persona within the present story. This sort of autocitation and ironic portrayal is possible only to the extent that he has recognized the historical and aesthetic distance of the story.

The space of artistic representation that Chaucer claims in his epic and legendary materials is also a domain of moral speculation. Just as the *Parliament* explores the moral conditions of eros and the embodiment of desire in figural agents, the later narratives turn to ethical and ontological questions. Boethius's *Consolation of Philosophy,* which Chaucer probably translated in the mid-1380s, brings a particular articulation of those questions into the Knight's Tale and *Troilus*; Boccaccio himself relies on Boethius, and Chaucer makes independent additions, such as Troilus's speech on predestination. The Monk's Tale, too, incorporates a Boethian view of mutability and Fortune in its definition of tragedy (Robertson "Tragedy"). The point, however, is that the poems address problems of moral being quite independently from any particular doctrine. The shift from the aestheticizing of the dream visions to the historical subject matter of the later narratives establishes history as a realm of ethical deliberation.

Cecilia's bitter exchanges with her judge in the Second Nun's Tale are a clear, if extreme, example of moral debate. "Chees oon of thise two: / Do sacrifice, or Cristendom reneye," Almachius demands (VIII.458–59), to which Cecilia answers, "Woltow that I reneye innocence, / To make me a wikked wight" (VIII.464–65). The Monk's story of Ugolino imposes a Boethian coloring on Dante's story through Ugolino's lament, "Allas, Fortune, and weylaway" (VII.2445). The horror of the predicament, its resonant portrayal of impotent human options before an unfolding doom, is rendered most effectively, however, through misperception. The Monk relates, "His children wende that it for hunger was / That he his armes gnow, and nat for wo" (VII.2447–48), and they propose, as in Dante (*Inferno* 33.61–63) to return the flesh he has given them as a sign of filial devotion: "Oure flessh thou yaf us, take oure flessh us fro" (VII.2451). Their offer is a grotesque restoration of social order made within an entire sequence of betrayals and transgressions.

The ethical dimension that Chaucer finds in historical subject matter is always, then, a contested terrain. Boethius may give a framework for the Knight's Tale, *Troilus,* and the Monk's tragedies, but he does not determine the moral or artistic meanings of the poems. We have seen, for example, that as early as the *Duchess* Chaucer introduces Boethian arguments, but leaves them problematic. So, too, Troilus's speech on predestination or Theseus's First Mover speech serve to formulate rather than answer the thematic questions of the poems. The past constitutes, in other words, a world of human behavior whose moral complexity needs to be investigated. The rivalry of Palamon and Arcite, set in the remoteness of Theban history, examines the nature of desire and its consequences for the competing values of love and friendship. The *Legend of Good Women* does not follow Cupid's simple program of praising feminine virtue; instead, it represents the contradictory, often unacknowledged, motives of human agents driven by different forms of love. If the historical distance of the past makes possible a space of aesthetic representation, it is representation whose meaning is kept open by the poet's art.

These directions in Chaucer's poetry are connected to the aesthetic speculations formulated in the early narratives. In discussing the *House of Fame* I suggested that the reduction of poetry to sound and truth to tidings was both a conceptual impasse and a moment of profound insight. It is an impasse because here Chaucer reaches the limit of his formalistic reasoning about the nature of poetry; the insight comes from realizing that poetry is not just instrumental but that it participates materially in the world and enjoys a perceptual access to it. Chaucer abandons an exclusively representational epistemology, in which poetry is sundered from the world and must operate at a finally unbridgeable distance; he takes up a position which acknowledges that some real continuity must exist between poetry and the world.

In this way, the epistemological and ethical dimensions of Chaucer's poetics find a common ground, for the concern with defining the terms of aesthetic representation in the dream visions depends at length on discovering a subject matter and theme of adequate scope and subtlety. I have suggested that the discovery occurs in the *Parliament,* specifically in the narrator's intention to dream "som thyng for to fare / The bet." This intention, echoing yet contrasting the resolve merely "to put this sweven in ryme" at the end of the *Duchess* (1332), helps establish the moral authority of poetry. The consequences become fully visible in the succeeding poems based on epic and legend.

Most of these poems can be classified under the category of "olde appreved stories" which Chaucer gives retrospectively in the Prologue to the *Legend* (F 21). Such stories, he elaborates, are "of holynesse, of regnes, of victories, / Of love, of hate, of other sondry thynges" (F 22–23). The thematic range is widened from the martial-erotic ideal of the book expressed in the *Duchess,* but these remain predominantly narratives with historical subjects. They are "approved," that is, "proven true," because they are part of human experience, and they "prove true" because they address the complexities of human experience with moral force. Furthermore, as the Prologue contends, the stories belong to the world of books, which deserve our credence and assure "that olde thinges ben in mynde" (F 18). Here Chaucer builds on the *Parliament*'s conceit of bringing new corn from old fields. The truth claim derives not simply from "assay" (the testing out of perception, as in the dream visions) but from prior texts, oral and written (as man "hath herd seyd or founde it writen," F 8). The story can be known as a species of experience and not just as an isolated wonder; "remembraunce" belongs to rational and not sensitive memory. The source of knowledge, as Chaucer develops his argument, finally narrows down to books; he says, "there we han noon other preve" (F 28). In the G version, the claim is reasserted, and "assay" and "preve" through reading become convertible. We should believe books, he says, "There as there is non other assay by preve" (G 28), for "the world of autours ... / Cristene and hethene" (G 308–9) offers a ground of moral authority.

The outcome of the theorizing that Chaucer begins in his early narratives is thus a deepened and enhanced sense of the way in which poetry inhabits the world. Poetry is at once a material product and a realm of moral experience whose complexity must be grasped. It is instrument and object, a means of reflection and a body of human wisdom. Even when, as in the case of Cleopatra's *Legend,* the precise source is difficult to identify and may be a compilation, poetry sustains the claim that "this is storyal soth, it is no fable" (702). It is not, however, a closed system or a moral formula. Writing—particularly, though not exclusively, writing about the past—suspends the determinate meaning of moralization. Representation exists in an essential tension with moral deliberation.

Writing also operates, as we have seen earlier, in the play of will and chance. As medieval literary theorists prescribed, the poet intentionally imagines the conceptual architecture of his poem, yet the "purpose" he intends sometimes gives way in the process to chance. It seems clear that the same thing occurs in the poems that follow the early narratives. Chaucer discovers only after he starts to imitate Boccaccio's epic style that his topic in *Anelida and Arcite* is Arcite's "slye wey" (48). Alceste's enigmatic comment suggests that the first version of the Knight's Tale may have had a different focus—"al the love of Palamon and Arcite" (F 420)—from the story of societal order that appears in the *Canterbury Tales. Troilus* is, in many respects, the story of the narrator's discovery of the possibilities and dangers of the poetic materials.

The *Legend of Good Women* takes as one of its recurrent themes the ways in which chance enters history and story. Excusing his translations of the *Filostrato* and the *Rose,* the narrator separates "what so myn auctour mente" from "myn entente," which was, he says, "To forthren trouthe in love and yt cheryce, / And to ben war fro falsnesse and fro vice / By swich ensample" (F 470–74). For the story of Dido, he takes, as in the *House of Fame,* the "tenor" from Vergil and Ovid, but reserves "the grete effectes" (929) to himself. He can therefore reject the substitution of Cupid for Ascanius or later the intervention of Mercury, saying of his source, "as of that scripture, / Be as be may, I take of it no cure" (1144–45). The original intention of embellishing the classical authors leads to the transgression—not mentioned in Vergil but certainly a pervasive topic in courtly literature—of a knight who betrays his promise "to be trewe / For wel or wo and chaunge hire for no newe" (1234–35).

Similarly, the question of Chaucer's own art is drawn into his speculations about the moral truths of the historical past. In the legend of Hypsipyle, Chaucer adds the motif of mediated desire by treating Hercules's praise of Jason as the means for inflaming Hypsipyle's desire. The encomium is, as the narrator says, "a shrewed lees" (1545) devised by the heroes "to bedote this queen" (1547), but it also bears more than a faint resemblance to the rhetorical effects that the poet seeks to make. Chaucer comes to discover his own ambiguous position in the legend of Phyllis, where Demophon repeats Theseus's betrayal of Ariadne. The poet is surfeited ("agroted," 2454) with writing about erotic treachery and steadily recedes from the task of reproducing his characters' words. He is reduced, however, to a warning that ironically puts his own position in question: "Be war, ye wemen, of youre subtyl fo, / Syn yit this day men may ensaumple se; / And trusteth, as in love, no man but me" (2559–61). His own motives in pursuing the "effectes" are inevitably implicated in the deliberation he conducts about "these olde appreved stories."

The prospect I have been sketching out builds on the artistic and conceptual achievements of Chaucer's early narratives. As stories and aesthetic reflections, the dream visions work toward a substantive appreciation of the nature of poetry. Their radical subjectivity operates within imagination and a world of antecedent writers, yet the great breakthrough occurs when Chaucer moves beyond the internal economy of images and wonders. The early narratives lead toward a kind of objectification, situating poetry in a domain of history, representation, and moral deliberation. But they do so without diminishing the power of their original critique. If the practical legacy of these poems consists in style, techniques of characterization, and themes, another part has to do with the characteristic vision they help to establish. The questions pondered in Chaucer's poems remain open, situated in ways that resist reductive answers; they neither fold back into subjectivity nor stand as dilemmas merely to be read off the surface of nature and history. The stories and experiments of the early narratives bring into all of Chaucer's poetry an extended meditation on the place of art, and they make it inextricably part of aesthetic meaning.

Notes

Preface

1. The linguistic question is discussed by Crépin 56–57, Vale, Coleman ("Culture"), and Fisher ("French Influence").
2. See the comments on literary taste in Burnley (6), Coleman (*Readers*), and Vale (47, 51).

Introduction

1. Burrow (*Writers* 12–23) and Edwards (*Ratio*) discuss the restructuring of Cicero's categories, particularly in John of Garland's *Parisiana Poetria*.

The Practice of Theory

1. Wimsatt ("Elegy" 119) uses the passage to argue for a spiritual meaning that balances the secular meaning of the *Book of the Duchess* by analogy to the double genres and twin meanings of the Canticles and Apocalypse in the Bible. The point of the line, however, is to emphasize the aesthetic effect of harmony rather than the spiritual meaning.
2. Gushee points out that the theory contained in musical treatises is determined by audience as well as critical doctrine. Gushee's observation applies as well to medieval literary theory. I contend (*Ratio*) that the precepts of literary criticism vary according to the author's view of his audience and that medieval literary theory is therefore not determinate; rather, it represents a literary thematic, a set of categories and topoi for discussing poetry, many of which become subject matter in their own right. Minnis takes an opposite view.
3. Kelly ("Scope" and "Theory") corrects Faral's overemphasis on the place of ornamentation in medieval poetics. Dronke ("Rhetoric") argues for the conceptual sophistication of medieval poetic theory, especially Geoffrey of Vinsauf's theory of invention. De Bruyne (2:26–27) notes that Geoffrey's architectural image borrows

Platonic terminology and has an aesthetic rapport with the Victorines and Cistercians; the comparison itself recurs throughout Aquinas's remarks on art. See Gallo and Jordan (*Shape*) for discussion of the aesthetic and rhetorical implications.

4. Wetherbee observes that "Chaucer has significantly altered the emphasis of his original. Geoffrey's equivalent to the 'hertes line' of 1068, 'intrinseca linea cordis,' is a wholly inner resource, a faculty of the 'interior man,' which traces in its archetypal form what is then, by a secondary process—the 'hand of the heart' giving place to that of the body—translated in an outward imitation. In Pandarus's case, by contrast, the 'hertes line' is sent '*out* from withinne' as the first stage of the creative process, which thus becomes a process not of preconception, but of reconnaissance. The point, I think, is that Pandarus has little or no inner life in the sense that Geoffrey's example implies and no archetypal preconception of what he seeks to realize" (*Poets* 78–79). Murphy ("Look") disputes whether Chaucer had firsthand knowledge of Geoffrey of Vinsauf, but see Dronke ("Medieval Latin" 170) for an alternate view.

5. Boethius makes a claim for verbatim translation in the opening remarks in the second edition of the commentary on the *Isagoge* of Porphyry: "This second task of exposition, which I have undertaken, will clarify the course of my translation, for I am afraid I have fallen victim in my translation to the fault of the faithful interpreter, in that I have rendered every word, expressed or implied, with a word. The reason for the present undertaking is that in these writing, in which knowledge of things is sought, there must be expressed, not a charm of translucent style, but the un-corrupted truth [*non luculentae orationis lepos, sed incorrupta ueritas*]." He goes on to say, "It seems to be me that I shall have accomplished a great deal to this end if books of philosophy should be composed in the latin language by painstaking and complete translation, until nothing more were missing from the literature of the Greeks" (McKeon 1:70). His remarks make it clear that fullness (*per integerrimae translationis sinceritatem*) is somehow essential to the task of matching the Greek sources. The phrasing consciously reverses the emphasis in Horace. Horace's *fidus interpres* does not strive for word-by-word translation, whereas Boethius is obviously content to bear the *fidi interpretis culpam* of rendering the passage *uerbum uerbo*.

6. I have emended Jenkins's text with the revisions proposed by Wimsatt ("French Poetry" 109–10) and Fisher (*Chaucer* 952–53). The passage is discussed by Glending Olson ("Art").

7. There is a great deal of commentary on Guillaume's apology for dreams at the beginning of the *Roman de la rose* (see recent discussion in Hult 114–37). My analysis reads the passage in terms of the medieval Square of Opposition, a set of logical relations in syllogistic logic. Guillaume's propositions can be located within the following array:

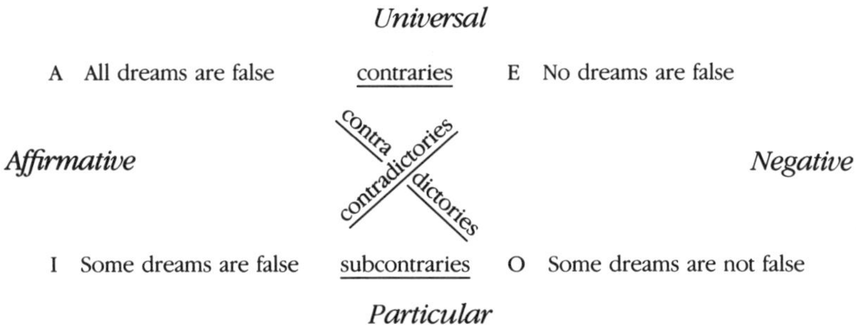

Universal

A All dreams are false	contraries	E No dreams are false

Affirmative   *Contradictories*   *Negative*

I Some dreams are false	subcontraries	O Some dreams are not false

Particular

A and E are universal propositions; I and O are particular. A and I are affirmative propositions; E and O are negative. According to the Square of Opposition, A and E are contraries, and I–O are subcontraries (the former pair cannot both be true and the latter pair cannot both be false). A–O and I–E are contradictories: the truth of one member of a pair forces the falsity of the other. For example, if the O proposition (some dreams are not false) is true, then the A proposition (all dreams are false) cannot be true. Guillaume's first subargument is valid: if the O proposition is true, then it follows that the corresponding A proposition cannot be true. Guillaume then tries to argue that if the O proposition is true, the E proposition must also be true. Here the reasoning can work only one way: if the E proposition is true, then the O proposition must be true (the truth of the universal proposition determines the truth of the particular proposition). But the reverse does not hold: the truth of the O proposition does not determine anything about the E proposition. It is at the point where Guillaume tries to go from the O proposition to the E proposition that Chaucer's translation emphasizes the force of Guillaume's asseveration ("moi ai ge fiance" 15) by doubling it: "For this trowe I, *and say for me*" (15, italics added) as if to mark the character of its special pleading.

The Narrator in Chaucer's Early Poems

1. Bethurum ("Narrator") and Elliott. Payne contends, "from the *Book of the Duchess* all the way through to the *Parson's Tale,* the docent who conducts us into, through, and back out of all those various dreams and fictions is a series of variations on a basic, invented *ethos:* the doubtfully hopeful minor academic writer trying his best to recover from his most recent disaster because he really does have something to say to us, even though neither his love life nor his bibliography would make that seem very probable" ("Realization" 281). Garbáty points out, however, "Chaucer did not mean to pose as an idiot, an absolute simpleton in the early poems" (98). It is not until the *Tales* that the narrator accuses "*himself* of having little wit. In the early poems the charge is always leveled against him by others, specifically by these unorthodox beings he has the ill luck to meet" (100). Garbáty's subsequent description of the narrator as "the reasonable man," a figure of uncomplicated common sense, minimizes the subtlety of an artistic persona within a courtly milieu, but the trajectory of this characterization indicates an important difference between the personae of the early poems and the narrative figure of the *Tales.*
2. Bethurum and Elliott see the narrator as a proxy figure; Mehl and Clemen argue that facets of Chaucer's historical personality enter the self-portrayal. The debate over the narrator of the *Canterbury Tales* was identified by the positions taken respectively by Donaldson ("Pilgrim") and by Bronson and Howard ("Man"). The most recent phase in the debate centers on C. David Benson's attack (*"Tales"* and *Drama*) on the dramatic principle in the *Canterbury Tales.*
3. It can be argued that by subordinating interpretive questions to the matter of tone Lawton simply relocates them outside of character and action in a vaguely defined kind of performance and that Jordan's rejection of narrative unity ignores the explicit procedures that medieval writers used to discover their materials. Their approaches properly caution, however, against taking the narrative persona as a fixed and determinate character. Kellogg gives a particularly fine expression of the narrator's position when he refers to "the withdrawn intelligence which does not exist from moment to moment, but encompasses the whole fabric of its work" (120).

4. Donner goes on to argue that subjectivity and objectivity are inversely related: "if the narrator is to be central to the events he describes, then he must be the sort of man whom one need not take seriously; only as he moves to the periphery of the action does he become the sort of man who might command respect" (190–91).
5. Bloomfield extends these views in "Chaucerian Realism."
6. Bertilak discloses at the end of *Sir Gawain and the Green Knight* that Morgan le Fay has devised, if not the entire adventure, at least the testing of Arthur's court by the Green Knight (lines 2456–62).

> Ho wayned me vpon þis wyse to your wynne halle
> For to assay þe surquidré, ȝif hit soth were
> þat rennes of þe grete renoun of þe Rounde Table;
> Ho wayned me þis wonder your wyttez to reue,
> For to haf greued Gaynour and gart hir to dyȝe
> With glopnyng of þat ilke gome þat gostlych speked
> With his hede in his honde bifore þe hyȝe table.

The relation of the scene to problems of narrative invention is discussed in Edwards (*Ratio*).
7. Discussions of the two theories of representation that Plato propounds can be found in Russell (99–112) and Urmson (125–36).
8. There is a good account of the theory of voices in Salmon. Strohm ("Persona" 293) doubts the effect of this particular system on medieval conceptions of the narrator. Minnis shows the application of the system of voices in late medieval exegesis (22, 57–58, 110–12, 189–90).
9. Though in practice a court professional, Machaut takes on a fully realized role as *poeta*. Kean observes, for example, that a miniature portrait of him shows the dress and bearing of a clerk, in much the same way as do portraits of Boccaccio and later Chaucer (1:25–26).
10. John Stevens repeats the point in a later essay: "In this singularly coherent courtly world the courtier, the lover *and the poet* were 'of imagination all compact.' To be a poet was a natural function of being a lover; the poet's 'facunde tong' was the courtier's discourse of love raised to the highest level; and his elegance and refinement in composition were direct symptoms of his courtliness" ("Music" 114).
11. John Stevens and Richard Firth Green stress the relation of literature to social history and social practice; Glending Olson (*Recreation*) examines the theoretical assumptions under which medieval writers sought to create works that produce pleasure.
12. Lawlor makes the same point in "Earlier poems": "I have suggested that Chaucer's is an art which springs from direct confrontation of a small audience, with whom his relationship is that of licensed entertainer. His gifts are those proper to a training in courts—an unerring eye for pretence, for that attempt 'to been estatlich of manere' which, whether in actual dress and deportment, or in the attempt to don the singing-robe of master-poet, must bring disaster, if, aspiring above its station, it aims merely 'to contrefeete cheere of court' " (62–63).
13. Guillaume de Deguilleville's *Pèlerinage de la Vie Humaine* is the source for Chaucer's poem; for a discussion of Chaucer's approach to translating it see David "ABC."
14. Middleton says, "In brief terms, poetry was to be a 'common voice' to serve the 'common good.' The realized presence of the poetic speaker in this literature became a stylistic means of expressing that purpose, and it produced a new kind of experientially based didactic poetry, tonally vivid and often structurally unstable" (95).
15. John Shirley (1366–1456) attributes "Lady" and "Pity" to Chaucer under the title "The

balade of Pytee by Chauciers," and he divides the two poems by a horizontal line in MS. Harley 78.

16. Charles J. Nolan, Jr., notes that Chaucer uses the conventions of legal pleading to suggest that the complaint entails personal as well as broader social consequences. Robbins says, "The action is all in the lover's mind, the allegory mirrors his own worst fears" ("Lyrics" 388).

Imagination and Memory (I):
The Book of the Duchess *and the Beginnings of Chaucer's Narrative*

1. See Spurgeon (1:38, 166) and Larry D. Benson (*Riverside Chaucer* 966). Recent studies of the historical context of the poem are by Robertson ("Setting"), Condren ("Context"), Palmer, and Condren ("Deaths"). Arguments for dating the poem some time well after Blanche's death are made by Robertson ("Setting"), Hill, and Pelen.

2. Wimsatt (*Chaucer* 12–13) proposes that the narrator's insomnia and the Ovidian tale (1–290) frame the dream; the dream constitutes a second frame in which the descriptions of the garden (291–442) and the hunt (1311–24) contain the elegy; the elegy in turn contains the knight's complaint (443–720) and his account of love (721–1310). Eldredge ("Structure") finds a principle of ring composition in which the dreamer's sorrow (1–43) and his decision to write a poem (1330–34) envelop the motif of reading (44–220, 1324–29); the dream (291–1323) is at the center of the composition. Ebel envisions three receding planes in the poem, related to one another by repetition of imagery and diction. Jordan ("Structure") emphasizes that Chaucer uses the techniques of rhetorical amplification and disposition.

3. Shoaf ("Notes") stresses "Chaucer's awareness that every poet must change the past even if and sometimes precisely because he perfectly understands it" (57). The concern with defining a work's relation to its predecessors preoccupies modern criticism from T. S. Eliot's "Tradition and the Individual Talent" to studies such as Harold Bloom's *Anxiety of Influence* and Edward Said's *Beginnings*. For Chaucer, Wimsatt argues that the relation extends in both directions: "The *Book of the Duchess* thus grew out of a French literary development and became an integral part of that development" ("*Lay*" 15–16).

4. *De doctrina christiana* 1.22; discussion in Robertson (*Preface* 65–113). Thomas Aquinas's divergence from earlier aesthetic theory is discussed by de Bruyne (3:281–86). Doob analyzes the conventions of madness. A more general notion of the psychological usefulness of fables appears in Giovanni Boccaccio, *Genealogie deorum gentilium* 14.9 (Romano 2:705–9). Hill identifies the dreamer's psychic condition as the "head melancholy" described in medieval medical treatises (36, 39–43).

5. De Boer ("Machaut") and Hoepffner (Machaut 3:xxxiv–xxxv) discuss Machaut's use of the *Ovide Moralisé*.

6. Crampton, Severs, and Wimsatt (*Chaucer* 12–13).

7. The former view derives from Kittredge (37–72) and the latter from Kreuzer and Bronson.

8. Baker ("Dreamer"), French, Martin Stevens, James Neil Brown. Cherniss ("Dialogue") identifies the black knight's poem with the first meter of Boethius' *Consolatio Philosophiae*. Ebel says that the dialogue between the narrator and knight aims "to elucidate the resonances of the Knight's opening eleven-line complaint and to raise to its highest power the testing of convention that is at the heart of the poem as a whole" (206).

9. Bronson (*"Book of the Duchess"*) and Lumiansky ("Bereaved Narrator") point out the resemblances between the figures; Severs contends that the narrator's illness is insomnia rather than lovesickness (28–32) and that the narrative persona is a "nonlover" (38). Robertson (*Preface*) argues, "the dreamer and the Knight are both aspects of the poet" (465); but he elsewhere suggests ("Setting" 190) that "the Black Knight and the dreamer represent two aspects, not only of Geoffrey Chaucer, but of everyone who loved Blanche."

10. The term is applied to Alceste in the *Legend of Good Women* (F 411, G 397) and the Parson in the *Canterbury Tales* (x.657).

11. Johnson similarly emphasizes the separation of emotion and convention. Shoaf ("Mutatio" 76–137) argues that Chaucer's "revisionary poetics" requires a thorough break from the language of poetic convention.

12. The gloss in Chaucer's translation notes that Boethius argues against the Stoic position: "But yif the thryvynge soule ne unpliteth nothing (that is to seyn, ne doth nothing) by his propre moevynges, but suffrith and lith subgit to the figures and to the notes of bodies withoute-forth, and yeldith ymages ydel and vein in the manere of a mirour, whennes thryveth thanne or whennes comith thilke knowynge in our soule, that discernith and byholdith alle thinges?" (*Boece* 5.m4.22–30). Fisher (*Poetry* 555n) cites the connection between the knight's self-portrait and Boethius's discussion.

13. Peck ("Theme" 73–89) adopts the scheme from St. Augustine's *De Trinitate*. Will, as a psychological category, designates the man in black's natural inclination for love ("his firste craft"); and the interplay of imagination, will, and memory makes it possible for him to identify White as the proper object of his desire. Ferster, emphasizing the hermeneutic rather than poetic dimension of will, regards Chaucer's narrator as a paradigm of will and intention: "When he looks, he looks with a purpose. His knowing and his willing are connected. Knowing requires willing because, when giving attention to something, we also have intentions toward it. If attention and intention are linked, what the narrator sees is influenced by what he wants to see" (55). The converse, however, does not hold true—willing does not require knowing—and though attention and intention are linked, their relation in a theory of knowledge is hierarchical. Peck ("Questions") points out that will played a dominant role in the intuitive and abstractive cognition of experience, according to the so-called "nominalist questions" that occupied a number of fourteenth-century English thinkers.

Imagination and Memory (II):
The House of Fame

1. The view is argued by Everett ("Reflections"), Payne (*Key* and "Rhetoric"), Shook, Wilson ("Grammar" and "Logic"), Grennen, Delany (*Fame*), Fyler, Boitani ("Labyrinth" and *Fame*), and Irvine. Jordan (*Poetics*) believes that it is not a determinant theme in the poem.

2. Sypherd and Curry discuss the conventions; Spearing proposes, "If we stand far enough back from the wonders of the Dreamer, we can easily recognize in *The House of Fame* the outlines of a *somnium coeleste*" (76). Additional discussion in Newman and Giaccherini.

3. Delany says, "Skeptical fideism offered a way of saving both faith and reason, for while faith was no longer to be supported by reason, neither was it to be denied out of hand" (*Fame* 21). Delany's point is extended and narrowed in Dickerson.

Eldredge (*"Via Moderna"*) suggests that a vein of skepticism remains in the narrator's attitude toward the new way: "What we have on this celestial journey then are two travelers on the *Via Moderna,* but one of them, we soon learn, is a less convinced modernist than the other" (115).

4. Carr cites the line by the Roman poet Lygdamus preserved in the *Corpus Tibullianum,* where it in fact opens *and* closes an elegy in the form of a dream vision which shares many features with the elegies of Propertius. The poem by Lygdamus is discussed in Edwards (*Ratio*).

5. Tisdale (254–55). Patch says the desert "seems to be the realm of despair for the lover" (320). Rowland ("Art" 167) treats the sterility of the desert not as a symbol but as a functional contrast that sets off and makes vivid the details of mnemonic systems. Boitani (*Fame* 189–91) treats the desert as part of a sequence of archetypal images in the poem. Irvine says it is "a literary wasteland" (860).

6. Leyerle regards the eagle as a source for the poem's thematic unity; Steadman stresses that the flight is an intellectual journey. Berry notes that the eagle is connected in late medieval iconographical sources not only with sight (hence contemplation) but also with air, which is the medium of sound in the poem.

7. *Boece* 3.m2.39–42: "Alle thynges seken ayen to hir propre cours, and alle thynges rejoysen hem of hir retornynge ayen to hir nature." The discussion in *Boece* 3.pr11 offers a more extended treatment, but Philosophy's point in that passage is to demonstrate man's inclination toward the good. Schless (55–58) discounts the influence of *Convivio* 3.3. Bennett (*Fame*) and Boitani (*Fame* 18–71) discuss the various sources and traditions bearing on Fame.

8. Various sources and analogues are suggested for the transformation of words into images: the Hebrew *Zohar,* Boethius, and Dante. See respectively Williams, Ziegler, Ruggiers ("Words"). Rowland ("Art") does not account for the fact that, although words and images are convertible and have an internal economy, words themselves also multiply.

9. Bennett (*Fame* 12–15), but Kendrick suggests that the Palais de Justice in Paris afforded closer parallels.

10. Additional discussion in Overbeck and Stevenson.

Intellect: The "Certeyn Thing" in the Parliament of Fowls

1. Deyermond points out that Ullman's Augustinian reading does not deal "with the particular ambiguity that impedes a wholly serious interpretation of the passage" (57). Ullman seems to load the argument by assuming that the opposite of Augustinian *intelligentia* must be the Thomistic *intellectus agens;* he says nothing of the passive, abstractive power of the soul. Marina Scordilis Brownlee extends Ullman's application of voluntarism to Juan Ruiz's theory of reading, which she correlates with the Archpriest's "affirmation of human pluralism" (78).

2. The political dimensions of the poem are stressed by Cowgill and Paul A. Olson. Kearney also emphasizes the connection between the love theme and political values.

3. Brewer (*Parlement* 18), but Gilbert argues for a connection between Neoplatonic metaphysics and a theory of love.

4. Goffin ("Heaven and Earth") and Lumiansky ("Chaucer's *Parlement of Foules*") emphasize the question of true and false felicity in the poem; Chamberlain associates love with concordia.

5. Heffernan offers an exegetical reading. See other discussion in Donaldson ("Venus")

and Emerson Brown ("Priapus"). Wimsatt ("Realism" 50) sees a connection between the two sons of Cupid in Alan of Lille's *De planctu naturae* and the two inscriptions over the gate to the park.

6. Ferster points out that the verbs associated with the two goddesses—*finden* and *devysen*—can combine the senses of discovery and constructing meaning (61).

7. Aers has extended Salter's argument by questioning the status of a reading that would affirm Nature's dominant role. The poem, he concludes, "has quite undermined such discourse and all claims to an impersonal and transcendental viewpoint" (14), for its poetic process moves continually in the direction of self-reflexivity and therefore subverts generalized and absolutist perspectives.

8. Quilligan makes the point about intertextuality: "Chaucer's process is essentially to transform the silent, unvoiced textuality of his allegorical sources into a dramatic, mimetic fiction of audible, voiced sound" (164).

9. Brewer (*Parlement* 113) denies any influence of Alan on Chaucer's poem. Eldredge ("Poetry") finds Alan's influence in the portrayal of Nature as a general principle and Venus as the particular.

10. Discussions of Alan's rationalization of sexuality appear in Cherniss (*Apocalypse* 49–71), Richard H. Green, Wetherbee ("Function"), Bloch (133–36), Leupin, and Ziolkowski.

11. Everett ("Visions" 101–9 and "Reflections" 160) emphasizes Chaucer's use of *contentio* (contrast) as a rhetorical device.

12. Dubs and Malarkey read the first stanza as an expression of the struggle to master technique and content. Jordan ("Question" 379) argues that the stanza is marred by a failure to maintain a tone of solemnity and high moral purpose.

13. Paul A. Olson believes Nature is "that figure who can reveal the meaning and institutional form necessary to the quest for the common profit in the same way that Beatrice can reveal the theological meaning of history, of Hell and Purgatory, and pull together the meaning of the fragments of imperial and papal life which Dante has viewed in Hell and in the lower Purgatory." Nature is "the vicar of God *in a civic sense;* exactly the sense which makes the king the vicar of God in the language of medieval ruler-praise" (58).

14. Jordan ("Question") and Leicester argue for the poem's essential fragmentation.

Bibliography

Aers, David. "The *Parliament of Fowls:* Authority, the Knower, and the Known." *Chaucer Review* 16 (1981–82): 1–17.

Alan of Lille. *De planctu naturae.* Studi Medievali, 3d. Nikolaus M. Häring, 787–879. 3d ser., vol. 19, fasc. 2, 1978.

———. *Alan of Lille: The Plaint of Nature.* Trans. James J. Sheridan. Toronto: Pontifical Institute of Mediaeval Studies, 1980.

Aquinas, Thomas. *Summa Theologiae.* Trans. Blackfriars of the English Province. 60 vols. New York: McGraw-Hill, 1969.

Augustine. *Confessions.* Ed. and trans. William Watts. Cambridge, Mass.: Harvard University Press, 1979.

———. *De musica.* Trans. Robert C. Taliaferro. Vol. 2 of *Writings of Saint Augustine.* New York: CIMA Publishing Co., 1947.

Baker, Donald C. "The Dreamer Again in the *Book of the Duchess.*" *PMLA* 70 (1955): 279–82.

———. "The Poet of Love and the *Parlement of Foules.*" *University of Mississippi Studies in English* 2 (1961): 79–110.

Barbi, Michele, ed. *La Vita Nuova di Dante Alighieri.* Volume 1 of the Edizione nazionale delle Opere di Dante. Florence: R. Bemporad & Figlio, 1932.

Barron, W. R. J. *English Medieval Romance.* New York: Longman, 1987.

Bartholomaeus Anglicus. *On the Properties of Soul and Body.* Ed. R. James Long. Toronto: Centre for Medieval Studies, 1979.

Baum, Paull F. "Chaucer's 'The House of Fame.'" *ELH* 8 (1941): 248–56.

Bennett, J. A. W. *Chaucer's Book of Fame.* Oxford: Oxford University Press, 1968.

———. *The Parlement of Foules: An Interpretation.* Oxford: Clarendon Press, 1957.

———. "Some Second Thoughts on *The Parlement of Foules.*" In *Chaucerian Problems and Perspectives: Essays presented to Paul E. Beichner, C.S.C.,* ed. Edward Vesta and Zacharias P. Thundy, 132–46. Notre Dame, Ind.: University of Notre Dame Press, 1979.

Benson, C. David. "The *Canterbury Tales:* Personal drama or experiments in poetic variety?" In *The Cambridge Chaucer Companion,* ed. Piero Boitani and Jill Mann, 93–108. Cambridge: Cambridge University Press, 1986.

———. *Chaucer's Drama of Style: Poetic Variety and Contrast in the* Canterbury Tales. Chapel Hill: University of North Carolina Press, 1986.

Benson, Larry D. "The 'Love-Tydinges' in Chaucer's *House of Fame.*" In *Chaucer in the Eighties,* ed. Julian N. Wasserman and Robert J. Blanch, 3–22. Syracuse, N.Y.: Syracuse University Press, 1986.

———. "The Occasion of *The Parliament of Fowls.*" In *The Wisdom of Poetry,* ed. Larry D. Benson and Siegfried Wenzel, 123–44. Kalamazoo, Mich.: Medieval Institute Publications, 1982.

———, ed. *The Riverside Chaucer.* Boston: Houghton Mifflin Company, 1987.

Berger, Harry, Jr. "Two Spenserian Retrospects: The Antique Temple of Venus and The Primitive Marriage of Rivers." *Texas Studies in Language and Literature* 10 (1968): 5–25.

Bernardus Silvestris. *The* Cosmographia *of Bernardus Silvestris.* Trans. Winthrop Wetherbee. New York: Columbia University Press, 1973. *See also* Jones.

Berry, Reginald. "Chaucer's Eagle and the Element of Air." *University of Toronto Quarterly* 43 (1974): 285–97.

Bethurum, Dorothy. "The Center of *The Parlement of Foules.*" In *Essays in Honor of Walter Clyde Curry,* 39–50. Nashville, Tenn.: Vanderbilt University Press, 1954.

———. "Chaucer's Point of View Narrator in the Love Poems." *PMLA* 74 (1959): 511–20.

Bevington, David M. "The Obtuse Narrator in Chaucer's *House of Fame.*" *Speculum* 36 (1961): 288–98.

Birney, Earle. "The Beginnings of Chaucer's Irony." *PMLA* 54 (1939): 637–55.

Bloch, R. Howard. *Etymologies and Genealogies: A Literary Anthropology of the French Middle Ages.* Chicago: University of Chicago Press, 1983.

Bloom, Harold. *The Anxiety of Influence: A Theory of Poetry.* New York: Oxford University Press, 1973.

Bloomfield, Morton W. "Authenticating Realism and the Realism of Chaucer." *Thought* 39 (1964): 335–58.

———. "Chaucerian Realism." In *The Cambridge Chaucer Companion,* ed. Piero Boitani and Jill Mann, 170–93. Cambridge: Cambridge University Press, 1986.

———. "Chaucer's Sense of History." *Journal of English and Germanic Philology* 51 (1952): 301–13.

———. "The Gloomy Chaucer." In *Veins of Humor,* ed. Harry Levin, 57–68. Harvard English Studies 3. Cambridge, Mass.: Harvard University Press, 1972.

Boccaccio, Giovanni. *Boccaccio on Poetry.* Trans. Charles G. Osgood. Princeton, N.J.: Princeton University Press, 1930.

———. *Genealogie deorum gentilium.* Ed. Vincenzo Romano. 3d ed. 2 vols. Bari: Laterza, 1951.

———. *Teseida delle nozze d'Emilia,* ed. Alberto Limentani. In *Tutte le Opere di Giovanni Boccaccio,* ed. Vittore Branca, 2:229–664. 12 vols. Florence: Mondadori, 1964.

Boer, C. de. "Guillaume de Machaut et *l'Ovide Moralisé.*" *Romania* 43 (1914): 335–52. *See also Ovide Moralisé.*

Boethius. In *Isagogen Porphyrii Commenta,* ed. Samuel Brandt. Corpus Scriptorum Ecclesiasticorum Latinorum. Vienna: Tempsky, 1906.

Boitani, Piero. *Chaucer and the Imaginary World of Fame.* Woodbridge, Suffolk and Totowa, N.J.: D. S. Brewer, 1984.

————. "Chaucer's Labyrinth: Fourteenth-Century Literature and Language." *Chaucer Review* 17 (1982–83): 197–220.

————. "Old Books Brought to Life in Dreams: The *Book of the Duchess,* the *House of Fame,* the *Parliament of Fowls.*" In *The Cambridge Chaucer Companion,* ed. Piero Boitani and Jill Mann, 39–57. Cambridge: Cambridge University Press, 1986.

————. "Style, Iconography and Narrative: The Lesson of the *Teseida.*" In *Chaucer and the Italian Trecento,* ed. Piero Boitani, 185–99. Cambridge: Cambridge University Press, 1983.

————. "What Dante Meant to Chaucer." In *Chaucer and the Italian Trecento,* ed. Piero Boitani, 115–39. Cambridge: Cambridge University Press, 1983.

Brewer, Derek. *Chaucer: The Poet as Storyteller.* London: Macmillan, 1984.

————. "The Relationship of Chaucer to the English and European Traditions." In *Chaucer and Chaucerians,* ed. D. S. Brewer, 1–30. University: University Press of Alabama, 1966.

————. *Towards a Chaucerian Poetic.* Oxford: Oxford University Press for the British Academy, 1974.

————, ed. *The Parlement of Foulys.* London: Nelson, 1960.

Bronson, Bertrand H. "*The Book of the Duchess* Re-opened." *PMLA* 67 (1952): 863–81.

Brown, Emerson, Jr. "Priapus and the *Parlement of Foulys.*" *Studies in Philology* 72 (1975): 258–74.

Brown, James Neil. "Narrative Focus and Function in *The Book of the Duchess.*" *Massachusetts Studies in English* 2 (1970): 71–79.

Brownlee, Kevin. *Poetic Identity in Guillaume de Machaut.* Madison: University of Wisconsin Press, 1984.

————. "Reflection in the *Miroër aus Amoreus:* The Inscribed Reader in Jean de Meun's *Roman de la Rose.*" In *Mimesis: From Mirror to Method, Augustine to Descartes,* ed. John D. Lyons and Stephen G. Nichols, Jr., 60–70. Hanover, N.H.: University Press of New England, 1982.

Brownlee, Marina Scordilis. "Autobiography as Self-(Re)presentation: The Augustinian Paradigm and Juan Ruiz's Theory of Reading." In *Mimesis: From Mirror to Method, Augustine to Descartes,* ed. John D. Lyons and Stephen G. Nichols, Jr., 71–82. Hanover, N.H.: University Press of New England, 1982.

Bruns, Gerald. "The Originality of Texts in a Manuscript Culture." *Comparative Literature* 32 (1980): 113–29.

Bruyne, Edgar de. *Études d'esthétique médiévale.* 3 vols. 1946; reprint, Geneva: Slatkine Reprints, 1975.

Bundy, Murray W. *The Theory of Imagination in Classical and Mediaeval Thought.* Urbana: University of Illinois Press, 1927.

Burlin, Robert B. *Chaucerian Fiction.* Princeton, N.J.: Princeton University Press, 1977.

Burnley, J. David. *Chaucer's Language and the Philosopher's Tradition.* Cambridge: D. S. Brewer, 1979.

Burrow, John A. *Medieval Writers and Their Work: Middle English Literature and Its Background, 1100–1500.* Oxford: Oxford University Press, 1982.

————. *Ricardian Poetry: Chaucer, Gower, Langland, and the Gawain-Poet.* London: Routledge & Kegan Paul, 1971.

Burton, Robert. *The Anatomy of Melancholy.* Ed. Floyd Dell and Paul Jordan-Smith. New York: Farrar and Rinehart, 1927.

Calin, William. *A Poet at the Fountain: Essays on the Narrative Verse of Guillaume de Machaut.* Lexington: University of Kentucky Press, 1974.

Carr, John. "A Borrowing from Tibullus in Chaucer's *House of Fame.*" *Chaucer Review* 8 (1973–74): 191–97.

Chamberlain, David. "The Music of the Spheres and the *Parlement of Foules.*" *Chaucer Review* 5 (1970–71): 32–56.

Chapman, Janet A. "Juan Ruiz's 'Learned Sermon.' " In *"Libro de Buen Amor" Studies,* ed. G. B. Gybbon-Monypenny, 29–51. London: Tamesis, 1970.

Cherniss, Michael D. *Boethian Apocalypse: Studies in Middle English Vision Poetry.* Norman, Okla.: Pilgrim Books, 1987.

———. "The Boethian Dialogue in Chaucer's *Book of the Duchess.*" *Journal of English and Germanic Philology* 68 (1969): 655–65.

Chrétien de Troyes. *Cligés,* ed. Alexandre Micha. Paris: Champion, 1957.

Cicero. *De inventione, De optimo genere oratorum, Topica.* Trans. H. M. Hubbell. Loeb Classical Library. Cambridge, Mass.: Harvard University Press, 1976.

———. *Somnium Scipionis.* In *Cicero: De re publica and De legibus,* trans. Clinton Walker Keyes, 260–83. Loeb Classical Library. Cambridge, Mass.: Harvard University Press, 1966.

Clanvowe, John. *The Works of Sir John Clanvowe.* Ed. V. J. Scattergood. Cambridge: D. S. Brewer, 1985.

Clemen, Wolfgang. *Chaucer's Early Poetry.* Trans. C. A. M. Sym. London: Methuen, 1963.

Clogan, Paul M. "The Textual Reliability of Chaucer's Lyrics: *A Complaint to his Lady.*" *Medievalia et Humanistica* n.s. 5 (1974): 183–89.

Coleman, Janet. "English Culture in the Fourteenth Century." In *Chaucer and the Italian Trecento,* ed. Piero Boitani, 33–63. Cambridge: Cambridge University Press, 1983.

———. *Medieval Readers and Writers: 1350–1400.* New York: Columbia University Press, 1981.

Condren, Edward I. "The Historical Context of the *Book of the Duchess:* A New Hypothesis." *Chaucer Review* 5 (1970–71): 195–212.

———. "Of Deaths and Duchesses and Scholars Coughing in Ink." *Chaucer Review* 10 (1975–76): 87–95.

Copeland, Rita. "Rhetoric and Vernacular Translation in the Middle Ages." *Studies in the Age of Chaucer* 9 (1987): 41–75.

Cowgill, Bruce Kent. "The *Parlement of Foules* and the Body Politic." *Journal of English and Germanic Philology* 74 (1975): 315–25.

Crampton, Georgia Ronan. "Transitions and Meanings in *The Book of the Duchess.*" *Journal of English and Germanic Philology* 62 (1963): 486–500.

Crépin, André. "Chaucer and the French." In *Medieval and Pseudo-Medieval Literature,* ed. Piero Boitani and Anna Torti, 55–77. Cambridge: D. S. Brewer, 1984.

Crow, Martin M., and Clair C. Olson. *Chaucer Life-Records.* Austin: University of Texas Press, 1966.

Curry, Walter Clyde. *Chaucer and the Mediaeval Sciences.* Nashville, Tenn.: Vanderbilt University Press, 1926.

Dahlberg, Charles, trans. *The Romance of the Rose.* Princeton, N.J.: Princeton University Press, 1971.

Dampier, William C. *A History of Science and Its Relations with Philosophy and Religion.* 4th ed. Cambridge: Cambridge University Press, 1971.

Dane, Joseph A. "Chaucer's Eagle's Ovid's Phaethon: A Study in Literary Reception." *Journal of Medieval and Renaissance Studies* 11 (1981): 71–82.

Dante Alighieri. *The Divine Comedy.* Trans. Charles S. Singleton. 3 vols. in 6. Princeton, N.J.: Princeton University Press, 1970–75. *See also* Barbi.

David, Alfred. "An ABC to the Style of the Prioress." In *Acts of Interpretation: The Text in*

Its Contexts, 700–1600, ed. Mary J. Carruthers and Elizabeth D. Kirk, 147–57. Norman, Okla.: Pilgrim Books, 1982.

Delany, Sheila. *Chaucer's* House of Fame: *The Poetics of Skeptical Fideism.* Chicago: University of Chicago Press, 1972.

———. "Chaucer's *House of Fame* and the *Ovide moralisé.*" *Comparative Literature* 20 (1968): 254–64.

———. " 'Phantom' and the *House of Fame.*" *Chaucer Review* 2 (1967–68): 68–74.

Deyermond, Alan D. "Some Aspects of Parody in the 'Libro de buen amor.' " In *"Libro de Buen Amor" Studies,* ed. G. B. Gybbon-Monypenny, 53–78. London: Tamesis, 1970.

Dickerson, A. Inskip. "Chaucer's *House of Fame:* A Skeptical Epistemology of Love." *Texas Studies in Language and Literature* 18 (1976): 171–83.

Donaldson, E. Talbot. "Chaucer the Pilgrim." *PMLA* 69 (1954): 928–36.

———. "Venus and the Mother of Romulus: the *Parliament of Fowls* and the *Pervigilium Veneris.*" *Chaucer Review* 14 (1979–80): 313–18.

Donner, Morton. "Chaucer and His Narrators: The Poet's Place in His Poems." *Western Humanities Review* 27 (1973): 189–95.

Doob, Penelope B. R. *Nebuchadnezzar's Children: Conventions of Madness in Middle English Literature.* New Haven, Conn.: Yale University Press, 1974.

Dronke, Peter. "Chaucer and the Medieval Latin Poets." In *Geoffrey Chaucer,* ed. D. S. Brewer, 137–54. Athens: Ohio University Press, 1975.

———. "Mediaeval Rhetoric." In *The Medieval World,* vol. 2 of *Literature and Western Civilization,* ed. Donald Daiches and Anthony Thorlby, 315–45. 4 vols. London: Aldine, 1973.

Dubs, Kathleen E., and Stoddard Malarkey. "The Frame of Chaucer's *Parlement.*" *Chaucer Review* 13 (1978–79): 16–25.

Ebel, Julia G. "Chaucer's *The Book of the Duchess:* A Study in Medieval Iconography and Literary Structure." *College English* 29 (1967): 197–206.

Eberle, Patricia J. "The Politics of Courtly Style at the Court of Richard II." In *The Spirit of the Court,* ed. Glyn S. Burgess and Robert A. Taylor, 168–78. Cambridge: D. S. Brewer, 1985.

Eckhardt, Caroline D. "The Art of Translation in *The Romaunt of the Rose.*" *Studies in the Age of Chaucer* 6 (1984): 41–63.

Economou, George D. *The Goddess Natura in Medieval Literature.* Cambridge, Mass.: Harvard University Press, 1972.

Edwards, Robert R. *The Montecassino Passion and the Poetics of Medieval Drama.* Berkeley: University of California Press, 1977.

———. *Ratio and Invention: A Study of Medieval Lyric and Narrative.* Nashville, Tenn.: Vanderbilt University Press, 1989.

Eldredge, Laurence. "Chaucer's *Hous of Fame* and the *Via Moderna.*" *Neuphilologische Mitteilungen* 71 (1970): 105–19.

———. "Poetry and Philosophy in *The Parlement of Foules.*" *Revue de l'Université d'Ottawa* 40 (1970): 441–59.

———. "The Structure of *The Book of the Duchess.*" *Revue de l'Université d'Ottawa* 39 (1969): 132–51.

Elliott, R. W. V. "Chaucer's Reading." In *Chaucer's Mind and Art,* ed. A. C. Cawley, 46–68. London: Oliver and Boyd, 1969.

Everett, Dorothy. "Chaucer's Love Visions, with Particular Reference to the *Parlement of Foules.*" In *Essays on Middle English Literature,* ed. Patricia Kean, 97–114. London: Oxford University Press, 1959.

————. "Some Reflections on Chaucer's 'Art Poetical.' " In *Essays on Middle English Literature,* ed. Patricia Kean, 149–74. London: Oxford University Press, 1959.

Faral, Edmond. *Les arts poétiques du XIIᵉ et du XIIIᵉ siècle.* Paris: Champion, 1924.

Ferster, Judith. *Chaucer on Interpretation.* Cambridge: Cambridge University Press, 1985.

Fichte, Joerg O. *Chaucer's "Art Poetical": A Study in Chaucerian Poetics.* Tübingen: Gunter Narr Verlag, 1980.

Fisher, John H. "Chaucer and the French Influence." In *New Perspectives in Chaucer Criticism,* ed. Donald M. Rose, 177–91. Norman, Okla.: Pilgrim Books, 1981.

————, ed. *The Complete Poetry and Prose of Geoffrey Chaucer.* New York: Holt, Rinehart and Winston, 1977.

Fleming, John V. *The Roman de la Rose: A Study on Allegory and Iconography.* Princeton, N.J.: Princeton University Press, 1969.

Fletcher, Angus. *The Prophetic Moment: An Essay on Spenser.* Chicago: University of Chicago Press, 1971.

Frank, Robert Worth, Jr. "Structure and Meaning in the *Parlement of Foules.*" *PMLA* 71 (1956): 530–39.

French, W. H. "The Man in Black's Lyric." *Journal of English and Germanic Philology* 56 (1957): 231–41.

Froissart, Jehan de. *Chroniques.* Ed. George T. Diller. Geneva: Droz, 1972.

————. *Oeuvres de Froissart: Poésies.* Ed. Aug. Scheler. Brussels: Victor Devaus, 1870.

Fry, Donald K. "The Ending of the *House of Fame.*" In *Chaucer at Albany,* ed. Rossell Hope Robbins, 27–40. New York: Burt Franklin, 1975.

Fyler, John M. *Chaucer and Ovid.* New Haven, Conn.: Yale University Press, 1979.

Gallo, Ernest. *The* Poetria Nova *and Its Sources in Early Rhetorical Doctrine.* The Hague: Mouton, 1971.

Garbáty, Thomas J. "The Degradation of Chaucer's 'Geffrey.' " *PMLA* 89 (1974): 97–104.

Geoffrey of Vinsauf. *Poetria Nova.* In *Les arts poétiques du XIIᵉ et du XIIIᵉ siècle,* ed. Edmond Faral, 194–262. Paris: Champion, 1924.

————. *Poetria Nova of Geoffrey of Vinsauf.* Trans. Margaret F. Nims. Toronto: Pontifical Institute of Mediaeval Studies, 1967.

Giaccherini, Enrico. "Una *crux* Chauceriana: i sogni nella *House of Fame.*" *Rivista di letterature moderne e comparate* 27 (1974): 165–76.

Gilbert, A. J. "The Influence of Boethius on the *Parlement of Foulys.*" *Medium Aevum* 47 (1978): 292–303.

Goffin, R. C. "Heaven and Earth in the *Parlement of Foules.*" *Modern Language Review* 31 (1936): 493–99.

Green, Richard Firth. *Poets and Princepleasers: Literature and the English Court in the Late Middle Ages.* Toronto: University of Toronto Press, 1980.

Green, Richard H. "Alain of Lille's *De planctu naturae.*" *Speculum* 31 (1956): 649–74.

Greenblatt, Stephen. *Renaissance Self-Fashioning: From More to Shakespeare.* Chicago: University of Chicago Press, 1980.

Grennen, Joseph E. "Science and Poetry in Chaucer's *House of Fame.*" *Annuale Medievale* 8 (1967): 38–45.

Guillaume de Lorris and Jean de Meun. *Le Roman de la Rose.* Ed. Félix Lecoy. 3 vols. Classiques Français du Moyen Age. Paris: Champion, 1965–70. *See also* Dahlberg.

Gushee, Lawrence A. "Questions of Genre in Medieval Treatises on Music." In *Gattungen der Musik in Einzeldarstellungen (Gedenkschrift Leo Schrade),* ed. Wulf Arlt, Ernst Lichtenhahn, and Hans Oesch, 365–433. Munich: Francke Verlag, 1973.

Hanning, Robert W. "Chaucer's First Ovid: Metamorphosis and Poetic Tradition in *The*

Book of the Duchess and *The House of Fame.*" In *Chaucer and the Craft of Fiction,* ed. Leigh A. Arrathoon, 121–63. Rochester, Mich.: Solaris Press, 1986.

———. "Poetic Emblems in Medieval Narrative Texts." In *Vernacular Poetics,* ed. Lois Ebin, 1–32. Kalamazoo, Mich.: Medieval Institute Publications, 1984.

Havely, N. R., ed. and trans. *Chaucer's Boccaccio: Sources of Troilus and the Knight's and Franklin's Tales.* Cambridge: D. S. Brewer, 1980.

Heffernan, Carol Falvo. "Wells and Streams in Three Chaucerian Gardens." *Papers on Language and Literature* 15 (1974): 339–56.

Henryson, Robert. *Poems.* Ed. Charles Elliot. 2d ed. Oxford: Clarendon Press, 1974.

Hieatt, Constance B. *The Realism of Dream Visions.* The Hague: Mouton, 1967.

Hill, John M. "The *Book of the Duchess,* Melancholy, and that Eight-Year Sickness." *Chaucer Review* 9 (1974–75): 35–50.

Hoccleve, Thomas. *The Regement of Princes and Fourteen Minor Poems.* Ed. Frederick J. Furnivall. Vol. 3 of *Hoccleve's Works.* E.E.T.S., E.S. 72. London: Kegan Paul, Trench, Trübner & Co., 1897; reprint, Millwood, N.Y.: Kraus Reprint Corp., 1978.

Horace. *The Odes and Epodes.* Trans. C. E. Bennett. Rev. ed. Loeb Classical Library. New York: Macmillan, 1929.

Howard, Donald R. *Chaucer: His Life, His Works, His World.* New York: E. P. Dutton, 1987.

———. "Chaucer the Man." *PMLA* 80 (1965): 337–43.

———. "Chaucer's Idea of an Idea." In *Essays and Studies 1976,* ed. E. Talbot Donaldson, 39–55, n.s. 29. London: John Murray, 1976.

Hult, David F. *Self-Fulfilling Prophecies: Readership and Authority in the First* Roman de la Rose. Cambridge: Cambridge University Press, 1986.

Irvine, Martin. "Medieval Grammatical Theory and Chaucer's *House of Fame." Speculum* 60 (1985): 850–76.

Jacobus de Voragine. *Legenda Aurea vulgo historia lombardica dicta.* Ed. Th. Graesse. 3d ed. 1890; reprint, Osnabrück: Otto Zeller Verlag, 1969.

Jenkins, T. A. "Deschamps' Ballade to Chaucer." *Modern Language Notes* 33 (1918): 268–78.

Jerome. *Epistulae.* Ed. Isidore Hilberg. 3 vols. Corpus Scriptorum Ecclesiasticorum Latinorum. 54–56. Vienna: Tempsky, 1910.

John of Garland. *The* Parisiana Poetria *of John of Garland.* Ed. and trans. Traugott Lawler. New Haven, Conn.: Yale University Press, 1974.

Johnson, William C., Jr. "Art as Discovery: The Aesthetics of Consolation in Chaucer's 'Book of the Duchess.' " *South Atlantic Bulletin* 40 (1975): 53–62.

Jones, Julian Ward, and Elizabeth Francis Jones, eds. *The Commentary on the First Six Books of the "Aeneid" of Virgil Commonly Attributed to Bernardus Silvestris.* Lincoln: University of Nebraska Press, 1977.

Jordan, Robert M. *Chaucer and the Shape of Creation: The Aesthetic Possibilities of Inorganic Form.* Cambridge, Mass.: Harvard University Press, 1967.

———. *Chaucer's Poetics and the Modern Reader.* Berkeley: University of California Press, 1987.

———. "The Compositional Structure of the *Book of the Duchess." Chaucer Review* 9 (1974–75): 99–117.

———. "Lost in the Funhouse of Fame: Chaucer and Postmodernism." *Chaucer Review* 18 (1983–84): 100–115.

———. "The Question of Unity and the *Parlement of Foules." English Studies in Canada* 3 (1977): 373—85.

Kane, George. *The Biographical Fallacy in Chaucer and Langland Studies.* London: H. K. Lewis, 1965.

Kean, Patricia M. *Chaucer and the Making of English Poetry*. 2 vols. Oxford: Oxford University Press, 1972.

Kearney, John A. "*The Parliament of Fowls*: The Narrator, the 'Certeyn Thyng' and the 'Commune Profyt.'" *Theoria: A Journal of Studies in the Arts* 45 (1975): 55–71.

Kellogg, A. L. "Chaucer's Self-Portrait and Dante's." *Medium Aevum* 29 (1960): 119–20.

Kelly, Douglas. *Medieval Imagination: Rhetoric and the Poetry of Courtly Love*. Madison: University of Wisconsin Press, 1978.

———. "The Scope of the Treatment of Composition in the Twelfth- and Thirteenth-Century Arts of Poetry." *Speculum* 41 (1966): 261–78.

———. "Theory of Composition in Medieval Narrative Poetry and Geoffrey of Vinsauf's *Poetria Nova*." *Mediaeval Studies* 31 (1969): 117–48.

Kendrick, Laura. "Chaucer's *House of Fame* and the French Palais de Justice." *Studies in the Age of Chaucer* 6 (1984): 121–33.

Kittredge, George L. *Chaucer and His Poetry*. Cambridge, Mass.: Harvard University Press, 1915.

Knopp, Sherron. "Chaucer and Jean de Meun as Self-Conscious Narrators: The Prologue to the *Legend of Good Women* and the *Roman de la Rose* 10307–680." *Comitatus* 4 (1973): 25–39.

Knowles, David. *The Evolution of Medieval Thought*. New York: Random House, 1962.

Kolve, V. A. *Chaucer and the Imagery of Narrative: The First Five Canterbury Tales*. Stanford, Calif.: Stanford University Press, 1984.

Koonce, B. G. *Chaucer and the Tradition of Fame: Symbolism in* The House of Fame. Princeton, N.J.: Princeton University Press, 1966.

Kreuzer, James R. "The Dreamer in the *Book of the Duchess*." *PMLA* 66 (1951): 543–47.

Krieger, Murray. "The Ekphrastic Principle and the Still Movement of Poetry; or *Laokoon* Revisited." In *The Play and Place of Criticism*, 105–128. Baltimore, Md.: The Johns Hopkins Press, 1967.

Lawlor, John. *Chaucer*. New York: Harper and Row, 1968.

———. "The Earlier Poems." In *Chaucer and Chaucerians: Critical Studies in Middle English Literature*, ed. D. S. Brewer, 39–64. University: University of Alabama Press, 1966.

———. "The Pattern of Consolation in *The Book of the Duchess*." *Speculum* 31 (1956): 626–48.

Lawton, David. *Chaucer's Narrators*. Woodbridge, Suffolk: D. S. Brewer, 1985.

Lazarus, Alan J. "Venus in the 'North-north-west'? (Chaucer's *Parliament of Fowls*, 117)." In *The Wisdom of Poetry*, ed. Larry D. Benson and Siegfried Wenzel, 145–49. Kalamazoo, Mich.: Medieval Institute Publications, 1982.

Leicester, H. M. "The Harmony of Chaucer's *Parlement*: A Dissonant Voice." *Chaucer Review* 9 (1974–75): 15–33.

Lenaghan, Robert T. "Chaucer's Circle of Gentlemen and Clerks." *Chaucer Review* 18 (1983–84): 155–60.

Lewis, C. S. *The Allegory of Love*. Oxford: Oxford University Press, 1936.

Leupin, Alexandre. "Alan of Lille's Grammar of Sex." *Diagraphe* 9 (1975): 119–30.

Leyerle, John. "Chaucer's Windy Eagle." *University of Toronto Quarterly* 40 (1971): 247–65.

Lumiansky, Robert M. "The Bereaved Narrator in Chaucer's *Book of the Duchess*." *Tulane Studies in English* 9 (1959): 5–17.

———. "Chaucer's *Parlement of Foules*: A Philosophical Interpretation." *Review of English Studies* 29 (1948): 82–89.

Lydgate, John. *Lydgate's Fall of Princes.* Ed. Henry Bergen. 4 vols. E.E.T.S., E.S. 121–24. Washington: Carnegie Institution, 1923.

Machan, Tim William. *Techniques of Translation: Chaucer's* Boece. Norman, Okla.: Pilgrim Books, 1985.

Machaut, Guillaume de. *The Judgment of the King of Bohemia (Le Jugement dou Roy de Behaingne).* Ed. and trans. R. Barton Palmer. New York: Garland, 1984.

———. *Oeuvres.* Ed. Ernest Hoepffner. 3 vols. Paris: Firmin-Didot, 1908–21.

McKeon, Richard. *Selections from Medieval Philosophers.* 2 vols. New York: Charles Scribner's Sons, 1929.

McLuhan, Marshall L. *The Gutenberg Galaxy.* New York: New American Library, 1969.

Macrobius. *Commentary on the Dream of Scipio.* Trans. William Harris Stahl. New York: Columbia University Press, 1952.

———. *Opera.* Ed. James Willis. 2 vols. Leipzig: Teubner, 1963.

Manning, Stephen. "Chaucer's Good Faire White: Woman and Symbol." *Comparative Literature* 10 (1958): 97–105.

Mathew, Gervase. *The Court of Richard II.* London: Murray, 1968.

Matthew of Vendôme. *Ars versificatoria.* In *Les arts poétiques du XIIe et du XIIIe siècle,* ed. Edmond Faral, 106–93. Paris: Champion, 1924.

———. *The Art of Versification.* Trans. Aubrey E. Galyon. Ames: Iowa State University Press, 1980.

Mehl, Dieter. *Geoffrey Chaucer: eine Einführung in seine erzählende Dichtungen.* Berlin: E. Schmidt, 1973.

———. *Geoffrey Chaucer: An Introduction to his Narrative Poetry.* Cambridge: Cambridge University Press, 1986.

Middleton, Anne. "The Idea of Public Poetry in the Reign of Richard II." *Speculum* 53 (1978): 94–115.

Miller, Jacqueline T. "The Writing on the Wall: Authority and Authorship in Chaucer's *House of Fame.*" *Chaucer Review* 17 (1982–83): 95–115.

Mills, Maldwyn, ed. *Six Middle English Romances.* Totowa, N.J.: Rowman and Littlefield, 1973.

Minnis, Alistair J. *Medieval Theory of Authorship: Scholastic Literary Attitudes in the Later Middle Ages.* London: Scolar Press, 1984.

Miskimin, Alice. *The Renaissance Chaucer.* New Haven, Conn.: Yale University Press, 1975.

Murphy, James J. "A New Look at Chaucer and the Rhetoricians." *Review of English Studies* 15 (1964): 1–20.

———. *Rhetoric in the Middle Ages: A History of Rhetorical Theory from St. Augustine to the Renaissance.* Berkeley: University of California Press, 1974.

Muscatine, Charles. *Chaucer and the French Tradition.* Berkeley: University of California Press, 1957.

Newman, Francis X. *"House of Fame,* 7–12." *English Language Notes* 6 (1968): 5–12.

Nolan, Barbara. "The Art of Expropriation: Chaucer's Narrator in *The Book of the Duchess.*" In *New Perspectives in Chaucer Criticism,* ed. Donald M. Rose, 203–22. Norman, Okla.: Pilgrim Books, 1981.

Nolan, Charles J., Jr. "Structural Sophistication in 'The Complaint Unto Pity.' " *Chaucer Review* 13 (1978–79): 363–72.

Norton-Smith, John, ed. *Bodleian Library MS Fairfax 16.* London: Scolar Press, 1979.

Offord, M. Y., ed. *The Parlement of the Thre Ages.* E.E.T.S. 246. London: Oxford University Press, 1959.

Olson, Glending, "Deschamps' *Art de dictier* and Chaucer's Literary Environment." *Speculum* 48 (1973): 714–23.

————. *Literature as Recreation in the Later Middle Ages.* Ithaca, N.Y.: Cornell University Press, 1982.

————. "Making and Poetry in the Age of Chaucer." *Comparative Literature* 31 (1979): 272–90.

Olson, Paul A. *"The Parlement of Foules:* Aristotle's *Politics* and the Foundations of Human Society." *Studies in the Age of Chaucer* 2 (1980): 53–69.

Otis, Brooks. *Ovid as an Epic Poet.* 2d ed. Cambridge: Cambridge University Press, 1970.

Oton de Grandson. *Oton de Grandson, sa vie et ses poésies,* ed. Arthur Piaget. Société d'Histoire de la Suisse romande, Mémoires et Documents. 3d ser., vol. 1. Lausanne: Payot, 1941.

Overbeck, Pat Trezger. "The 'Man of Gret Auctorite' in Chaucer's *House of Fame." Modern Philology* 73 (1975): 157–61.

Ovid. *Metamorphoses.* Ed. and trans. Frank Justus Miller. 2 vols. Loeb Classical Library. Cambridge, Mass.: Harvard University Press, 1958.

Ovide Moralisé. Ed. C. de Boer. 5 vols. Amsterdam: Noord-Hollandische Uitgevers-Maatschappij, 1936.

Palmer, J. J. N. "The Historical Context of the *Book of the Duchess:* A Revision." *Chaucer Review* 8 (1973–74): 253–61.

Patch, Howard R. "Chaucer's Desert." *Modern Language Notes* 34 (1919): 321–28.

Payne, Robert O. "Chaucer and the Art of Rhetoric." In *Companion to Chaucer Studies,* rev. ed. Beryl Rowland, 342–64. New York: Oxford University Press, 1979.

————. "Chaucer's Realization of Himself as Rhetor." In *Medieval Eloquence: Studies in the Theory and Practice of Medieval Rhetoric,* ed. James J. Murphy, 270–87. Berkeley: University of California Press, 1978.

————. *The Key of Remembrance: A Study of Chaucer's Poetics.* New Haven, Conn.: Yale University Press, 1963.

————. "Making His Own Myth: The Prologue to Chaucer's *Legend of Good Women." Chaucer Review* 9 (1974–75): 197–211.

Peck, Russell A. "Chaucer and the Nominalist Questions." *Speculum* 53 (1978): 745–60.

————. "Chaucerian Poetics and the Prologue to the *Legend of Good Women.* " In *Chaucer in the Eighties,* ed. Julian N. Wasserman and Robert J. Blanch, 39–55. Syracuse, N.Y.: Syracuse University Press, 1986.

————. "Theme and Number in Chaucer's *Book of the Duchess.*" In *Silent Poetry: Essays in Numerological Analysis,* ed. Alistair Fowler, 73–115. New York: Barnes and Noble, 1970.

Pelen, Marc M. "Machaut's Court of Love Narratives and Chaucer's *Book of the Duchess.*" *Chaucer Review* 11 (1976–77): 128–47.

Poirion, Daniel. *Le poète et le prince: l'évolution du lyrisme courtois de Guillaume de Machaut à Charles d'Orléans.* Paris: Presses universitaires de France, 1965.

Quilligan, Maureen. "Allegory, Allegoresis, and the Deallegorization of Language: The *Roman de la rose,* the *De planctu naturae* and the *Parlement of Foules.*" In *Allegory, Myth, and Symbol,* ed. Morton W. Bloomfield, 163–86. Harvard English Studies 9. Cambridge, Mass.: Harvard University Press, 1981.

Rand, E. K. *Ovid and His Influence.* New York: Cooper Square Publishers, 1963.

Reames, Sherry L. "The Cecilia Legend as Chaucer Inherited It and Retold It: The Disappearance of an Augustinian Ideal." *Speculum* 55 (1980): 38–57.

Reiss, Edmund. "Chaucer and His Audience." *Chaucer Review* 14 (1979–80): 390–402.

Robbins, Rossell Hope. "The Lyrics." In *Companion to Chaucer Studies,* rev. ed. Beryl Rowland, 380–402. New York: Oxford University Press, 1979.

————. "The Middle English Court Love Lyric." In *The Interpretation of Medieval Lyric,* ed. W. T. H. Jackson, 205–32. New York: Columbia University Press, 1980.

Robertson, D. W. Jr. "The Historical Setting of Chaucer's *Book of the Duchess.*" In *Mediaeval Studies in Honor of Urban Tigner Holmes, Jr.,* ed. John Mahoney and John Esten Keller, 169–95. Chapel Hill: University of North Carolina Press, 1965.

———. *A Preface to Chaucer: Studies in Medieval Perspectives.* Princeton, N.J.: Princeton University Press, 1969.

Robinson, F. N., ed. *The Works of Geoffrey Chaucer.* 2d ed. Boston: Houghton Mifflin, 1957.

Rowland, Beryl. "The Art of Memory and the Art of Poetry in the *House of Fame.*" *Revue de l'Université d'Ottawa* 51 (1981): 162–71.

———. "Bishop Bradwardine, the Artificial Memory, and the *House of Fame.*" In *Chaucer at Albany,* ed. Rossell Hope Robbins, 41–62. New York: Burt Franklin, 1975.

Ruggiers, Paul G. "Words into Images in Chaucer's *Hous of Fame:* A Third Suggestion." *Modern Language Notes* 69 (1954): 34–37.

Ruiz, Juan. *Libro de Buen Amor.* Ed. and trans. Raymond S. Willis. Princeton, N.J.: Princeton University Press, 1972.

Russell, D. A. *Criticism in Antiquity.* London: Duckworth, 1981.

Said, Edward. *Beginnings: Intention and Method.* New York: Basic Books, 1975.

Salmon, P. B. "The 'Three Voices' of Poetry in Mediaeval Literary Theory." *Medium Aevum* 30 (1961): 1–18.

Salter, Elizabeth. *Fourteenth-Century English Poetry: Contexts and Readings.* Oxford: Clarendon Press, 1983.

Sands, Donald B., ed. *Middle English Verse Romances.* New York: Holt, Rinehart and Winston, 1966.

Scattergood, V. J. and J. W. Sherborne, eds. *English Court Culture in the Later Middle Ages.* London: Duckworth, 1981.

Schless, Howard H. *Chaucer and Dante: A Revaluation.* Norman, Okla.: Pilgrim Books, 1984.

Seidenspinner-Nuñez, Dayle. *The Allegory of Good Love: Parodic Perspectives in the* Libro de Buen Amor. Berkeley: University of California Press, 1981.

Severs, J. Burke. "Chaucer's Self-Portrait in the *Book of the Duchess.*" *Philological Quarterly* 43 (1964): 27–39.

Shepherd, Geoffrey T. "Make Believe: Chaucer's Rationale of Storytelling in *The House of Fame.*" In *J. R. R. Tolkien, Scholar and Storyteller: Essays in Memoriam,* ed. Mary Salu and Robert T. Farrell, 204–20. Ithaca, N.Y.: Cornell University Press, 1979.

Shoaf, R. A. "Mutatio Amoris: Revision and Penitence in Chaucer's *The Book of the Duchess.*" Ph. D. diss., Cornell University, 1977.

———. "Notes Toward Chaucer's Poetics of Translation." *Studies in the Age of Chaucer* 1 (1979): 55–66.

Shook, Lawrence K. *"The House of Fame.*" In *Companion to Chaucer Studies,* rev. ed. Beryl Rowland, 414–27. New York: Oxford University Press, 1979.

Simmons, J. L. "The Place of the Poet in Chaucer's *House of Fame.*" *Modern Language Quarterly* 27 (1966): 125–35.

Singleton, Charles S. *See* Dante Alighieri.

Spearing, A. C. *Medieval Dream-Poetry.* Cambridge: Cambridge University Press, 1976.

Spitzer, Leo. "Note on the Poetic and the Empirical 'I' in Medieval Authors." *Traditio* 4 (1946): 414–22.

Spurgeon, Caroline F. E. *Five Hundred Years of Chaucer Criticism and Allusion, 1357–1900.* 3 vols. Cambridge: Cambridge University Press, 1925.

Statius. *Silvae and Thebaid.* Ed. and trans. J. H. Mozley. 2 vols. Loeb Classical Library. New York: G. P. Putnam's Sons, 1928.

Steadman, John M. "Chaucer's Eagle: A Contemplative Symbol." *PMLA* 75 (1960): 153–59.

Stevens, John. *Music and Poetry in the Early Tudor Court.* London: Methuen, 1961.
———. "The 'Music' of the Lyric: Machaut, Deschamps, and Chaucer." In *Medieval and Pseudo-Medieval Literature,* ed. Piero Boitani and Anna Torti, 109–29. Cambridge: D. S. Brewer, 1984.
Stevens, Martin. "Narrative Focus in *The Book of the Duchess:* A Critical Revaluation." *Annuale Medievale* 7 (1966): 16–32.
Stevenson, Kay. "The Endings of Chaucer's *House of Fame." English Studies* 59 (1978): 10–26.
Strohm, Paul. "A Note on Gower's Persona." In *Acts of Interpretation: The Text in Its Context, 700–1600,* ed. Mary J. Carruthers and Elizabeth D. Kirk, 293–98. Norman, Okla.: Pilgrim Books, 1982.
———. "The Social and Literary Scene in England." In *The Cambridge Chaucer Companion,* ed. Piero Boitani and Jill Mann, 1–18. Cambridge: Cambridge University Press, 1986.
Suetonius. *Suetonio* De Poetis *e biografi minori.* Ed. Augusto Rostagni. Turin: Chiantore, 1944.
Sutherland, Ronald, ed. *The Romaunt of the Rose and Le Roman de la Rose: A Parallel-Text Edition.* Oxford: Blackwell, 1968.
Sypherd, Wilbur Owen. *Studies in Chaucer's* Hous of Fame. Chaucer Society, 2d ser., vol. 39. London: Kegan Paul, Trench, Trübner & Co., 1907.
Tatlock, J. S. P. *The Development and Chronology of Chaucer's Works.* 1907; reprint, Gloucester, Mass.: Peter Smith, 1963.
Thiébaux, Marcelle. *The Stag of Love: The Chase in Medieval Literature.* Ithaca, N.Y.: Cornell University Press, 1974.
Tisdale, Charles P. R. *"The House of Fame:* Virgilian Reason and Boethian Wisdom." *Comparative Literature* 25 (1973): 247–61.
Traversi, Derek. *Chaucer: The Earlier Poetry.* Newark, Del.: University of Delaware Press, 1987.
Trevisa, John. *On the Properties of Things: John Trevisa's Translation of* Bartholomaeus Anglicus De Proprietatibus Rerum: *A Critical Text.* Ed. M. C. Seymour. 2 vols. Oxford: Clarendon Press, 1975.
Ullman, Pierre L. "Juan Ruiz's Prologue." *Modern Language Notes* 82 (1967): 149–70.
Urmson, James O. "Plato and the Poets." In *Plato on Beauty, Wisdom, and the Arts,* ed. Julius Moravcsik and Philip Temko, 126–36. Totowa, N.J.: Rowman and Littlefield, 1982.
Vale, Juliet. *Edward III and Chivalry: Chivalric Society and Its Context, 1270–1350.* Woodbridge, Suffolk: Boydell Press, 1982.
Vance, Eugene. "Chaucer's *House of Fame* and the Poetics of Inflation." *Boundary 2* 7 (1979): 17–37.
Watts, Ann. "Chaucerian Selves—Especially Two Serious Ones." *Chaucer Review* 4 (1969–70): 229–41.
Wetherbee, Winthrop. *Chaucer and the Poets: An Essay on* Troilus and Criseyde. Ithaca, N.Y.: Cornell University Press, 1985.
———. "The Function of Poetry in the *De planctu naturae of* Alain of Lille." *Traditio* 25 (1969): 87–112.
Wickham, Glynne. *Early English Stages.* 3 vols. London: Routledge and Kegan Paul, 1959.
Williams, Jerry Turner. "Words into Images in Chaucer's *Hous of Fame." Modern Language Notes* 62 (1947): 488–90.
Wilson, William S. "Exegetical Grammar in the *House of Fame." English Language Notes* 1 (1964): 244–48.

————. "Scholastic Logic in Chaucer's *House of Fame*." *Chaucer Review* 1 (1966–67): 181–84.

Wimsatt, James I. "The Apotheosis of Blanche in the *Book of the Duchess*." *Journal of English and Germanic Philology* 66 (1967): 30–42.

————. "The *Book of the Duchess:* Secular Elegy or Religious Vision?" In *Signs and Symbols in Chaucer's Poetry,* ed. John P. Hermann and John J. Burke, Jr., 113–29. University: University of Alabama Press, 1981.

————. *Chaucer and the French Love Poets: The Literary Background of the* Book of the Duchess. University of North Carolina Studies in Comparative Literature, no. 43. Chapel Hill: University of North Carolina Press, 1968.

————. "Chaucer and French Poetry." In *Geoffrey Chaucer,* ed. D. S. Brewer, 109–36. Athens: Ohio University Press, 1975.

————. *Chaucer and the Poems of "CH" in University of Pennsylvania MS French 15.* Cambridge: D. S. Brewer, 1982.

————. "The *Dit dou bleu chevalier:* Froissart's Imitation of Chaucer." *Mediaeval Studies* 34 (1972): 388–400.

————. "Machaut's *Lay de Confort* and Chaucer's *Book of the Duchess*." In *Chaucer at Albany,* ed. Rossell Hope Robbins, 11–26. New York: Burt Franklin, 1975.

————. "Realism in *Troilus and Criseyde* and the *Roman de la Rose*." In *Essays on Troilus and Criseyde,* ed. Mary Salu, 43–56. Cambridge: D. S. Brewer, 1979.

Windeatt, Barry A., ed. and trans. *Chaucer's Dream Poetry: Sources and Analogues.* Totowa, N.J.: D. S. Brewer–Rowman and Littlefield, 1982.

————, ed. *Troilus and Criseyde: A New Edition of "The Book of Troilus."* New York: Longman, 1984.

Winny, James. *Chaucer's Dream-Poems.* New York: Barnes and Noble, 1973.

Woods, Marjorie Curry, ed. *An Early Commentary on the* Poetria Nova *of Geoffrey of Vinsauf.* New York: Garland, 1985.

Yates, Frances. *The Art of Memory.* Chicago: University of Chicago Press, 1966.

Ziegler, Julian. "Two Notes on J. T. Williams' 'Words into Images in Chaucer's *Hous of Fame.*'" *Modern Language Notes* 64 (1949): 73–76.

Ziolkowski, Jan. *Alan of Lille's Grammar of Sex: The Meaning of Grammar to a Twelfth-Century Intellectual.* Speculum Anniversary Monographs. Cambridge, Mass.: Mediaeval Academy of America, 1985.

Zumthor, Paul. "The Great Game of Rhetoric." *New Literary History* 12 (1981): 493–508.

Index

About the Author

Robert R. Edwards is Professor of English and Comparative Literature at the State University of New York at Buffalo. He is the author of *The Montecassino Passion and the Poetics of Medieval Drama, The Poetry of Guido Guinizelli,* and *Ratio and Invention: A Study of Medieval Lyric and Narrative.* He is Chair of the Department of English at Buffalo.

Library of Congress Cataloging-in-Publication Data

Edwards, Robert R., 1942–
    The dream of Chaucer : representation and reflection in the early
narratives / by Robert R. Edwards.
        p.   cm.
    Bibliography: p.
    Includes index.
    ISBN 0-8223-0871-1
    1. Chaucer, Geoffrey, d. 1400—Criticism and interpretation.
    2. Dreams in literature. 3. Visions in literature. 4. Narration
    (Rhetoric) I. Title.
PR1933.D74E39   1989
821'.1—dc19   88-7925CIP